"I trust Tiffany Yates Martin with the editing process even more than I trust myself. Read this book and steal her secrets!"

—**Kelly Harms,** *Washington Post*–**bestselling author of** *The Overdue Life of Amy Byler*

"Tiffany Yates Martin is an exceptional editor, so of course her advice and counsel in *Intuitive Editing* is exceptional as well. Whether you're a seasoned author looking to fine-tune your craft, pacing, or tension or just starting out and looking for guidance on building overall structure and engaging characters, this book is a must-read that will take you from idea to finished manuscript, which is what every writer hopes for."

—*New York Times*–**bestselling author Allison Winn Scotch**

"We've always asserted that Tiffany Yates Martin has a superpower— the ability to make any manuscript shine. Now she's sharing her editing secrets in her how-to guide, *Intuitive Editing*, and it's a must-have for any writer. She'll push you to delve deeper into your characters, to connect the dots of your storylines. Trust us—don't revise another novel until you've absorbed every word of this book."

—**Liz Fenton & Lisa Steinke, authors of** *The Two Lila Bennetts*

"This book is a must-have tool every author needs in their toolkit. When you are ready to go deeper, to dig into the revision process, using Tiffany's *Intuitive Editing* strategies will help you take your writing to the next level."

—*New York Times*– **and** *USA Today*–**bestselling author Steena Holmes**

"*Intuitive Editing* belongs on every author's bookshelf. Martin's advice goes way beyond the 'how-to' of editing and provides a big-picture strategy for making your work shine. It is the next-best thing to having a top-notch developmental editor in your corner. Best book on editing or writing that I have ever read."

—**Bette Lee Crosby,** *USA Today*–**bestselling author of** *Emily, Gone*

"Martin is more than an insightful editing guru; she understands the writer's mind. Packed with straightforward, practical advice, *Intuitive Editing* will up the game of aspiring and seasoned authors alike. Martin breaks down the multifaceted tasks of revision into a GPS route to a polished manuscript. Indispensable!"

**—Sonja Yoerg, *Washington Post*–bestselling author
of *True Places and Stories We Never Told***

"Authors, if you can't be lucky enough to have Tiffany as your editor, then *Intuitive Editing* is the next-best thing. Her advice is sound, thoughtful, no-nonsense and given with the compassion that every author and their book deserves."

—Elisabeth Weed, literary agent, the Book Group

"I've worked with literally dozens of editors in my career, and Tiffany Yates Martin is one of the very best. She has pushed and cajoled and teased me into my best work ever, and I'm telling you now...buy this book right now and USE it. With Tiffany's guidance, you, too, will discover depths to your work that you never knew existed."

**—Barbara O'Neal, *Wall Street Journal*, *Washington Post*, and
#1 Amazon Charts bestselling author of *When We Believed in Mermaids***

"*Intuitive Editing* takes the daunting task of revising fiction and transforms it into an approachable and—dare I say it?—exciting process. I walked away from this book with a powerful self-editing action plan and newfound confidence in my ability to successfully revise my stories. I'd recommend this gem of a book to any writer eager to overcome the overwhelm of the editing process."

**—Kristen Kieffer, author of *Build Your Best Writing Life*
and founder of Well-Storied.com**

"I always know when I work on a manuscript with Tiffany Yates Martin that I'll love my story more when we finish. She has a unique approach to illuminating exactly what aspects should be enhanced or tweaked. Martin puts the magic of her editorial genius in your hands with *Intuitive Editing*. Loaded with tips and techniques designed to help delve deeper into your story, this guide is a must-have in any author's craft book arsenal."

—Kerry Lonsdale, *Wall Street Journal*– and *Washington Post*– bestselling author of the Everything series and *Last Summer*

"I love this book! I love its clarity, its meticulousness, and, yes, its intuitiveness. I love how much emphasis there is on making sure that what is on the page actually matches the story in your head. And I especially love the humanity of it all, the compassion and understanding that radiates from this book for the arduous and indeed sometimes mysterious journey the writer faces in undertaking substantive revisions. It really is like having a good friend, who is also a tremendous editor, holding your hand through the process!"

—Sherry Thomas, author of the Lady Sherlock series and *The Magnolia Sword: A Ballad of Mulan*

"*Intuitive Editing* offers fresh, approachable, clear guidance to making your work the best it can be. It's an excellent tool that will help writers not just with editing but with the writing process itself."

—Annelise Robey, literary agent, Jane Rotrosen Agency

"For writers like me—who love drafting but yearn to hide when it comes time to polish all that rough material into a story that shines—*Intuitive Editing* is a godsend. I've worked with Tiffany Yates Martin for years and have always marveled at her unparalleled editorial vision. Now she's distilled that magic into one concise guide that doesn't just make editing doable; it actually makes it an enjoyable part of storytelling."

—Camille Pagán, *Washington Post*–bestselling author of *This Won't End Well* and *Life* and *Other Near-death Experiences*

"*Intuitive Editing* is a book that should be on every writer's bookshelf. Tiffany's approach is straightforward, her information essential for every writer, and her knowledge and ideas will fire the imagination and enhance every story. Intuitive Editing helps to clear the debris and allow you to take control of your story to make it shine. A must-read."

—**Sejal Badani, *USA Today*–, *Washington Post*–, and *Wall Street Journal*–bestselling author of *Trail of Broken Wings* and *The Storyteller's Secret***

"'Good writing multitasks,' states Martin in this masterful, comprehensive and indispensable guide for writers who wish to hone their craft and make their stories shine. Indeed, her book on self-editing multitasks as well, serving as a master class in creating story, a clear guide to honing a draft into a polished yet personal gem, as well as a reference that writers will keep on their shelves to turn to again and again."

—**Jess Montgomery, author of the Kinship historical mysteries**

"Tiffany Yates Martin is a master editor. Drawing on her years of experience working with a wide range of authors, she shares her razor-sharp skills in this must-read for all writers. Whether shaping, polishing, or digging deep inside the visceral components of your story, Tiffany's intuitive approach, complete with tools and techniques, is sure to take your writing to the next level. I've written six books. I still hear Tiffany's voice in my ear *every single time* I sit down to write. Do yourself a favor and buy this book."

—**Rochelle Weinstein, *USA Today*–bestselling author of *Somebody's Daughter* and *This Is Not How It Ends***

"*Intuitive Editing* is the most helpful writing book I've ever opened. I had trouble reading to the end, because every few pages I'd want to get up to dive into my current manuscript and fix a problem! There were so many great aha moments thanks to the clear examples. Keep this book close at hand."

—**Victoria Helen Stone, bestselling author of *Jane Doe***

"As any writer will tell you: Writing is the easy part—it's editing that is tough. Well, not anymore. *Intuitive Editing* will guide new writers through what can be a daunting process. For experienced writers it provides the perfect checklist, offering an invaluable 'helicopter' view. Yates Martin is the editor with the magic touch. In this book she shares insight drawn from decades of experience and a sheer love of books. If you are writing or thinking of writing, this book is a must-have."

—**Amanda Prowse, international bestselling author of *The Girl in the Corner* and *The Things I Know***

"Tiffany Yates Martin has accomplished an unlikely feat: a book about editing that is as effective and handy with the broad themes as it is with the nitty-gritty. She has distilled all her years of experience into digestible and entirely practical advice on a wide range of topics—comprehensive and complete, and yet she drills down into the weeds on just about everything. *Intuitive Editing* is insightful, readable, entertaining, and authoritative. Simply put, this book will make you a better writer."

—**Andy Abramowitz, author of *A Beginner's Guide to Freefall***

"A creative and specific guide for writers, fiction and nonfiction alike—fun, easy to read, covers all the topics we need to think about, and it's not boring. That's a gift. A fabulous guide!"

—**International and *USA Today*–bestselling author Kaira Rouda**

"Tiffany Yates Martin's *Intuitive Editing* is a treasure box full of gems for writers at all stages of their careers. I wish I had this resource before I started writing my first novel. The chapter on POV alone is worth the price of admission. It would have saved me hours of confusion and rewrites. With tools for storytelling (developmental editing) and word craft (line editing) *Intuitive Editing* is accessible, funny, and packed full of information. I have no doubt that Ms. Martin's editing has improved my novels. Do yourself a favor—read *Intuitive Editing* to learn her tricks of the trade so you can improve your own writing."

—**Laila Ibrahim, bestselling author of *Yellow Crocus* and *Paper Wife***

"A good editor is critical to the process of writing a book, and I can say from direct experience that Tiffany Yates Martin is one of the best. A true 'book whisperer,' she's intuitive, insightful, and passionate about the work. Having access to her knowledge and expertise through the pages of *Intuitive Editing* is the next-best thing to having her real voice in your ear."

—**Barbara Taylor Sissel, bestselling author of *Tell No One***

"Tiffany Yates Martin has given an immeasurable gift to writers—expert help on the all-important stage of editing. In a crowded field of craft books, this stands out by digging deep into what happens after the writing. With copious examples of familiar favorites and probing questions that will help a writer take an honest look at their work, Martin's book will be one that you'll want to read and reference again and again. Be prepared to roll up your sleeves! And to be wowed by what is possible."

—**Camille Di Maio, bestselling author of *The Memory of Us***

"The absolute last word on editing. While reading *Intuitive Editing*, I found myself taking copious notes, applying Tiffany's advice, and improving my manuscript. Tiffany Yates Martin is brilliant. Read her new book before you write another word of your own."

—**Marilyn Simon Rothstein, author of *Lift and Separate* and *Husbands and Other Sharp Objects***

"*Intuitive Editing* is the new must-have for authors at all levels. Page after page, this book is a strategic guide to editing fiction or nonfiction into as clear, clean, and creative a work as possible. Chock-full of Martin's professional editing experience, teachable moments, and resources, *Intuitive Editing* is primed to become a new classic."

—**Amy Sue Nathan, author of *The Last Bathing Beauty***

"Everything I know about crafting a story I learned from Tiffany Yates Martin. If you're going to revise your own manuscript, you need *Intuitive Editing*. You may not realize it yet, but trust me, you do."

—**Camilla Monk, author of the Spotless series**

"I always knew there had to be a better way to tackle editing, and Tiffany Yates Martin's inspiring approach flipped a switch in my brain. *Intuitive Editing*'s wise and illuminating advice helps writers cut through the clutter and confusion of rough drafts to find the true core of their stories. Essential reading for anyone who wants to take their work to the highest level possible."
—**Karin Gillespie, author of *Love Literary Style*
and the Bottom Dollar Girl series**

"Tiffany always has the magical ability to both psychically tap into my dream version of a book and to rigorously analyze the structure needed to help me achieve my vision. I'm not certain how I feel about my secret weapon going public in this essential guide, but I do know that any writer who doesn't have *Intuitive Editing* in her arsenal is going onto the field unarmed."
—**Sarah Bird, author of *Daughter of a Daughter of a Queen***

"Before I read *Intuitive Editing*, I thought I was a pretty good storyteller. *Intuitive Editing* showed me all the ways I could be even better, and, just like Tiffany's feedback, did so in an approachable and straightforward way. Better still, the more I read, the more I itched to go back to my work-in-progress. She kept my wheels spinning and my creative juices flowing. Suitable for the beginning novelist as much as it is for the seasoned."
—**Elisa Lorello, bestselling author of *Faking It* and *Ordinary World***

"Writers (and first drafts), rejoice! This book is nothing short of a novice editor's dream come true."
—**Ania Ahlborn, bestselling author of *Brother* and *Within These Walls***

"If you're a writer, here is the live-in editor that you've been looking for—just the right balance of cheerleader, literary critic and even therapist. Truly, if I could recommend only one book to help writers improve their abilities to see what's still lacking in their manuscripts, this would be the one. I very well may be sleeping with *Intuitive Editing* under my pillow."
—**Joy Jordan-Lake, bestselling author of *A Tangled Mercy***

intuitive EDITING

A Creative & Practical Guide to Revising Your Writing

TIFFANY YATES MARTIN

For the storytellers,
who illuminate the world.

CONTENTS

INTRODUCTION

E diting your own writing can feel like doing your own brain surgery: No matter how good you may be at the technical procedure,
it's all but impossible to be quite so adept when you turn the scalpel
inside your own head.

But self-editing *is* an accessible skill you can develop and hone just
like the craft of writing, and in this book I'll show you how to evaluate your own manuscripts with an objective eye and create a clear,
actionable blueprint for making your story more compelling, effective,
and engaging.

While editing and revision may not seem as glamourous or exciting as initially spinning your story onto the page, it's my favorite part
(obviously). I've spent my entire career in the publishing industry, and in
more than twenty-five years as an editor I've worked on literally hundreds of books, with major publishers as well as directly with authors at
every stage of their careers, from *New York Times, USA Today, Washington Post*, and *Wall Street Journal* bestsellers to first-timers, and I promise
you every one of them came away from the editing process happier with
their story. A good edit is exhilarating—not the act of tearing down,
as many think of it, or a long, painful slog up Revision Mountain, but
the creative, intuitive art of building up, deepening, developing, homing
in on the story you set out to tell. It's like the world's greatest treasure

hunt—combing through the map you created in your first draft and finding the gold. It's where the magic really happens.

But as in pretty much every area of life, "genius" takes a mix of both right brain and left, inspiration and perspiration—creativity and craft. Editing a first draft into something polished and publishable is the real work of writing, and often what separates career authors from hobbyists. To be clear, if writing is your hobby and your creative outlet there's not one thing on earth wrong with that—it's a beautiful form of self-expression. But if you hope to enter the hypercrowded market of published books, editing is how you make your books competitive.

The approach I take in this book is the one I take in my own editing work with authors. It's not about finding the "right" way to tell your story based on outside expectations, or the market, or what the latest craft book or writing "guru" says you should do. *Intuitive Editing* is designed to help you find the most effective way to tell the story on the page that's as true as possible to the dream of it in your head. To find the best version of your vision.

How to Use This Book

Editing intuitively is about growing your story and bringing it fully to life in a way that taps into your creativity and lets it flow instead of binding it with externally imposed "rules." I've never been a fan of writing and editing guides that offer any type of one-size-fits-all dogma. Rigidly following a predetermined methodology is the very opposite of creativity. In my experience there are no hard-and-fast "rules" in any creative arena (in fact, you'll see that when I use the word in this book it's always in quotes). That's the beauty (and agony) of any art—it's fluid, organic, and every creation is as unique as the artist's fingerprint. Writing, editing, and revising are subjective processes and every author has to find the approach that's right for her. The only real "rules" are the ones that serve you and your story best.

Intuitive Editing is organized to help lead you through every step of editing your own work in a way that makes the most sense for *your* story, *your* style, *your* voice. You can use this book as a troubleshooting guide to jump right to the areas you know you're struggling with, or you can assess your manuscript as a whole, like an editor does, and see how effectively it's working. Storytelling is like a Jenga puzzle, where every piece affects the overall structure, so all these elements work in tandem.

For that reason it's impossible to separate out each chapter's subject into a discrete, self-contained package; every storytelling element impacts every other element, so you'll see questions of motivation and goal discussed in the Character chapter, but also in Stakes and in Plot. You'll see questions of suspense addressed in the Suspense and Tension chapter, but also in Showing and Telling and in Momentum and Pace. Storytelling is a web where each element is intrinsically connected to every other element.

First we'll talk about how to gain objectivity about your writing and approach the edit. Then in each of the book's three main sections—Macroedits, Microedits, and Line Edits—I give you the tools I use to evaluate and analyze authors' manuscripts so you can assess your own work with the same objective, intuitive approach, from the big picture to the smaller details and all the way to the nuts and bolts of polishing and streamlining the prose itself.

Every chapter has two main sections:

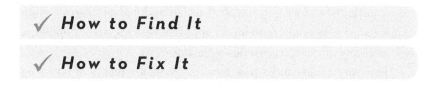

✓ *How to Find It*

✓ *How to Fix It*

In the first we look at how to spot the areas in your story that could be stronger and more effective with a bit more development or polish; then I show you specific, actionable techniques to effect those improvements on the page.

I often preface what tend to be my extremely long, in-depth editorial letters to authors by warning them that I tend to ask a lot of questions—perhaps more than they ever wanted to consider. But it's through asking yourself questions that you can really analyze with the objectivity of a professional editor and find the right path forward for *your* story. So I've loaded up each chapter with the kinds of questions I ask authors in our edit about every aspect of their story.

Throughout I've used copious examples, mostly from works many people are likely to be familiar with, like classics, fairy tales, and bestsellers. I also incorporate examples from TV and film, both because they tend to be widely seen and because the contained format—a half hour, an hour, two hours—is a highly useful way to see storytelling theories in distilled "packets" that often make it easier to take in the gestalt at a single sitting. I also offer examples drawn from real manuscripts—the details may be changed, but the principles are culled and hybridized from my work with hundreds of authors.

Finally, in part IV I offer specific suggestions for how to solicit and process feedback, how to approach the edit, and the ins and outs of hiring a professional editor.

The theories and practices I offer aren't exclusive to fiction; the same storytelling elements apply to narrative nonfiction and memoir as well: your protagonist is the subject or main player in the narrative, the minor figures your supporting characters; the plot is the actual events you're writing about; stakes, suspense, show and tell, voice—all elements of story also apply to these genres. And part III, which looks at fine-tuning your prose, is also universal to writers. Together these techniques will help you find the story you intended to tell and make it as compelling and polished as possible, with lots of specifics, reasons, and examples, as well as plenty of clear, actionable suggestions.

This isn't a book about how to write; there are plenty of books out there about writing. (Some of my favorites are listed on the Resources page of my website, www.foxprinteditorial.com.) And it's not "the last book on editing you'll ever need." Read widely and take what works for you, your process, and each particular story.

Intuitive Editing isn't meant to replace the value of an objective professional editor, beta reader, or critique group either, but to put tools in your writer toolbox. These are skills that can be learned and used by writers of every level, whether just starting out or multipublished—the only prerequisite is a deep love of story and a dedication to your craft. Like Waldo, once you begin to see these things in your writing, you can never unsee them.

Writing your first draft is like mining a rough diamond from virgin earth. But editing is what turns it into a jewel, polishing all its facets so it can really shine. I'm passionate about the process and the way it can transform a story—and I hope by the time you've worked with the techniques in this book, you will be too.

Think of *Intuitive Editing* as a user manual to help you make your story as effective and compelling as it can be—a practical, usable, adaptable set of techniques for editing your own work with confidence, creativity, and skill.

approaching
THE EDIT

"Start by doing what's necessary; then do what's possible,
and suddenly you are doing the impossible."
—Francis of Assisi

Learning to see the areas in your own manuscript that may need more development or clarification is just one of the challenges of editing your own work—one I'll offer specific suggestions for throughout the book. But equally important—and often confusing—is knowing *how* to actually go about addressing them and revising once you do.

Not all editors work the same way, but to give you an idea of how an edit generally looks, here's how I approach a manuscript.

Years ago there was an episode of the sitcom *Murphy Brown* where the news team, for various reasons, was taking turns driving as they carpooled to work. When fastidious anchorman Jim took the wheel, for a long moment he simply sat there staring at the dash. The other characters grew impatient and began exhorting him to move, but deadpan Jim brushed them off, stating, "I'm familiarizing myself with the vehicle."

I always think of that scene when I start a new editing project (or rent a car). The first thing I do with a manuscript is a cold read to "familiarize myself with the vehicle"—to get my feet planted in the story. I don't even do this on a computer but on my e-reader, so I'm literally not doing anything but simply reading the story as if it's a published book, without focusing specifically on technical elements—staying in "reader brain" rather than "editor brain." Until I have an overview of the story's world, characters, plot, theme, arcs, etc., I can't analyze how well the story holds together and works as a whole, let alone on the individual storytelling elements. This read is indispensable for me.

At that point I ask myself specific big-picture questions about the story to assess how effective it is, and circle in on what may not be working as well as it could. In parentheses next to some of the questions I consider below are the storytelling elements each one reflects. At this stage, as I consider the story on this broad overview level, most of these are macroediting elements.

- Is there a central story question (plot, character)?
- Who are the protagonists, and are they the engine of the story (character, plot, stakes)?
- Do I feel I know them—that they're real people (character)?
- Do I care about them? Why or why not (character, stakes)?
- Does the story keep propelling the reader forward? If not, where did my focus lag (stakes, character, plot, momentum and pace, suspense and tension)?
- Are the story events believable (plot)?
- Are there extraneous story events, or loose ends (plot, character)?
- Does it all tie together cohesively (plot)?
- Does the story take me on a clear journey? Are the characters changed somehow by the end of the story? Was that change a direct result of the story events (character, plot)?

This big-picture overview heavily informs my second read—the slow, meticulous edit pass—as I embed comments liberally where I see something the author might clarify or develop or trim based on the first-read impressions as well as how those impressions develop as I do this much closer read. At this point I'm taking a magnifying glass to the macro story elements (character, stakes, plot), but I'm now also circling in on microedit areas, considering the story's effectiveness not just overall, but scene by scene, line by line. Some of the questions I might ask myself are:

- Does each scene feel immediate—am I as a reader brought directly and viscerally into it (character, point of view, showing and telling, suspense and tension)?
- Are the characters open to me as a reader? Do I understand their reactions, share their thoughts, feelings, what they make of what they're experiencing? Am I living vicariously through them (character, showing and telling, point of view)?
- Is it vivid and visual? Do I "see" the story? Do the characters and events feel tangible and real (show versus tell, point of view)?
- Does the story seem to lag in specific places? Did I lose interest anywhere (stakes, momentum and pace, suspense and tension, character, showing and telling, point of view)?

I'm also examining the prose itself for places it may not be conveying what the author intended, or where the meaning is unclear or ambiguous, or the pace stalls, or it feels redundant (voice, line editing).

At this stage I'm inserting comments everywhere a story question or concern leaps out at me—where readers may feel confused or uninvested or disengaged. I'm also jotting brief overview notes in a separate Word doc, sometimes cutting-and-pasting key sentences that spark a thought or idea I want to expand on in my overview notes, and I usually wind up with pages of extremely rough notes and these pasted excerpts. I'll then use these as a guideline for writing my editorial letter—a thorough, minutely detailed, exhaustive (sometimes painfully exhaustive) overview of every single element of the story—not only those areas that could use a bit of shoring up or fleshing out, but what's working well. It's equally important for authors to know where the story succeeds, not only for morale amid what usually winds up being 5-10K words of constructive feedback (though that's important), but also so they get a complete picture of how the story holds together.

The editorial letter is the "wide shot," in film parlance, that gives the author my overall impressions, which the embedded comments build on by showing specific places where these ideas jumped out at me and why, and suggesting ways to address those areas—the close-up shots. Together the letter and the embedded notes create a thorough report on how well every part of the manuscript is serving the story, offer a lot of questions (like, a *lot*) meant to spark the author's ideas for how to address areas that could use more development or clarification, and in tandem they serve as a very clear road map for an author to follow in tackling revisions. Between the two the edit thoroughly addresses every storytelling element.

At that point I always tell authors to sit with the feedback for a day or two, consider what resonates for their story, and then take what works and toss what doesn't. The edits aren't meant to be prescriptive, but rather illuminative, holding up a mirror to every crevice of the manuscript so the author can see what she has and how it may be coming across, and decide which parts of the feedback serve her intentions for the story. An editor's job isn't to impose her own vision, but help the author achieve his as clearly, effectively, and satisfyingly as possible.

*But...*as thorough, detailed, and specific as this way of working allows an editor to be in assessing an author's manuscript, it's almost impossible to approach your own edit that way. If anything authors are *over*familiar with their story, which is why it can be so hard to see what's actually on the page the way an objective reader can, rather than what the creator is subconsciously filling in. And it's really difficult to ask yourself hundreds (literally) of open-ended questions about your own manuscript as you read without slipping into "writer brain" and starting to try to answer them and fix as you go. That's usually a recipe for losing all your hard-won objectivity and finding yourself so deep in the rabbit hole you can't see daylight.

The main focus in editing your own work lies in two areas: achieving the objectivity needed to assess analytically how well the story is working (editing), and addressing in a productive, efficient, effective way those areas that may need more development or polish (revising). I generally advise authors to break these down into two separate processes.

Attaining Objectivity

When you've spent weeks, months, even years writing a story, it lives in your head. Even when you're away from it, it's constantly churning in the background like a pot left to simmer on a back burner. When you're drafting you're in creation mode, weaving a tapestry thread by thread. You are creating something out of nothing.

But when you edit you are assessing what you have already created and fine-tuning it. As editor Susan Bell says in *The Artful Edit,* "We write into a void; we edit into a universe." It's like sculpting: Writing is the heady, inspired act of sheer creation, taking an amorphous chunk of stone and carving form from it—discovering the statue inside of it, to paraphrase Michelangelo. Editing is a different skill, using different tools as the artist shapes, chisels, sands, polishes…painstakingly, patiently doing the meticulous detail work and smoothing the rough edges to go from "general human shape" to "the David."

To oversimplify, creation is right-brained; editing is left-brained. Your job is to find a way to shut off writer brain and open the tap on editor brain—get out of the wild unfettered id and into the objective, assessing superego. (Note the conspicuous absence of ego, which is of little use in either writing or editing.)

But how do you do that with a world you've immersed yourself in so completely for so long? Over the years I've found a few techniques that seem to work for authors:

TIME/DISTANCE

Without doubt, the most effective way to achieve distance from your writing is to step away from it—for as long as possible. Put it in a (metaphorical) drawer (i.e., stash it in a file folder you don't open), write another manuscript, move, get married, have children, go walk the Camino de Santiago.

This may not always be feasible.

If you're on deadline from your publisher, or for a contest, or with an agent, or you just want to "git 'er done," you can't always take the weeks, months, years away that automatically bring you back to the story with fresh eyes. But even days can be effective—especially if you distract yourself from the story as thoroughly as possible. Go on vacation; work on another project; serve as carpool mom for the neighborhood kids. Even if all you do is take a day to hike with your dog or go to a spa or binge-watch movies, if you can find a way to take a complete mental break from the story, often you'll come back to it with some measure of objectivity.

NEW PLACE/ENVIRONMENT

The act of reading/editing your story in a place other than where you wrote it can alter your perception from creator mindset. If you normally sit at your desk at home to write, then when you begin to edit go to a coffee shop, or the library, or Spain. Even just moving to another area of your house is effective. The brain is a creature of habit, and if you have disciplined yourself as a writer to sit down and write when you enter your working space (and good for you if you have!), then it will automatically kick into writer brain as soon as you do. Trick that little bugger and shake things up. Bonus points if you have the luxury of dedicating a whole second space of your home only to editing and revising—it will train your brain the same way you did to create the habit of writing.

READ ALOUD; HAVE IT READ TO YOU

A lot of authors swear by this technique—hearing your story out loud automatically puts you in the mindset of taking the story in, rather than creating it, and allows you to hear what's actually there rather than filling in the blanks. Reading it aloud yourself is helpful, but better still is to have it read to you. If you don't have the most accommodating partner or children or friends on earth who'll spend hours doing it, record your own amateur audiobook of the manuscript and then play it back (you get a bonus perspective there—reading it aloud from the page does offer a different take). Or you can use a TTS (text to speech) program like AudioBookMaker or Natural Reader or Zabaware or others (there are many free/inexpensive software programs for this). Microsoft Word even has a TTS feature built right in (look in the Review menu for the Speak/Read feature), as does Scrivener (Edit: Start Dictation) within the app.

USE A DIFFERENT FONT OR DIFFERENT NAME

As ridiculous as it sounds, these can be surprisingly effective ways of instilling mental distance. Changing the font from what you usually write in gives the manuscript just enough foreignness that it can help reset your brain (I know one author who swears by the much-maligned Comic Sans, which she says also allows her not to take the read too seriously).

Putting a different author name on the cover page and headers seems like the most ludicrous mental chicanery ever, but again, often it can somehow flip a switch in your mind that lets you take a step back from the story. Don't use a real author's name, or your pen name if you use one; make up a name. This little trick may not work for you, but it's easy to execute (and undo), so it might be worth a try.

PRINT IT OUT

As anyone who's ever written longhand or on a typewriter versus a computer can attest, there's something different about hard copy versus virtual copy, almost a different region of your brain that comes into play. This is another one of those nebulous, why-would-it-possibly-help suggestions that may or may not work for you, but if you've got a ream of paper to spare, print that sucker up, grab yourself a beverage and a lounge chair, and read it like a top Hollywood agent looking for his next hot property.

READ IT ON AN E-READER

When you load a Word doc into most e-readers it formats like a regular e-book, and something about seeing your industry-standard Times New Roman double-spaced work-in-progress all professional and prettied up plays good tricks on your perception, with the added bonus that our brains are usually trained for enjoyment reading when we pick up our e-readers, so you're automatically in the right frame of mind.

$$\cdot \cdot \# \cdot \cdot$$

Try any or all of these techniques, even in combination (e.g., read on your e-reader in a new location), to come to your familiar story with the freshest eyes possible—and just enjoy this initial cold read.

I always advocate trying to do this read in as few sittings as possible—one is ideal, if you can magically find a big chunk of time in your busy life, but if not multiple sittings are okay; just do them as close together as you can, and the fewer, the better. The idea is to get a cohesive picture of what you have, and it's most effective to do that by taking the story in as close to a whole as possible.

How to Evaluate Your Manuscript

Congratulations! You've just completed the easy part. Now it's time to start the climb up Revision Mountain. Keep your head down, take it step by step, and you *will* get to the top. Or as Anne Lamott says in her lovely book about writing by the same name, take it bird by bird.

Now that you've gotten what might be your first complete overview of what you have, what do you think? Did you enjoy the story? Did it draw you in? Overall were you pleased with what wound up on the page as compared to the story you set out to tell? Before you even start a close analysis, put the manuscript down and let your general impressions coalesce—how well did your story hold together for you?

If there were places that jarred, or where you felt you'd missed the mark of your intentions, or you were pulled out of simply enjoying the story on its face, what were they? Write those story elements or parts of the manuscript down in a separate document—very briefly. What jarred you about them? Did the strong, fearless heroine you envisioned come across as too passive or unmotivated? Were there places where you felt disengaged, impatient to get on to "the good stuff" you knew was coming? Was there part of the plot that made total sense in your head, but on the page it felt as if you'd left something out? Don't *think* too hard about anything at this stage—I think of this as *feeling* the story; for now you're just working in general terms. Try to stay in that reader mind, layman's mind, that you so painstakingly achieved in the cold read. You're not analyzing this as a skilled craftsperson yet—for now just let it play in your head the way you do after watching a TV show or movie or reading someone else's book. (If you're like many creatives, you probably can't simply enjoy a story without parsing out what you felt worked and what didn't.)

Did you notice any loose threads? Did any characters feel too bland or one-dimensional, or did you not like or relate to them as much as you wanted to? Was there a sense of urgency or momentum that kept you turning pages (or not)? Did the emotional moments affect you? Did the end leave you feeling satisfied? Don't think; *feel* the story.

These are just a handful of examples of the kinds of questions to ask yourself, the various impressions you might have from your initial read. Don't grab onto any of them right now or try to solve them (or beat yourself up over them, equally important). Simply let the story you just read percolate in your head, and make very brief notes of any areas that struck you as not working as well as you intended. I always liken this feeling to a woodworker running her hand along a piece of furniture she's just created—where are the rough spots that may need smoothing? That's all you're doing for now—feeling for those spots. We're not ready to start sanding yet.

If you can stand to wait, don't open the document up yet to actually start working—go about your business for a day or so and just let the story keep simmering on a back burner of your mind (it will). As new impressions occur to you (they will), briefly jot those into your notes as well. Don't get too involved in it still, though, and don't trouble yourself over how to fix it. Right now you're the building inspector, not the handyman.

I want to pause a moment here to talk about your psyche.

Many authors beat up on themselves during editing and revision: *How could I miss the mark so badly? I'm an idiot. Who told me I could write?*

This is an early draft. As no less a writer than Ernest Hemingway famously (and piquantly) said, "The first draft of anything is shit." It's *supposed* to suck to some degree. If it weren't every author would toss off a draft and call it done—and there'd be no such job description as "editor." A story draft that needs some work is not a reflection of your talent or skill—it's simply the fact that art is a process, and when you're deep in the creative trance it's impossible to also objectively evaluate your creation as you go. If you are, chances are you're fettering your creativity, or trying to write to a formula or some external idea of "story," hampering the fire and life and voice and individuality in your work. Write like a dog; edit like a cat—meaning it's okay to get all wonderfully slobbery and over-excited when you're drafting; when you edit you'll take on that cool feline calculation.

Don't expect your first draft—or second, or fifth—to be perfect, any more than an actor expects a first table read to be ready for an audience, or a violinist would expect to play a new piece of music with the nuance and expression that will grow into it as he rehearses and rehearses and rehearses. Beating yourself up for failing to fully achieve your artistic vision on your first swing shuts down the very part of you that can achieve it. Be gentle with your artistic soul. Nurture your talent and inspiration and skill. If you planted a seed in the ground, you wouldn't stomp out the first tendrils that unfurl because they aren't a flower yet. Be kind to yourself, friends—and respect and admire the rich turf you've sown and that first beautiful green shoot. Now it's time to grow.

THIS IS A NORMAL PART OF THE PROCESS. I'd be willing to put a fairly substantial bet on the fact that nearly any novel you've ever admired or loved has gone through rounds and rounds of editing and revision. What looks so smooth and effortless in final execution is anything but; just as with most any art, it's the product of painstaking effort. I work with bestselling, multipublished authors who go through exactly this same process with each and every book—multiple edit passes and revisions, sometimes as many as five or six, and that's *after* they've done however many revisions already on their own before even turning it in for editing. This is normal. You are normal.

Please don't denigrate your own work or ability. The subconscious hears it and internalizes it. Most of us would never say such harsh things even to someone we hated. Artists face so much judgment and criticism; the one person they must always be able to count on to believe in them and their talent is themselves. So be your own champion—always. Take yourself seriously and own your talent, but also know that the other part of the equation—often the major part— is hard work and practice.

And now...back to that process.

After you've sat with your impressions of your story for a day or two, it's time to tackle the revisions. As you address these areas, though, don't start at the beginning and work your way through the story over and over and over on every edit pass. That's the instinctive way many authors approach editing, and it's counterproductive—it usually results in either a beautifully polished, tight, compelling first third or so, with ever diminishing returns on the rest of the manuscript as those elements gradually begin to fall apart...or a technically well-developed first act, but one that lacks life and voice and then slowly unravels as the story goes on.

Why? Because each time you go "back to one," in film terms, and start from the beginning, you're losing that freshness and objectivity for the whole. You get so enmeshed in those early pages you revise the daylights out of them, which might make them fantastic or might over-work them and edit out all their personality and style. And by the time you progress on to the other parts of the story—the dreaded sagging middle and the climax and resolution—you are back in the center of the forest, unable to see a path out. And at that point, friends, when you've trodden the trail into the thicket so many times it's worn flat, it's almost impossible to move forward and forge your way through the underbrush to the other side.

So rather than this seemingly logical progressive approach from beginning to end, when editing your own work I advocate a version of master editor Sol Stein's "triage" method, which is pretty much what it sounds like: You take the most critical cases first. Start with the bleeders.

What that means is this: In the notes you jotted down after you finished your cold read, and in the impressions you've had since as it percolated, what struck you as the main parts of the story that aren't quite where you want them or aren't yet as effective as they can be? Most often these will fall in the macroedit areas, the main tent poles of story: character, plot, or stakes. If this foundation for your story isn't solid, then none of what you build on top of it matters yet. Readers have to connect strongly with fully developed, three-dimensional characters we invest in, who want something desperately and doggedly pursue that thing despite setbacks and challenges in the course of the plot, and have something big to gain by succeeding (and/or lose by failing) at stake.

As counterintuitive and willy-nilly as it may seem, try simply going directly to those parts of the story and shoring them up. If your characters lack motivation, for instance, or need fleshing out, go back to individual scenes and encounters and strengthen those areas. If you notice a breach in logic in how your character got from one scene to the next, a missing step, go in and insert that—in fact if there are any scenes you realized you need to add, write and insert them at this stage. Need to amp up stakes? Cherry-pick those areas and salt in whatever words or sentences or paragraphs you need to pump up the volume. In this first stage of revision you're filling in those blanks in the foundational story elements that might not have made it from your head to the page.

Once you feel fairly solid about these essential building blocks of your story, now you can focus on the microedit elements. Again going directly to areas of concern, you might drop more bread crumbs of tension in certain parts of the story, or amp up the suspense where perhaps you let it defuse. Perhaps you kept readers at arm's length from your characters' direct experience by slipping into a distancing, weak, or uncertain point of view—dig a little deeper in those places to let us in. Maybe you've "told" crucial parts of the story that would be much stronger with "show" (or vice versa—sometimes show is a pace killer). Fix 'em.

Now that you've patched up every chink you found on that first cold read, it's time to test the dam. Take another objectivity break for a day or two, and then go back and once again enjoy your manuscript like a book—do another cold read. This is when you get to see how well your repairs are holding up, whether they addressed the issues you spotted in your first go-around, and what more may need to be done in those areas, as well as take a closer-angle lens to the story.

Again, try not to get too bogged down as you're reading—these early cold reads are your greatest chance for objectivity, at least imminently, and as soon as you stop to plow through chronologically and address issues you lose that distance. Try to simply take in this second read as you did the first…and then go back and triage again. And again. And again. Editing isn't a one-and-done pursuit—remember the image of the sculptor or woodworker patiently making pass after pass after pass of the work until every shape is sharply defined, every rough area smooth and polished.

Once you feel confident you've taken care of all the critical cases— the foundation of your story and its support structure—you can start at the beginning and work forward just as you might finish building a house by installing the drywall and flooring room by room, completing the final structural work as you go.

Now it's time for the sexy part of editing, the cosmetic work: line edits, where you shine the flashlight on your actual prose. This is the HGTV-makeover part—and a lot of authors want to dive right to this stage. But there's no point painting over walls that are cracked or unstable, or hanging curtains before you've installed the windows. Hold off on polishing your prose till you've made sure everything else is as solid as you can make it. Think of it as your reward for the hard work of structural editing.

To review, here's the whole system for how I recommend most effectively approaching a self-edit:

1. Gain objectivity
2. Read like a reader
3. Make brief notes
4. Address foundational issues—macroediting
5. Address the support elements of the story—microediting

6. Regain objectivity and reread
7. Repeat
8. Repeat
9. Repeat
10. Polish with line edits

When you first try it, this approach to revision may feel a little scattershot or haphazard, as if you're spot-patching gaps but aren't sure whether the dam will hold. But before you can fill up the reservoir and find out, you have to take care of those obvious holes—if you don't it's guaranteed to leak.

As you're working this way you may find—and likely will—that there's some overlap. Sometimes the most immediately gaping wound won't be a macroedit area, but a microedit. It's fine to start there—but once you've stanched the bleeding from the most critical cases, go back to the macroedits and make sure everything is stabilized. The guy who's missing a limb probably needs attention before the one with the bullet in his arm.

Try not to get discouraged if you find that your first draft—or second, or third, or eighth—still isn't quite the finished version of your story. Again, this is perfectly normal—some stories take longer to shake out. I work with a lot of authors who call themselves "revision writers," meaning they truly find the story in editing. It's part of their creative process—they vomit that first draft onto the page and then they hunker down and flesh it out. With each pass your story will deepen and develop, tighten and smooth. With each pass your storytelling instincts will sharpen; you will ever more deeply master and hone the craft elements of fiction; and you will not only make your story better and more effective, but grow as a writer.

This book is organized based on this approach. Part I addresses macroedits: character, stakes, and plot. Part II talks about microedit areas: suspense and tension, point of view, showing and telling, pace, structure, and voice. Part III looks at the prose itself with line edits.

Each chapter focuses on a single storytelling element, with a brief explanation, examples, and the How to Find It and How to Fix It sections.

At the end we'll talk about getting feedback from editors, beta readers, and crit partners, and how to use it in tackling revisions, but for now let's concentrate on what you can do on your own to make your story the best version of your vision.

PART I
MACROEDITS

chapter one

CHARACTER

H ere's the most important truism about storytelling: **Readers don't care what's happening unless we care who it's happening to.**

Character is the heart of story. It's why we get invested: because characters, whether people or Hobbits or Skynet or farm animals if we're reading *Charlotte's Web*—*any* sentient soul—are the lens through which we live a story. It's the difference between hearing news about a disaster or tragedy and seeing the faces of those directly affected by it, between dry facts and vivid *story*.

A character's experience becomes the reader's experience; we travel on their backs, in their heads, behind their eyes. We will invest in a story even where nothing really happens if we are sufficiently invested in the characters (as James Joyce and nine seasons of *Seinfeld* prove). Human beings are actually hardwired to relate to the world through the filter of our own perception—and vicariously, therefore, through the filter of the characters in a story. (For the neuroscience of it, read Lisa Cron's terrific *Wired for Story*.)

The most enduring works in history tend to be the ones defined by the vividness and appeal of their central characters: Othello, Cyrano de Bergerac, Jay Gatsby, Jo March, Atticus Finch, Jane Eyre, Don Quixote, Nancy Drew, James Bond, Sherlock Holmes.

And that's why of all the craft elements you may hone in your writing, learning to create well-developed, three-dimensional, relatable characters and taking them on a meaningful journey is the most important skill you will ever master.

Even knowing this, though—even having done extensive work in developing and defining your characters—the hard part is determining how much of it is actually on the page. Your characters might feel utterly real to you, their motivations and backstories fully fleshed out, but if you haven't shown that clearly in your manuscript they may feel opaque or underdeveloped to readers. We need a sense of their history, context, surroundings, interactions, dynamics with other people, fears, loves, desires, beliefs, who these people are in the world. You have a single medium—words—with which to create fully dimensional characters who feel as real as flesh and blood.

Whether and where you've conveyed your characters believably and fully on the page is one of the trickiest things to spot in editing your own writing. These people are already real to you—they may have been living in your head for months or years, so how do you know whether you're mentally filling in the blanks or you've put enough information in the story itself so that your readers feel they know them as well as you do?

Let's start with the basics of creating character, and then we'll look at how to determine whether you've conveyed key character elements to the reader and, if not, how to fix it.

The Foundation

The answers to three key questions form the basis of character—your protagonist's "point A" at the beginning of the journey we will travel with her:

- Who is this character—broadly and granularly?
- What drives her, and why?
- What's in her way?

WHO IS THIS CHARACTER?

Who your character is at his "point A" comprises both his broad external qualities as well as his specific internal ones—you can think of it as your character's situation when we first "meet" him. Don't get lost in the weeds here with exhaustive detail: "My character was raised by a single mom who suffered from depression and he had to learn to take care of himself. As a child, he…" We're not looking for a full bio right now; think of this as a slightly more intimate answer to the classic job-interview question, "Tell me about yourself." We just want the essence crystallized down: Harry Potter is a lonely, unassertive, but goodhearted orphaned boy living unhappily under the stairs in his unkind aunt and uncle's house; Celie from *The Color Purple* is a poor, self-effacing and resigned abused African-American teenage girl in the rural South in the early 1900s; Frodo Baggins is a Hobbit contentedly living in the Shire, whose main traits are goodness of heart, authenticity, and honesty.

Who a character is comprises a vast array of traits and situations; for our purposes at this point, boil your answer down to what is directly germane to his central journey in *this* story. For instance, if I'm writing the story of a plucky editor writing a long-dreamed-of guide to editing for writers, summing up who I am relative to that story would encompass that I'm both analytical and creative, a career editor with experience at every level of publishing who loves helping and teaching authors. It wouldn't necessarily include that I love dogs and the outdoors, was raised by a single mother in the South with my two siblings, used to be an actor, etc. Those things might come up at some point in the story of me writing this book, but they are not intrinsic to that central arc—for now focus on only the traits that essentially define your character's main journey in the slice of her life you're presenting in this story.

You should be able to succinctly sum up who your protagonist is at the core when we first meet him. He may foundationally change as a result of what he experiences in the story, and what he wants may evolve, but his basic situation and nature *before* embarking on the journey are what we're after for now.

WHAT DRIVES YOUR CHARACTER, AND WHY?

This is deeper than a character's goal and motivation, which we'll talk more about in the Stakes chapter. What drives your character includes that, but it also encompasses her underlying constitutional makeup: what has led her to where she is in life when we first meet her, and what makes her want what she wants, both at the beginning of the story and as it develops. This is a key component of what creates character arc—and your central story question.

If I were to ask what drives you, for instance, chances are good at least part of your answer would be "to write a book." But that's actually your *goal*—part of what's driving you, yes, but the core answer lies deeper than that. *Why* do you want to write a book? Maybe you have a particular story you've always dreamed of telling, or you love books and want to create them, or you want to change the world. Now dig even deeper than that. Why do you want tell *this* particular story, and why does it have to be in a book format, rather than a magazine article or blog post or just scintillating party conversation? Or why does your love of books dictate in you a need to create one yourself? Or what makes you want to change the world, and what do you want to change about it, and why is this the path you have chosen to do it?

Keep digging—we're still not at the core of what drives you to write. Let's take the first motivation above—that there's a particular story you want to tell—and say you want to write the story of a woman in an abusive relationship who finds the strength to break free and define her life on her own terms. Why that story? Maybe it reflects your own experience, or you read about a true story like that and it piqued your creative fancy, or you want women to know they can find the courage to assert themselves. Keep digging: Why does *that* motivation speak to you? Maybe it stems from your deeply held belief that we all have the right and the requirement to forge our own life path and not be intimidated or frightened or bullied away from it. *Now* we've dug down to the source—*that's* what drives you.

Let's try the same excavation process again, this time with the last motivation above—that you want to change the world. Why with a book? Perhaps you've been profoundly affected or changed by a book yourself and you realize the power of the written word to reach people on the deepest levels, and a book that might become a bestseller is a powerful way to reach lots of them. What do you want to change about the world? Maybe you want to help people realize that we're all the same, regardless of race or gender or class. Why is that message important to you? Perhaps you have a foundational belief in fairness and equality—*that's* what drives you.

I think of defining what drives your character like digging a well—you can't make a shallow hole in the ground and expect to hit a spring; you have to keep excavating deeper, under the topsoil, under the subsoil, under the loam and sand and gravel and clay till you finally hit the source.

What drives your character should be clear early in the story, even though it may evolve. A character who strives for nothing, who passively accepts her situation, doesn't engage readers for long. Harry Potter is initially driven by the longing to be seen and appreciated, to matter; Celie writes letters to God in the desperate hope of finding some caring ear. Even in characters who begin seemingly content or accepting, like Frodo, we must see some inkling of a longing for more: Frodo actually dreams of exciting adventure beyond the Shire, like his cousin Bilbo Baggins, even though he deeply loves his community—and it's both these drives that will factor into his journey: his willingness to take the ring into parts unknown in order to save and preserve his beloved Shire.

The character's *goal* may evolve along the journey of the story: Harry very quickly wants to go to Hogwarts, and then his goals shift throughout the story with each new situation he faces; Celie begins to long for (and seek) a life, voice, and love of her own; Frodo must take the ring to Mount Doom. Or it may not: Gatsby wants Daisy; Captain Ahab wants that damned whale. And immediate goals may change while the ultimate goal remains constant, as with Harry Potter, whose über-goal in the series becomes defeating Voldemort even as he faces more immediate goals on the path to that destination. But what lies underneath each goal and a character's immediate motivation to achieve it—in other words, what is *driving* your character—should be clearly defined and evident from very early in the story.

WHAT'S IN HER WAY?

At this stage, when we're assessing the foundation of your character and how effectively he is conveyed on the page, this question isn't necessarily about the story antagonist. For now we're looking just at why your character is where he is right now, at the beginning of his arc. What's holding him back from the journey of *this* story that he needs to go on? Harry Potter is treated like a third-class citizen in his aunt and uncle's house; Celie is abused by her father; Frodo is happy in the Shire in his nice, comfortable home.

But as we did with what drives your character, we want to dig deeper and see where this internal obstacle stems from. You may have heard this referred to as a character's fatal flaw or her wound or her misbelief, or the ghost, or the lie your character believes, but all share a basic idea: At some point your protagonist(s) formed an incorrect or maladaptive idea or behavior to "survive" in the world, often as a result of some shortcoming or trauma or formative event, and it's this maladaptation that directly causes or impacts the journey she takes in the story. Harry Potter has never known love and has little confidence in himself. Celie is too numb and disenfranchised to dream of or think she can expect better than her current situation. Frodo relishes creature comforts and simple pleasures, like friends and food, that keep him contentedly stuck.

Once you determine that you've built a challenge or flaw into your main character(s), consider how it manifests: Creating or mentioning a character's wound without showing its impact on his life is just lip service and doesn't resonate with the reader. It's not enough to say a character had an abusive or neglectful mother; we must see how that has manifested in who she has become when we join her in the course of this story: Perhaps she has come to close herself off to other people and relationships, or always overcompensates to be the "good girl" and earn people's regard, or in turn abuses her own daughter, etc. And this flaw must be unavoidably revealed and confronted during—and/or cause— the events of the story.

In Angie Thomas's bestseller *The Hate U Give*, for instance, when we meet sixteen-year-old protagonist Starr she has learned to bifurcate her life to fit into her two distinct identities: the street-savvy version of herself in her inner-city black neighborhood, and the carefully curated face she presents at her exclusive, mostly white high school. But when her unarmed best friend Khalil is shot by police in front of her, Starr must wrestle with whether to testify as a witness in the high-profile trial, bringing her two separate worlds into a direct collision…and ultimately determining whether she can integrate them.

So what is your protagonist's Achilles' heel, or the misconception or internal conflict that is intrinsically related to the journey she travels? What lesson must he learn from the events of the story; what mistaken conception will she reevaluate; what flaw is brought to light (which the character either addresses or is vanquished by) as a direct result of the events of the story? That's what's really standing in his way—it's what has created the situation your character is in when we meet him, and what will underlie all his challenges and obstacles as he travels the path of the story.

If you found you couldn't answer these three foundational questions about your main characters clearly and specifically, you may need to do a bit more development before diving into editing or revisions—there are plenty of wonderful resources for doing that, some of which I've listed in the Resources section of my website (www.foxprinteditorial. com). If you already have considered and developed these answers, the next step is to find out whether you've conveyed them clearly and effectively on the page.

✓ How to Find It, How to Fix It

This chapter, like a handful of others, combines the "How to Find It" and "How to Fix It" sections, because evaluating and developing character are too intrinsically connected to try to parse them apart: finding it often is fixing it.

Starting with the foundational questions above, for each one ask yourself, "How does the reader know the answers?" In other words, where on the page have you shown these character elements to us?

That doesn't just mean where have you said it—stated outright that your character works at an ad agency, for instance, or was brought up on a ranch, or is selfish. Those are merely facts, and facts don't create character; clarity, specificity and depth, and immediacy do. For each key character trait you want readers to understand, ask yourself three questions:

- Is it clear?
- Is it specific?
- Is it vivid?

IS IT CLEAR?

This is step one in evaluating how well you've conveyed character: In other words, did you do the work of character building and put the information on the page? When evaluating this in your own work it's easiest to start with the basics of the characters' situation and then circle in: For instance, say your protagonist is an ad executive—where and how does the reader know that? Or he's from Billings, Montana, and grew up on a dude ranch—where in the manuscript would a reader glean that info? Or he feels stifled at his corporate job—where have you shown or told us that, whether directly or indirectly?

Now look a little deeper, to their key character traits. How does the reader see on the page what you see in your head? If your protagonist is selfish, what indicates that to someone "meeting" her on the page for the first time? Or how would readers pick up on the fact that a character feels intrinsically unworthy, or is desperately lonely, or believes life is just suffering to be borne?

To evaluate this in your own story, watch for where you're making **assumptions**: For instance, let's say your protagonist is a disheartened single mother who dreams of a better life. Perhaps in an early scene you set out to establish her unhappy situation by showing her grocery shopping, with her kids throwing a tantrum, and she's near tears, and thus you feel you've shown she's frustrated and demoralized. But what readers actually take from that may be simply that she or her kids are having an unusually bad day. What makes us understand this is her overall situation? It could be as simple as her thinking, "Why couldn't she ever do even the simplest tasks without someone having a major meltdown?" Or maybe an older woman walks by and says sympathetically, "Bad day?"

and our protag mutters, "Bad life," sending the woman scurrying off with a frown. Or maybe the protagonist says to her kids, "I told you I'd start leaving you in the car if you can't behave!" Notice that these are all small, subtle adds, but they clearly convey to the reader the nuance of what you mean—they make it clear.

The key as you're evaluating whether you've shown what you meant to show on the page is to try to remain as much in editor brain as possible—as soon as you slip back into writer brain it becomes exponentially harder to see what's actually on the page because the creator in you defaults to the fill-in-the-blanks mind-set. It's similar to why we can't see ourselves clearly and objectively, the way others do; we're looking through a lens of our vulnerabilities, fears, insecurities—products of the decades of the "backstory" of our lives that only we know. And just as so many of the difficulties we face in relationships and life result from assuming others understand what we really mean and how we really feel, characters who seem flat, underdeveloped, or unrealistic often result from authors making the false assumption that readers understand what's going on inside the characters, even if they haven't shown it.

Start evaluating how well you've conveyed character right after your initial cold read, where you simply read as a reader. What jumped out at you about the characters as you read? Jot down any specifics you can remember that evoked a sense of who these people are—whether it's a scene of your ad exec protagonist working on a prime campaign in his office, or your selfish heroine leaving her sister collapsed by the side of the street when she twists an ankle in a marathon they were running together because she is determined to make her best time, or your Montana boy who likens his success with a woman to lassoing his first steer. Try not to fill in all the rich details you know in your head—simply focus on what concrete specifics jumped out at you from your first objective read that conveyed to you the character traits and attributes you wanted to convey.

As you go back into the manuscript for your first edit pass, keep that same evaluating eye out. Where and how do you convey significant information about your characters? It can help to briefly note where you see on the page anything that creates a sense of character—this might be a line of dialogue, a specific reaction to a situation, an action, exposition about the character, etc.—and what you meant it to convey.

For example, when a wife grasps her husband's hand on his way out the door and soulfully tells him, "I love you," that might show that she's a very loving and demonstrative person, or that she's insecure and desperate for reassurance, or that she fears she's losing him and is trying to hold on. The husband's reaction is another place to note character—does he return the pressure, cup her face, and echo the sentiment? Extricate his hand and grunt? Do tears fill his eyes as he says, "I love you too" through a constricted throat? Or does he not react at all? What was your intention with that moment? Keep it simple: Just note the action or description and what it's meant to show about your character—for example, "Wife goodbye, page 45: feeling insecure; husband indifferent."

You can create this list in another document or use Track Changes to insert it right into the manuscript, or both. A separate list of the traits you spotted allows you to determine whether you left out key character traits altogether, but using Track Changes serves as a series of clear signposts for taking the next steps in evaluating how well you've conveyed character: checking for specificity and depth.

IS IT SPECIFIC?

Let's say I want to describe to you a painting. If I say, "It's an impressionist water landscape," yes, that's a factual description, but is it real to you, tangible, visual? You may be imagining such a painting, but you're filling in all the blanks and it may or may not be anything like what I intended to convey. If tell you it depicts a water landscape with a bridge, your mental image may sharpen, but you're still making a lot of assumptions that I may or may not be describing: Is this a beach scene, or a lake or creek or river? Is the water calm or choppy, muddy or clear, wide or narrow? What portion of it are we seeing, what view? A huge bridge, like the Golden Gate or the Brooklyn? A covered bridge? Even if I say it's a Monet water lily painting, that helps sharpen the image, but it's still not very specific—Monet painted 250 of those, and they vary considerably in color, style, and scene; you might picture any one of them, rather than the one I'm trying to describe.

If I want this painting to be real and vivid and visual to you, I have to get pretty granular: "This oil painting shows a small arched Japanese footbridge stretched over a still pond papered with water lilies and bracketed by green thickets of reeds, painted in the loose, spontaneous brushstrokes of the impressionist style in vivid shades of royal blue and kelly green with pops of yellow and pink." Now you may start to "see" what I'm describing in detail, even if you don't know Monet's *Water Lily Pond #2* painting. This is the kind of specificity and depth creating fully fleshed characters requires.

Let's go back to our discouraged single-mom protagonist dreaming of a better life. Have you presented this description in specific, concrete terms?

- What has beaten her down, and why?
- What does "a better life" mean to her, specifically?
- What does she think keeps her from getting it?
- What *actually* keeps her from getting it, or what fear, wound, or misapprehension makes her think she can't or makes that situation true?

Watch for where you're **vague or generalized**—for instance, you may show (or tell) readers that your single-mother protagonist is frustrated or feels unhappy with her life situation, but we may not understand what that looks like in practice, what that specifically means to her. Is it a total lack of free time? The fact that she hasn't had a shower in a week? That she can't date? That she hates the tiny apartment that is all she can afford for her family? That she can't stand having someone tugging on her or calling "Mommy" all the time, or having to think of someone else first every single moment of every single day? Or just that she had other dreams for herself that she fears she may never achieve now?

What are those dreams, exactly—what does the "better life" she imagines look like? Is she living in a mansion eating bonbons while the nannies take care of her kids? Living in a house of her own with a picket fence and a dog for the kids? Performing on Broadway? Going out dancing, a different man on her arm every night, kid-free?

Why does she feel she can't have that, exactly—because of the dead-end job that is all she's qualified for, and working to support her kids keeps her from training for something better? Because she can't afford it? Because of her no-good ex who left her on her own with the kids? And what's underneath *that*, exactly—other people have accomplished their goals with kids. What's holding her back? Maybe she's afraid she'll be unable to properly care for/support her kids if she goes back to school or pursues a career, or that she'll fail, or that people will think she's a bad mother. And what core fear or wound or misbelief is underneath *that*? Perhaps she thinks she's stupid, or not good enough, or it's selfish to want something for herself, or she puts more stock in what other people think than in what she feels.

Each one of these specific details colors readers' impressions of her and her situation in a different way, and lacing in those concretes paints a much clearer, fuller picture. As the creator you may have all these ideas and specifics in your head as you're writing, but comb your manuscript for whether, where, and how you've conveyed those concrete details to the reader—and if you don't find them, dig down into the character and pave those details in.

IS IT VIVID?

Even if you've thoroughly fleshed out your characters and infused your story with all the right specificity and detail, they may still not spring to life on the page. Your characters are the vehicle in which readers ride through the story; we experience it directly only insofar as they experience it and share it with us. We want to live inside their heads, behind their eyes, which means letting readers deep into your characters' actions, reactions, motivations, emotions, beliefs, thoughts, etc. As an author you have to pull back the curtain and invite readers behind the public carapace we've all developed over our deepest and truest selves, intimately into your character's psyche. If we aren't inside the character's head we aren't part of the story—we're on the outside looking in, just distant observers safely removed from the action, and it doesn't have a deep impact on us.

Watch for where you're **distant or removed**, rather than immediate and visceral. Think of it this way: Would you rather watch someone's vacation slide show as they narrate all that they did? Or be on that vacation and experience it? The latter is what great fiction does for us—puts us there with the characters, lets us live the scenes through their eyes, in their heads.

That's not to say we want big chunks of inner monologue or navel gazing. We just need a glimpse of what's going on inside the protags, how they are interpreting things, processing them, what impact events have on them, what it makes them feel or think in response, what they decide to do next. If the reader isn't privy to their innermost thoughts, feelings, reactions, then we see the physical movements, hear the words, but it's as if we're in a "long shot" in a movie, far away, rather than in close-up, where we see the minutiae that tells us what's going on inside and between characters.

Giving us that visceral, vivid portrayal of your characters means mining and revealing their actions, reactions, motivations, emotions, beliefs, and thoughts—even in an objective point of view (more on this in the Point of View chapter). I don't mean you have to painstakingly delineate every internal monologue they have; just let us get a sense of who they are, how events strike them, why they do what they do, how they feel and react when something bad or good happens. Let us see the dynamics between characters, their interactions—all the rich undercurrents of a scene that happen underneath the surface events and action: the expressions, glances, pauses, tones, body language, the things they say—and don't say—and all that it means. Let us in—meaning let us into the characters' direct experience and perspective.

Are you showing us the characters' behavior and reactions, or just describing them? Give the reader a sense of immediacy, a "you are there" feeling, by letting us experience the scene as the characters do, instead of simply telling us about it. Dramatizing important scenes directly rather than summarizing the action will bring the story to life more fully. Rather than summing up or skimming through character interactions, slowing down and putting us directly in the scenes will amp up our involvement, the stakes, and our investment. Let us witness directly how your characters talk to each other, what they say (and don't say), the undercurrents and subtexts, whether they ever really connect or always talk superficially, whether they're warm and vulnerable with each other and show their true feelings, or are short and prickly and guarded, etc. Be intimate and immediate; show more and summarize less.

Just like an iceberg, most of our communication with others occurs below the surface level of the words we say. Think about a fraught exchange you've had with your spouse, your kids, your parents. Yes, the words matter, but what's really going on is under the surface—what you're thinking and feeling as your exchange goes on; your reactions; your physiological responses; what you get from the other person, their expressions, gestures, body language, tone, volume—all tells you so much more, creates the "vibe" between you, suggests what they may be thinking and feeling. Think about the pauses and silences that are anything but empty—they may be filled with self-recrimination, or angry thoughts, or tension as you wait for the other person to answer you or flail for your own answer. You may be glaring at each other or avoiding each other's stares; moving apart or leaning together; your jaw may be clenched, giving you a headache, or you may feel bonelessly relaxed.

I call this layer of interaction that's deeper and more revealing than dialogue the nonverbals: facial expressions, body language, tone and volume, gesture, weighted silences, eye contact, etc. If you want to see how crucial they are in character dynamics, try closing your eyes during a high-stakes or high-conflict scene in a movie or TV show and see how much you're left wondering about: the full depth of what's actually passing between the characters, what they're feeling, how they're reacting. Now watch the same scene with your eyes open but the sound turned off and see how much clearer the underlying dynamics of the scene are with *only* those nonverbals, no words. Great scenes offer both, but authors often neglect the intangibles. Offer us your characters' inner landscape to build depth and let readers really come to know and understand them; dig deeper and show us the whole dynamic, all these nonverbals and undercurrents and subtexts. Use these in addition to the characters' words and actions not simply to convey information at face value, but to reveal and develop who they are and their arc, and push the story forward.

Let's say our single mom is about to walk into the doctor's office to hear a diagnosis about one of her children. You could simply convey the information through the dialogue, but then you lose all the rich depth and resonance you could create for readers, and you miss the chance to further the story, raise stakes, and develop the characters and plot.

For example, what is your POV character feeling as she walks in— are her hands icy cold, her heart beating too fast? How does the doctor look, sound? What's his tone? Expression? Body language? Does he seem in a hurry for her to leave—to discharge his info and go? Or is he wearing a compassionate expression and leaning back in his chair as if he has all the time in the world for her? Or both—a strange dichotomy? And how does that impact the protag's feelings, her reactions?

As the doctor begins to speak and confirms her worst fears, does she make an involuntary noise in her throat, her stomach drop to the floor? Does she worry she may throw up, fighting the rising nausea because she's determined to be strong, or to hear the doctor out fully for her child's sake? Does she feel dizzy, unable to think about the implications? How does the doctor react to her reactions? Does he pick up on her upset? Does it concern him or not faze him at all?

You don't have to fill in *all* these blanks in a scene, but showing more of the rich subtext and undercurrents not only conveys info beyond just the dialogue and basic action, but begins to reveal something of these characters and their relationship, shows how high the stakes are, creates layers of tension—all while moving the story forward and painting a much fuller picture that involves the reader viscerally. You can do this with every single scene—not necessarily to this point, of course, as this is likely a key emotional scene, but adding more depth, more layers, and more dimension to draw the reader in viscerally and directly throughout.

And just because we may be focused on one topic of conversation or action or have one primary thing on our minds, even if we're all alone other reactions and feelings generally worm their way in. You can weave in these layers throughout as well. It raises stakes and tension still further, for instance, if as she learns her child's diagnosis the woman's mind instantly flitters to what these expenses mean for her already strained budget, or how she'll pay for it, or how she can take time off work to care for her child. She may remember a brief flash of the day her child was born and how happy she felt, or the way she's already watched her child suffering in pain and now knows how much worse it's going to get. She might think in fury of her ex who left them all behind, and resent that he's off living a carefree life while she and her child will struggle with this. All these other elements can color the scene even more, making it richer, deeper, more complex—and thus more interesting to the reader.

Even if your character isn't demonstrative, or is suppressing his full range of emotions, or is a taciturn or controlled person, you can still let us into his inner life—the visceral reactions, feelings, thoughts that reveal the full person inside, even if he doesn't show any of it. Even if your writing style is lean, spare, and subtle, you can let us in. Inner life isn't about melodrama or histrionics; it's about inviting the reader behind the scrim your character presents to others; we get to go "backstage" and see what's actually going on. We experience a story through the character's *direct visceral experience*. Dive deep and let us see that.

Other key character questions

DO YOUR CHARACTERS EXIST IN THE WORLD?

Characters can't exist in a vacuum. We need an understanding of how they move about in the world, where they came from, who and what surrounds them, what their daily life consists of, what relationships they have and what they're like. Characters are a tapestry of threads that make up the full picture; weaving in only a few colors leaves out the texture and layers that make them spring fully to life.

Often authors will know the facts about their characters—"she's a free-spirited artist who never wanted to be a wife or mother and leaves her family to pursue her art"—but we don't see the full picture of who they are on the page. Remember, facts are not character. To make sure you're conveying your character three-dimensionally, look for whether and where you fill in **concretes and context**.

As the story unfolds and we walk this path with your protagonist, we need specifics about his life, rather than generalities, and we need a sense of the full person he is, not just the part of him that directly pertains to the arc that we focused on in the one-line summary earlier in the chapter when we were looking at the essence of who your character is relative to the central story. Earlier I used myself as an example, and mentioned a few elements of my life that weren't germane to the story of an editor working on a long-dreamed-of editing book. But as a story develops and the characters take shape in the world you *do* bring in that kind of context and detail: my dogs, my upbringing, my past career as an actor may all work their way into my story at some point.

For instance, with our above character—the free-spirited artist who takes off to pursue her artistic career—in what way is she free-spirited, exactly? Do you mean that she rejects accepted societal strictures, that she follows her heart or gut in all decisions, or that she ruthlessly tramples on other people's feelings in the name of being true to herself? How does that manifest? For instance, growing up did she insist on wearing a feathered tutu and a baseball cap to school every day? Or did she miss her sister's important soccer championship because she got lost in working on an art piece? Or does she live in a commune and sell hemp soap for a living? Was she always a bit outside the norm? With everyone and in every aspect of her life, or just in certain areas? If she became free-spirited over the years, when did it start, and what touched it off? What was her upbringing like? Was she raised by a narcissist, for instance—or the opposite, parents who let their worlds revolve around her to the detriment of their own evolution? What was the family dynamic like?

How does she feel about her art? What does it mean to her, or what need does it fill? How did being a wife and mom not fill that need, or keep it from being filled? What did that look like in her life as a wife and mother? How does she feel after she leaves her family? Does she miss them? Think about them? Feel guilty? Freed? All of this together? How does that manifest—is she unable to sleep at night, thinking about the way her daughter looked the day she walked out, wondering what she looks like now, what she's like, what she's doing? Or does she throw herself into all the things she couldn't do then—late nights, partying, painting at all hours—and shudder at the thought of how caged she once was, or feel a rush of gratitude for being able to pursue these things, or numb herself out with drugs and alcohol and faceless lovers?

These are just some of the types of questions you can ask yourself as you look for whether your characters are fully faceted and real. You won't necessarily answer them directly and then plop the info into the story in big chunks of pace-killing exposition or info dump, but rather, once you've done the full, rich work of character development, the answers will serve as bread crumbs you drop throughout the story, little clues and context you lace in as you move the story forward that give a clear, concrete, visceral sense of who your character is in the world.

Here's an example of how you might do that: To show what her life is/was like before she rededicates herself to her art, perhaps we see this woman trying to make a complicated dinner before her husband gets home with his boss, while her two-year-old watches a blaring TV. The husband calls and says they're leaving the office now, and to make sure she looks nice "for a change" or "not like you don't own a mirror." Maybe she snaps at him, or maybe she meekly agrees, or maybe she pastes a big smile on her face and says, "See you soon—love you!" and then the moment she hangs up we see the expression fall away.

For just a moment the woman loses herself in the way the rich red-orange of the paprika looks against the snowy white flour when she dumps it in, how it mingles into the softest of peach colors, and she's overtaken by the memory of the thick scent of paint squeezed from tubes, the visceral pleasure of swabbing a brush in the glistening swirls, and the satisfaction of mixing burnt umber and raw sienna to create just the perfect flesh tone.

And then there's a sharp clatter and her toddler screams, the woman jumps, startled, and flour and paprika explode across the kitchen as she turns to see her child has fallen from her booster seat, red-faced and wailing with a cut on her forehead, minutes before her husband and his boss are due to arrive. We see her reaction—a tide of panic, a rush of guilt and shame; perhaps she feels inadequate or like a failure as a mother as she bandages the wound, or she's stricken with unbearable remorse for letting her baby get hurt. Perhaps later, as she scrubs away the mess on hands and knees like a drudge, tears fill her eyes as she remembers the wild, carefree girl she used to be in her artist's studio, dreaming of Paris.

You could simply sum up this character's backstory in a few lines inserted into the story—she left her husband and family for her art—but look how vividly we've conveyed a great deal about her and her situation simply by instead briefly showing her in the context of that external life and exploring her related inner life. This scene might appear as a flash of memory she has within whatever the present-day story is, or come out in context of a conversation with another character about her past, or even serve as a flashback chapter or prologue (we'll talk more later about the dreaded prologue), but notice how in this example even as we fill in backstory we're moving the story dynamically forward: There is action; there's urgency (getting dinner ready before the husband gets home), high stakes (his boss will be with him), conflict (the call with her husband), an obstacle (her toddler's accident, the mess). And we're also gaining deep and detailed insight into who this woman is through the way she reacts to her husband's attitude, both to him and about him; through her nostalgia for who she once was in her daydream into her old artistic life; through the constitutional creativity in her in the way she makes art out of something as pedestrian as flour and spices; through her feelings about her present situation in her reactions to her husband, the mini-crisis, her assessment of her life as it is. In a relatively brief and minor scene we've taken the roughed-out form of this character—the basic facts—and layered in so many brushstrokes of color in the portrait of who she is that fill her in and add dimension and detail and bring her to life.

This applies equally to characters who are perfectly happy or at least at a tolerable or content status quo overall at their point A, before some plot event occurs to shake them out of their comfort zone. For instance, let's say you open your story with your protagonist on his way home from a business trip where he signed the company's biggest client ever, catching a flight just in time to make it home for his engagement party that night.

Readers still need context and clarity for the character to come to life: What's his business, and what does it mean to him? Does he love his job or hate it? Is he good at it or does he struggle? Is he "the closer" who always brings in the big clients, or is this big deal an anomaly? Does he define himself by work success, or is it just a paycheck to let him live the life he wants? Did he earn this sale, or was it just luck? Was anything riding on this deal—a promotion, a commission he desperately needed, or his entire job? Is his fiancée supportive of his work, or is she indifferent to it? Is he looking forward to the engagement party, or feeling drained at having to be "on" all night after being "on" for days wooing the client? Did they plan the party together, or is this her idea and he hates having to make a big deal of it? Maybe he's dreading it because she invited dozens of her friends, and outside of business associates he had no one to invite? Or maybe her family disapproves of him and he's eager to get there with news of this deal to show them his worth. Or maybe he can't wait to show this woman off at the party and lock it down. Again, there are dozens of questions like this you can ask yourself to see whether you've paved in concretes and context to clearly, viscerally show readers who he is and offer a full and vivid picture of his life.

Let us see not just a sketch of who your characters are, but the rich tapestry of them as a whole person: who and what shaped them, what their lives are like outside just the central plot line, their personal goals, dreams, longings, challenges, fears, preoccupations, beliefs, history. Every one of us is so complex—if you can put more of that dimension and those kinds of specifics on the page, you make that fully fleshed character in your head just as real to us too, and he comes to life for us.

IS YOUR CHARACTER CONSISTENT?

Once you've established who your characters are—where they come from, how they were raised, what they believe, their socioeconomic situation, their experiences, etc.—watch for **consistency** and **cohesion**. Do they think, act, react, behave, observe, speak, etc., in ways that are true to their background, the experiences they've had, their personality—innate and acquired—their particular demons and foibles?

A wallflower isn't suddenly going to go ask the cutest boy at the prom out onto the dance floor—unless that's a deliberate choice she's making for a specific reason, ideally directly related to her arc: Maybe she's decided fortune favors the brave and she girds her metaphorical loins and approaches the boy she's had a crush on, or maybe her friends pressure her into it, or she's moving the next day and figures what does she have to lose? But it needs to be a choice the author makes to serve the story and the character arc. A research scientist isn't going to speak in substandard English—"I ain't got no idea"—unless that's a deliberate character choice you make for a specific reason: He's making fun of a character he thinks is beneath him, for instance, or when he's drunk his carefully learned persona slips and reveals his rural Deep South roots.

Watch the vocabulary you use, even outside of a character's dialogue or direct thought. In deep point of view every bit of narrative in that character's POV section is filtered through his perspective, so your descriptions and exposition should also reflect that through word choice, imagery, phrasings. The artist character might use more descriptive, figurative language even in her narrative sections; our research scientist would likely be more precise and literal—again, unless that's a specific choice you make to reveal something intrinsic about the character: Maybe part of your artist's arc is that she's constantly underestimated by people who dismiss her as a flaky creative and ignore her considerable intellect, so she whips out those five-dollar words to keep people off balance; maybe part of the research scientist's journey is that she hides a thwarted poet's soul. Be conscious of the choices you make for your characters and use them purposefully.

Different characters see the world differently too—the artist might see art in paprika and flour; the research scientist might wonder if this paprika originated from Mexico or Hungary, or what the capsaicin content is—or she might not pay attention to it at all as she focuses on exact measurements to get the recipe just right. The artist might describe a bird overhead as a brushstroke of Payne's gray against a wash of blue, while the research scientist might glance up and register the migratory flight of a slate-colored junco.

Characters' background and beliefs inform their thoughts, actions, and feelings. Your staunchly traditional social worker is likely to react differently to a gay couple looking to adopt than he would to a heterosexual one—unless that's a deliberate choice you make to illustrate a specific aspect of or change in your character. A deeply spiritual or religious character might not casually say "Oh, my God." Your job is to know your characters so fully and deeply that you understand how their makeup affects every nuance of the way they engage in and react to the world, and to show readers that on the page.

ARE YOUR CHARACTERS MULTIFACETED?

Remember the old melodrama shtick where a bow is used to represent a hero, a bad guy, and a damsel in distress? "You must pay the rent!" says the villain, the bow denoting his mustache (which clearly indicates how evil he is); "I can't pay the rent!" wails the helpless damsel with the bow in her hair. "I'll pay the rent!" cries the hero, sailing in to save the day with his snazzy bow tie. These archetypes are so broadly and simplistically drawn they are comical—but you may be surprised how often these black-and-white stereotypes can creep into your own writing without your realizing it.

And they're dull. Deadly dull.

Good and bad, the most fascinating, memorable characters have layers and lots of shades of gray. Ask yourself whether each main character has flaws and shortcomings as well as strengths, and look for where you've introduced **contrasts** and **ambiguity**.

Human nature is fascinating to us precisely because of its facets—we are good and evil, kind and cruel, brave and cowardly, and every other dichotomy you can think of. We are vast and contain multitudes! Characters who don't display this full range of emotion and attributes come across as flat, unidimensional—and worse, unrealistic. With protagonists this is often called "Mary Sue syndrome"—an idealized character who is entirely good with no discernible flaws. We don't recognize ourselves in characters like that.

It's that constant internal tension between these opposing forces that creates so much wonderful narrative tension. Think of Iron Man. Tony Stark is genius-level smart; he wants to do the right thing and defeat bad guys; he's resourceful and, in his Iron Man suit, unnaturally strong. But he's also arrogant, a womanizer, not a team player, etc. Yes, he's a good guy, but he's no saint. Gillian Flynn grew a publishing phenomenon out of her two complex, deeply flawed, fascinatingly layered protagonists in *Gone Girl*.

Even authors who take care to give complicated facets and layers to their "good guys" may fall into the common trap of creating "bad guys" who are unremittingly bad. But the same guidelines that govern heroes also go for villains: The best, most memorable ones are dense stews of good and evil—evil (as it's perceived by the protagonist) just happens to be the predominant flavor.

Khan from *Star Trek* and Loki from the *Avengers/Thor* are delicious villains: They are bad, yes, and you want the good guy to defeat them, but they also have their good qualities, and in some ways you can understand why they act as they do—even sympathize. Khan's entire race was nearly wiped out by the Federation, and he's trying to protect the few who are left; he is a strong, brave, protective leader of his people. Loki has been passed over and treated like a second-class citizen by his father all his life, despite his real intelligence and gifts and his desperate craving for Odin's approval and love; and Loki even helps the "good guys" sometimes, though at other times he's trying to destroy them. This is wonderful, tasty ambiguity, and it's what makes characters like these so unforgettable—and popular. Why did people love Hannibal Lecter, the most hideous of villains? He was also intelligent, hilarious, cultured, and even likable in some ways. Juicy stuff.

Villains never think they are villains—they feel justified in their actions based on their own backstory. They may be no less a villain, but there's a certain amount of humanity there, gray area—ideally we can relate to them on some level. That's infinitely more powerful than a one-dimensional, mustache-twirling bad guy. And "heroes" are just ordinary people trying to make the right choices—with all the foibles, flaws, and failings each of us carries inside us.

Black-and-white is boring for readers, and it's not realistic. We're complicated—no one is all good or all bad. Good people may cheat on their wives. Horrible people may have children they love and take wonderful care of—and most of us are somewhere in the middle, a mix of good and bad, hopefully trying to lean more toward the good. That's where compelling characters reside, in that gray area.

WHY SHOULD THE READER CARE?

Authors often make the mistake of assuming that if they have an interesting enough setup and plot, readers will automatically be invested. But we won't unless we care about the characters and what happens to them. Your job is to show us—fairly quickly—why we should, to make your characters **engaging** and **relatable**.

Your characters don't have to be likable, but it's one way to invest readers in them. That doesn't mean making them uniformly good—it means there's something inherently appealing to us about who they are: whether their sense of humor, sincerity, kindness or goodness, love or passion for something or someone, etc.

If you're going for likability, you might check whether you have inadvertently set up a character to be *un*likable by giving him traits that may distance a reader, even if you have created other sympathetic or likable qualities in him. Overcoming these flaws can of course be part of the protag's journey, but there are some traits readers often find hard to forgive, such as casual thoughtlessness or cruelty (especially to those weaker or in a "punch down" position: animals, children, servers, clerks); abuse; extreme narcissism or obliviousness of others' feelings and desires; self-indulgence, self-pity, or victimization without any effort or at least desire to be strong. Weakness in and of itself isn't a negative—in fact it can make a character greatly sympathetic. But we have to see her fighting, trying, striving—or at least aware of her inability to be strong at that moment for some reason, like depression or grief (or handcuffs).

But as the success of shows like *Breaking Bad*, *House of Cards*, and *The Americans* demonstrate (or stories like *Lolita*, *American Psycho*, or even *Catcher in the Rye*), protagonists don't have to be likable to engage us as readers. You can still invest the reader in them as long as we have something to root for—like the possibility or hope of redemption (*Leaving Las Vegas*) or comeuppance (*Gone Girl*), or the character's dedication to a righteous or relatable cause like seeking justice, righting a wrong, solving a mystery, even seeking vengeance for a grave wrong (*The Girl on the Train*). Or perhaps the character represents the lesser of two evils in the story (like Dexter), or we can admire their intelligence or cleverness (Ignatius J. Reilly in *A Confederacy of Dunces*) or their fierce and resourceful determination to pursue even an unadmirable goal (like Francis Underwood or Michael Corleone), or their sheer charisma (like Hannibal Lecter, or the mesmerizing titular sociopath in Victoria Helen Stone's Jane Doe series). These are powerful ways to invest readers in a character, whether or not we like him.

Readers will also invest in a character if we feel sympathy or empathy for him—if we can relate to his situation, struggle, challenges, pain. In Khaled Hosseini's *The Kite Runner*, protagonist Amir can be entitled, cruel, dismissive, and resentful of Hassan, the disadvantaged son of his family's caretaker who is raised almost as a brother with the privileged Amir and offers Amir nothing but unconditional love and support—and Amir commits an appalling betrayal of Hassan. Yet we can sympathize (perhaps empathize) with the lack of love Amir feels from the father he idolizes, his feeling that his father loves Hassan more, his inadequacy and pain, and we stay invested in his journey.

Even a "bad" character may invest us if we see him fighting his dark side or demons. For instance, spoiled, self-centered Darcy spends a lot of time in Emily Giffin's *Something Blue* ranting about her former best friend who stole her fiancé, but also realizes her own part in her broken relationships, and the meaning of friendship. Kristin Bell's character in the TV show *The Good Place* begins as a morally reprehensible soul mistakenly sent to heaven, but comes to genuinely want to learn to be a good person.

You can also show your character craving or fighting for something better for herself or others, like Katniss working for a better life for her family and to save her sister Prim in *Hunger Games*, or the father in Cormac McCarthy's *The Road* who will do any terrible thing and make any sacrifice—including his soul—for his son.

Finally, you can hook readers by showing a character willing to give up or actually sacrificing a self-focused goal for someone or something else, or for the greater good, like Cyrano de Bergerac sacrificing his own happiness for his love Roxane's.

IS THE PROTAGONIST THE CAPTAIN
OF HER OWN SHIP?

Remember when the Big, Bad Wolf decided not to eat Little Red Riding Hood and let her run safely back to her family? Or when the alien stayed behind on the Nostromo and Ripley escaped with her life? Or when Jerry Maguire was so happy that Dorothy came to find him and forgive him and they lived happily ever after?

No. You don't, because stories in which the protagonist isn't the engine of his or her own destiny don't impact readers or become classics. Riding Hood is clever enough to notice those big ears and eyes and teeth; Sigourney Weaver kicked that monster's ass; and Jerry Maguire had her at hello.

In the same way that the antagonist must directly or intrinsically cause or worsen what happens to the protagonist, your protagonist must directly affect or engineer his own destiny. If he doesn't he isn't the hero; he's a passenger in the story. Look for where your hero has **agency** and **directly drives the story**.

Even experienced authors can inadvertently slip into the trap of having a protagonist who's a passenger, rather than the captain of the ship—for example with a main character who lacks motivation and drive and passively reacts as story events happen *to* her or around her; or a story with fabulous secondary characters who wind up actually driving the story action; or with a brilliantly conceived, action-filled plot where the protagonist isn't a direct acting force affecting the outcome.

Even if the protagonist's journey involves discovering his strength or drive, it's the hero (it's right there in the name) who must be the one acting (in other words, *being active*...again, right there in the name) to effect and affect the events of the story, and of his own destiny. We read to watch a protagonist take the wheel and get where he wants to go—not passively sit back and let others steer his ship. Regardless of how many car chases, explosions, or grand romantic moments you create, a hero who isn't working to claim his own destiny is dull and unengaging, and it's a very tough sell to get readers to stay invested.

One reason readers and movie audiences loved *The Martian*, largely a single-character, single-setting book and movie, was that it was almost entirely a story about a protagonist's endlessly creative, ferociously determined efforts to forge his own fate. A character must actively be striving for something, and she must have agency—meaning, as Merriam-Webster defines it (emphasis mine), "the capacity, condition, or state *of acting or of exerting power*; a person or thing through which power is exerted or *an end is achieved*."

That's not to say every protag must be a get-'er-done Type A hero. You can have a damsel (or a dude) in distress or even stuck in place as long as we see them at least *trying* to save themselves, or with a burning, fierce desire to change their situation, like stodgy Walter Mitty who dreams of wild adventure; or indecisive Hamlet who burns to take action; or frustrated wife and mother Nora in Ibsen's *A Doll's House* who aches for something more than domesticity.

But there's a reason there's no genre for "Boy meets girl; boy loses girl; boy mopes around till girl comes back and they live happily ever after." A character who merely passively awaits his fate is someone we may pity, but likely won't empathize with, and empathy is what keeps readers hooked. We must root for your protagonist—it's why we read—and we can't do that if she's not carrying her own ball down the field. She has to be the engine of her own story, not a helpless victim or passive freight.

IS EVERY MAIN CHARACTER ESSENTIAL?

This question can be a hard one to examine, especially after you've painstakingly created a story and a cast of players for it, but extraneous characters are like overgrown underbrush in the forest: they slow the path, get in the way, and take up excess energy for the reader to navigate.

Take a look at every single character and make sure each one is essential to that scene, that moment, or the story as a whole. That doesn't mean everyone is a main player; it simply means that if you focus on the checkout girl as the hero buys chewing gum and dedicate a chunk of ink to an exchange between them, it needs to serve the story: whether it reveals something new about our main character, offers information we need, or furthers the plot. Remember the holy grail of storytelling: Every single scene, every single line, everything in your manuscript should move the story forward.

As an example, here are the characters in the first chapters of Dan Brown's *The Da Vinci Code*:

- **The curator**'s death is what sets the rest of the story's events in motion; he is essential. Further, he's carrying a secret he's desperate not to have die with him and leaves it in a code for protagonist **Robert Langdon**, the one man he knows can decipher it.
- **The albino** is the man's killer and one of the story's chief antagonists, and thus intrinsic to the story; in addition, he is a mindlessly devoted acolyte under the orders of the über-antagonist, "**the Teacher**," who also appears in the early chapters.
- Langdon is the protagonist, so obviously he's essential, but he also specializes in religious symbolism and codes, and there are symbols all over the murder scene. Plus his being named by the murder victim means he is compelled to solve the crime to exonerate himself.
- **The concierge** who calls Langdon to tell him he's been summoned by the police inspector allows the author to show a bit of who Langdon is in his first scene, to invest readers, and to convey the stakes and urgency of the inspector's appearance at the hotel. In contrast, Brown then uses Langdon's musing about an anonymous "**hostess**" at a lecture honoring Langdon for his work to fill in backstory and context, but the flashback feels heavy-handed and clumsy, defusing that urgency and stalling pace in this chapter. This character inclusion doesn't serve the story; Brown could have found a more organic way of establishing Langdon's stature and knowledge.
- **The lieutenant** from the French Judicial Police who bangs on Langdon's hotel door to summon Langdon to his captain further ups the stakes and builds anticipation in the reader.
- **Fache**, the captain of the Judicial Police who is awaiting Langdon at the crime scene, is investigating the murder; clearly he's essential. He's also, we later see, a member of a religious society that is tied into this killing. He is driven to protect his society's secret and determined to pin the murder on Langdon, all of which is intrinsic to the plot and drives it forward.

Almost every character plays a key role, and helps propel the story and the plot and/or develop character. Notice that it's the single character who doesn't that winds up stalling story momentum.

It's a worthwhile exercise to list all your main and major supporting characters in this way and determine how each one serves an essential role in the story. If any don't, either excising them or making them intrinsically serve the story will improve pace, heighten stakes, and deepen reader involvement.

Sometimes combining characters can significantly strengthen a story. Bestseller Robert Crais tells a story about one of his early mysteries where he realized in a revision draft that the minor character of the protagonist's secretary could be combined with the character of one of the murderer's victims, thus making the peripheral secretary an intrinsic part of the story and greatly raising stakes on the murder with this personal connection to the main character. Look for whether combining some of your secondary characters might make these minor characters more memorable, real, fleshed-out, and intrinsic.

DOES YOUR CHARACTER CHANGE?

It's not enough to create an interesting protagonist, even if you give her a fascinating backstory and a riveting plot. We must see how a character is *affected* by the events of the story—how she changes and grows throughout it, whether emotionally, mentally, idealistically, philosophically, spiritually, etc. If she doesn't we have no reason to take the journey with her—it's like packing your bags and taking a long plane trip, only to get off and find yourself right back in your hometown where you started. **Your characters must end somewhere different from where they began, and this change must be brought about directly as a result of the story events.** This is the spine of story.

You defined each of your main characters' point A with the three foundational questions—where they are in life when we first meet them. Can you succinctly state their point B—where they are at the end, how they have changed or grown?

As with the character's point A, her point B will usually be both internal and external: The character's situation has tangibly changed, but so has her initial internal misapprehension or obstacle. For instance, our stifled single mom may be enrolled in college, with a new job she loves and a love interest (external), having realized that only through pursuing her own dreams can she set an example for her kids to learn they deserve to follow theirs (internal).

Or maybe only one or the other element has shifted by her point B: Realizing that she deserves more than she's gotten out of life, she's decided nothing will stand in her way and dumped the kids with her mother so she can set out for New York—her external situation changed but her internal one hasn't; she's merely committed to the longings she wasn't acting on at the beginning. Or vice versa: She finally understands that family is what matters most to her, regardless of the cost, and learns to find contentment in the life she has—she's in the same place as point A externally, but her internal perspective has shifted. Each of these examples tells a very different story, but all involve some change in the character's point B from her point A: in other words, the character arc. Check to make sure that by the end you've shifted your character's situation—internal, external, or both.

Consider each of your protagonists this way if you have more than one. How is each one different at the end of the book than at the beginning—in other words, how are they changed by the path we just traveled with them? This is the reason we read. Without a character arc you have a series of events, but no story.

James Bond Never Changes

Remember how I said there are no hard-and-fast "rules" in writing? Invariably when I present character arcs at workshops, someone mentions a bestselling book or hit movie or TV show where the hero doesn't change: James Bond, Sherlock Holmes, Jack Reacher, or a host of other characters who basically are exactly the same person at the end that they were at the beginning, no lessons learned, no worldview shifted.

In certain genres—especially where the focus is on the action, like thriller or mystery—readers will still invest in a story with a static character as a protagonist. Symbologist Robert Langdon in *The Da Vinci Code* is a fascinating solver of puzzles and we do invest in Dan Brown's bestseller because of the sheer suspense the author creates. But the character is whisper-thin; we know little of him beyond this treasure hunt, and care just about that much, but watching him ingeniously solve each clue makes for a great ride and that's what we signed up for.

Although even in these types of stories, modern writers seem to be realizing that showing some character growth and change can raise stakes and increase audience investment—more recent James Bond movies have him wrestling with childhood trauma and tragically lost love, and Sherlock Holmes is having a marvelous renaissance in countless incarnations and genres as writers explore other facets of the iconic character.

Alternatively, you can create a character whose lack of change, or their refusal or inability to do so, is essential to the story in that it brings about the story's consequence: whether it costs him or her something positive or desirable or necessary (*Leaving Las Vegas*); or it results in a negative consequence like failure or death (Captain Ahab); or it's a commentary on human nature (Forrest Gump). Some characters don't significantly change themselves, but they serve to bring about change. For instance, Romeo and Juliet, it could be argued, have the ultimate character journey: from life to death. But fundamentally neither one constitutionally changes by the time they die, and they "fail" to achieve their goal—to be together as they want to—because of the rancor of their families' feud. Yet their suicides do change the other main characters in the story—the members of the Capulet and Montague families—and that shift in their attitudes as a direct result of the teenagers' deaths succeeds in ending the feud, and *that* gives the protagonists' journeys (and thus the story) meaning.

The character arc is also where your protag's internal misapprehension—the thing that stands in his way that we defined earlier—directly comes into play: It's often precisely what he must overcome to successfully achieve his goal. For example, in Tayari Jones's book *An American Marriage*, upscale executive Roy loses all the privileges he has taken for granted when he is imprisoned for a rape he did not commit, but it's this injustice and hardship that force him to reevaluate his casual attitudes toward his own formerly privileged life and his relationships and makes him the man he never would have become otherwise. In *The Kite Runner*, Amir must face his lifelong feelings of inadequacy and shame before he is able to find peace and forgiveness for his betrayal of his best friend. Can you identify in your manuscript whether and how your character's central shortcoming or internal obstacle is intrinsic and essential in the change she undergoes in the story?

WHAT'S WORKING AGAINST YOUR CHARACTER?

Even with beautifully crafted characters, without obstacles for them to contend with your story is simply a series of vignettes. Readers don't invest in a story where interesting people live happily ever after unless we've seen them earn the privilege; conflict is essential.

What's working against your character is different from what we established above as what stands in his way. The latter is the internal obstacle initially keeping your character stuck at their point A at the beginning of the story. Think of what's working against him as the external oppositional people, situations, or forces he encounters on the journey toward his point B. That includes the story antagonist, but it can also include other obstacles that hinder your character's journey; layering in oppositional forces can add dimension to a story, increase juicy narrative conflict, and raise stakes.

In Toni Morrison's *Beloved*, for instance, protagonist Sethe is literally haunted by her past: After she escapes the brutal slave plantation where she was abused, trauma from a horrific act she committed out of desperation is what stands in her way at the beginning of the story in the form of what's keeping her stuck. But her past also becomes what's working against her as her main external antagonist in the form of the young girl they call Beloved who turns up on her doorstep, who Sethe (and many other characters) believes is the incarnated spirit of her dead daughter. And there are also other key oppositional forces in Sethe's journey: the institution of slavery and its legacy; the cruel slave owner she fled from, and her ostracism by her community. Even her initial allies, her youngest daughter and her partner, come to work against her goals—her daughter by wanting to co-opt Beloved's affections for herself, and her partner when he rejects Sethe after learning of her past.

To look for whether you've created strong oppositional forces to work against your character, ask yourself:

- What obstacles present themselves along your protagonist(s)' journey that hinder him from reaching his goals?
- How does each of those forces impede the protag along his arc (his or her journey from point A to point B)?
- Does encountering this obstacle directly further your protagonist along his arc—whether in overcoming it or in failing to overcome it?

Some of these antagonists may be people—as with the character of Beloved, Sethe's youngest daughter, her partner, and the former slave owner—and some may be situations or forces—slavery itself, the community's shunning of Sethe.

Once you've identified those antagonistic forces, examine whether each actually serves as a roadblock in the character's pursuit of her goals. A bad boss may be an unpleasant thing, for instance, but he isn't an antagonist for your story unless we see him directly hindering your protagonist from what she wants in some way: He is actively holding her back from advancing to the position she strives for, or he undermines her in front of a client whose account she desperately needs to sign, or she fears losing her job if she reports him for sexual harassment. Then make sure that facing that roadblock is essential in the character's progression along her arc: the protagonist must find a way to thwart her boss to attain the goals she wants, or through facing his opposition she must discover a new goal that drives her further along her arc.

chapter two

STAKES

I f character is the vehicle in which readers travel along the path of your story, stakes are the engine. **Your characters must want something desperately, and there must be consequences—meaningful ones— if they don't achieve that goal**, no matter your genre (and yes, that includes nonfiction and memoir). If these basic elements aren't strongly established then a character has little to gain or lose, and readers are unlikely to deeply invest in his journey.

Story stakes are high only insofar as you make us care about your characters, and make the characters care about the outcome. Break every other "rule" of storytelling—some of the most extraordinary and original stories smash storytelling convention—but fail to create high stakes and readers will stop turning the pages (or never get hooked in the first place).

When I use the word *stakes* I mean more than what is tangibly at risk for a character. High stakes doesn't mean someone must die, or a character must lose everything, or the world must be in danger of ending. While those are objectively high-stakes events, by themselves that's not what pulls a reader in and makes her care about a story.

I mean it in a broader context: how important something is to the protagonist, how much the character (and thus the reader) cares—a personal interest or involvement, and the more personal and involved, the better. If you want your reader to invest, the character must *want* or *be in danger of losing* something he or she *cares enormously about.*

Human beings are human-being-oriented: meaning that witnessing aliens raining fire upon a city is sad, but it's much more affecting if we see the *faces* of the individual people running from the destruction. More affecting still if we focus on one of those fleeing people stopping to res-cue her small child...and even more personally affecting if that person is known to us and we care about her—if we have a personal connection or investment. It's simply human nature.

Consider a betrayal from a work colleague versus one from the coworker you are secretly dating. Or showing up for a blind date with a stranger versus one with the man you just cut off and flipped off in traffic, or the one you just had a job interview with, or the one who dumped your sister, or the ex you never got over. Each of these choices and motivations changes the stakes—not necessarily what is to be lost or gained but what importance and deeply personal resonance does each choice hold. Each one adds layers, impact, and meaning.

Even with major-stakes world-is-ending stories, when we are really engaged it's because the author has invested us deeply in the specific and intensely personal stakes of his or her protagonist. Although of course we want the world to be saved, it's Will Smith we're really rooting for in the original *Independence Day* (and also in *I Am Legend*...and in *I, Robot, Men in Black, Suicide Squad*—basically if a disaster is coming, you want Will Smith on your side). We care about *his* character and *his* personal stakes, and that becomes the vehicle we ride into the story on, the close-angle lens that focuses the bigger picture of saving the world.

But the same principles also apply to other genres of fiction, where the future of the world may not be at stake, there's not much call for heavy artillery, and stories are often much more intimate.

Some of the most affecting stories are about seemingly minute events: In Julia Claiborne Johnson's powerful *Be Frank with Me*, what's at stake to the protagonist is simply a very unusual boy's happiness. In Graeme Simsion's *The Rosie Project*, the stakes involve just one lonely man's love life. In the film *Priscilla, Queen of the Desert*, all the traveling performers ostensibly have to do is get that RV across the desert to do a drag show—but really it's about one of the characters finally meeting his son. Objectively, big deal, right? But that personal investment creates compelling stakes for the viewer because the film makes us feel how important that goal is *to him*. Your job as the author is to draw us so fully into the protag's subjective experience that we deeply and directly invest in her goals, even if they have little apparent objective value.

These are gross simplifications of each story, and the stakes evolve and rise as each one develops. But why do we invest deeply in these stories despite the objectively modest scale of their stakes?

In each case, it's because *the character profoundly cares about what is at stake*. And the author (or filmmaker) *has made us profoundly care about those characters*. The objective stakes have become highly *sub*jective—and the author has made us care about that subject. And while the explicit desires of each character may be intensely specific, they hit on universal human desires like love, redemption, happiness, belonging, security. It's those universal commonalities that allow us to directly relate to and invest in your character's journey.

Stakes are tightly interconnected with every other element of story. They are the fulcrum on which everything else balances.

Stakes are directly tied to **character**, because we can't care about someone who isn't real to us, to whom we can't relate, with whom we feel no sympathy or empathy. So building three-dimensional, fully realized characters is essential to creating high stakes that will deeply invest readers.

But so is a well-crafted **plot**; exquisitely drawn characters who are simply living out their daily lives with no obstacles or challenges or goals lie flat on the page: They want nothing, they do nothing, and so nothing rides on the outcome of their lives—there is nothing at stake.

Stakes are also closely tied to **motivation** and **goal**—the more a character wants (is motivated by) the goal (what he or she wants), the higher the stakes. They are closely tied to **conflict, tension**, and **suspense**, all of which amp up stakes (and vice versa). They are tied to **point**

of view (lack of strong voice or identification lowers stakes), to **pace** (leisurely pace often equals low stakes), and even to your prose itself (a single mother showing up with her baby on the doorstep of the father saying, "I can't do this" is different from one saying "I can't do this alone"). Fail to create high stakes and much of the rest of your story structure collapses.

How's that for pressure? ☺

✓ *How to Find It*

Sometimes it's hard to see where stakes in your story may not be as high as they could be, often because of the fill-in-the-blanks trap. It's easy to assume readers understand what is truly at stake for a character when you have an exhaustive knowledge of the world of the story—but how do you make sure readers see that too?

Look for areas where you may be making assumptions that the reader will understand why a character cares about something. For instance, it's not enough to simply show a character in danger of losing a job or a relationship or some other personal desire. We need to know *why* it matters so desperately to him—specifically, concretely, viscerally.

So often authors make low-stakes choices thinking they are high-stakes: "She can't lose this job because she needs money"; "He needs this woman to get information about a spy ring"; "She's leaving her husband because she doesn't love him anymore."

When I was an actor (another lifetime ago—but see? I told you minor details could be woven in to flesh out character), the best piece of acting advice I ever got was that what separates great actors from good ones is that great actors always make the strongest possible choices. So do great writers.

How much stronger might your story be if, for instance, your protagonist doesn't just need money, but she worked years to attain her coveted position at this particular prestige firm, or a recent scandal has made her unhirable anywhere else, or she can't lose health care for her special-needs child and there's a recession? What if the man isn't just using the woman for something he needs to know about the spy ring, but he also finds himself powerfully drawn to her, or they have a hookup and she gets pregnant with the child he thought he could never have, and getting what he wants from her means losing everything else? What if the woman leaves her husband not because she doesn't love him anymore, but despite the fact that she desperately *does*?

In Steena Holmes's novella *Stillwater Deep*, a woman is contemplating exactly the latter scenario when she's unable to get past the secret her husband kept from her for years, as well as his cowardice during a senseless, deadly shooting in the small-town elementary school where he is the principal. It would have been easy for Holmes to stop there with the stakes—that plot gives her plenty to work with. But she raises them higher by showing the very real love between the two, and the torment Charlotte, the protagonist, feels over wanting to reach for her husband— her best friend and source of strength—in coping with the tragedy, yet feeling alienated from him by her anger and disappointment over his betrayal and his actions. Then Holmes raises stakes still further when Charlotte learns there's more to the story, and how much she herself has contributed to the demise of their marriage.

By layering on top of her reasons for leaving her husband the real, powerful love Charlotte still bears him, Holmes raises the stakes enormously. Now Charlotte is leaving something of great value to her— because of an equally strong or stronger motivation (her anger, her pride, her guilt). So rather than the relatively low stakes of a character walking away from something she feels negative or ambivalent about, we see strong conflicting yet mutually exclusive desires—what master editor Sol Stein calls a crucible, one of the most powerful elements of compelling fiction.

In every situation, however big or small, the stronger a character's motivations, desires, and choices, the more engaging, dramatic, and compelling the scene. Readers feel what your characters feel. Give them the strongest emotions you can—the highest stakes possible, the greatest tension, the biggest conflicts, the deepest hole you can throw your characters in and then make them claw their way out of. Whenever you have a chance to make things stickier or clean them up, go for sticky. Don't take the easy way out—force your character to face the most complicated path instead. That's what makes for a book we can't put down.

Some writers fear—rightly so—that amping up stakes might result in melodrama. But complicating and raising the stakes doesn't mean slapping in willy-nilly a sick child or pregnant mistress or literal ticking time bomb. As in the above example, don't think in terms of adding more exciting *stuff.* Think in terms of adding more *meaning.*

As you consider your own story, see if you can identify, specifically, what's at stake for each protagonist and main supporting character, both externally and internally. These goals may shift throughout the course of the story—what a character wants on page one may not be what he wants by page one hundred, so try writing down each separate internal and external goal (though the internal ones are less likely to shift, as they are usually central to a character's journey in the story).

External goals are concrete and tangible—Frodo taking the One Ring to Mordor, Harry Potter vanquishing Voldemort, Romeo getting Juliet: the physical representation of what the character desperately wants to achieve (or avoid). They give readers something clear and concrete to root for.

Internal goals are squishier, but they are often the true driving force behind a character's arc, and the most compelling stories have both. Frodo wants to protect the Shire and preserve the Hobbits' way of life—security, comfort, happiness; Harry Potter wants a family/community—in other words, acceptance and love—and security, for himself, his loved ones, and the world; Romeo wants to love and be loved. Internal goals are what give meaning to the external goals that help create and amplify stakes—an external goal without that deeper driving force often falls flat and fails to really hook readers. Even in a Will Smith disaster movie, saving the world isn't actually the goal—it's rescuing his family or keeping them together, i.e., love and security—i.e., universal goals that nearly every reader can relate to. If you define clear external and internal goals for your characters and tie those internal goals to some universal goal—even if the characters themselves are not consciously aware of those goals—you will have your readers at hello.

✓ *How to Fix It*

But what does that look like, practically? Start, as I mention above, by clearly defining what's at stake for each character through answering a few concrete questions.

- What does your character want desperately (goal)? (Note: Your protag's goal may shift from the beginning of the story; do this exercise for each goal.)
- Why does he want it (motivation)?
- What does he stand to gain by succeeding in attaining it/lose by failing?
- What makes it urgent? Why must he achieve the goal *now*?

Are these answers clearly on the page? If not (or if you're not sure, which means probably not), then your story stakes may not be high enough or not be coming across.

Using the above questions, see if you can list as many ways as you can think of to raise the stakes higher. Be as exhaustive as possible and as crazy as you want to, even raising the stakes to the point of ridiculousness; this is just an exercise, but sometimes it can shake an idea loose and offer a glimpse into ways you could organically raise stakes and draw your reader in more deeply.

Here are a handful of specific suggestions for ways to raise stakes, with examples of novels that incorporate each one.

ADD LAYERS AND RESONANCE BY CREATING BOTH INTERNAL AND EXTERNAL STAKES

What a character wants or fears losing should be both external (Cinderella going to the ball) and internal (winning the prince—i.e., the universal goal of love). For the strongest punch and maximum stakes, great stories incorporate both.

Camille Pagán: *Life and Other Near-Death Experiences*—Libby is diagnosed with an inoperable brain tumor the same day her husband drops a bomb on their marriage. She fights for love and happiness (universal internal goals) by determining to live what life she has left as completely as possible on her own terms, decamping to a gorgeous tropical island and embarking on a budding relationship (external goals), despite her fear of experiencing another heartbreak (internal stakes), ties to her family and friends (internal and external stakes), as well as certain looming loss (external stakes).

PAINT IN SHADES OF GRAY

Black-and-white heroes (and villains) are dull for readers and seem inhuman—none of us are all good or all bad, but a fascinating mix of both. Creating shades of gray raises the stakes enormously—it gives us much more to root for, empathize with, relate to. A hero who might regress into alcoholism, for instance, instantly raises the story's stakes. A villain who might show signs of potential redemption also heightens stakes. Both these situations raise reader investment and involvement—now we are rooting for (or against) these characters in very tenuous circumstances, which creates tension and suspense... which raises stakes.

Emily Giffin's *Something Borrowed* **and** *Something Blue*— Both books are wonderful studies in shades of gray for protagonists/ antagonists: good-girl Rachel steals her best friend's fiancé, and vain, self-absorbed Darcy reveals a core of goodness and heart.

ADD CONFLICTING DESIRES/GOALS

This is part of the crucible I referred to earlier—pit something the character wants desperately against something else she also wants desperately—and make the two mutually exclusive. In **John Steinbeck's** ***Of Mice and Men***, George's lifelong protection and care for Lennie, his mentally challenged best friend, faces a seemingly insurmountable obstacle when (spoiler!) Lennie accidentally kills a woman: Lennie has become dangerous and must face the consequences of his actions, yet George knows Lennie's gentle soul and that he didn't mean to hurt her. But as a lynch mob closes in on Lennie there is no way George can reconcile both things, and he's forced to make an agonizing choice. *That's* a crucible, and that's where great, unforgettable fiction resides.

William Styron's *Sophie's Choice* is another classic and overt example of this—Sophie is forced to choose which of her children will live, an impossible choice that defines her entire arc in the story. Other good examples are **Pat Conroy's** *Prince of Tides*, where Tom Wingo must choose between the wife he built a life with and the psychologist he's come to love while digging into his sister's most recent attempted suicide; or in the film world *The Wrath of Khan*, where Spock (or Kirk, depending which version you're watching) chooses the good of the many over the good of the one and sacrifices himself for the *Enterprise* crew; or *Titanic*, when Jack chooses Rose's survival over his own and their chance to make the life together that they planned (despite the arguable premise that that door might have held them both...).

ADD MEANING AND LAYERS, AND CONTINUE TO UP THE ANTE AS THE STORY DEVELOPS

Stakes must be real and significant from the outset—but they should continue to evolve and heighten throughout the story. If a man kills his wife and her lover, is it stronger if he does it out of wounded pride and anger, or also a desperate, painful unreturned love for her? And what if he then learns that the man he killed was never actually her lover? And that his wife never stopped loving him? Or that she was pregnant? Create more investment in readers by continually layering in more meaning and impact for characters.

Richard Yates's *Revolutionary Road* is a great example of this. April and Frank Wheeler seem to have it all at the story's opening, but decry the emptiness of their middle-class American lives. But when April suggests they move to Paris the facade begins to fall away, revealing ever more severe cracks in their foundation and creating ever higher stakes: Frank is stifled at his job, April by the strictures of her life as a housewife and mom that made her give up her acting career; their marriage is far more troubled than we at first see, including infidelity and violence; and finally, an unexpected development forces them into horrific choices that have tragic consequences.

BE INTENSELY PERSONAL, AND INTENSELY SPECIFIC...

Have you ever read a story or seen a movie where a murder or tragedy happens, or the character experiences some kind of great loss, or even a great win—yet you're left unmoved and aren't sure why? It's either because we don't yet care enough about the character, or they don't care enough about what is at stake—or both. We root for even small, personal stakes when a character we are invested in cares enormously about a deeply personal, highly specific thing (have I hammered that home enough...?). Even if the protagonist is sublimating or denying what she wants, the reader must see it. Be granular, not generic; concrete rather than amorphous; highly personal and deeply specific.

In **Khaled Hosseini's** *The Kite Runner*, much of the stakes of the early part of the story revolve around a kite-fighting tournament, a popular event in the characters' Afghanistan town involving competing kites—not something most readers would normally feel a deep investment in. But the tournament in the story represents much more than just winning a game (external goal) for upper-class Amir, who competes on a team with his best friend, his father's servant's son Hassan. Winning the prestigious tournament allows Amir the chance to finally attain what he's hungered for all his life: his father's attention and approval (internal goal). But it leads to a tragedy and a foundational betrayal of his friendship with Hassan that will haunt Amir for the rest of his life, becoming a major part of the character's motivation for the present-day portions of the story.

...BUT ALSO BE UNIVERSAL

Yet this highly personal and specific thing should resonate with readers on a universal, relatable, empathetic level. Sympathy isn't enough—you must tap into the reader's own feelings through those of the character.

Whether we have any familiarity or even interest in Kabul, whether we care about kite fighting or even sports in general, whether we can understand the class divisions of 1970s Afghan society or the experience of young boys, most people can relate to the craving to be seen and loved for who we are by those we love most. We can relate to betrayal and its consequences. *The Kite Runner* hits on such common human goals and motivations: love, belonging, family (and conversely, the universal aversion to feelings of shame, remorse, guilt). The universality of these desires is what gives Hosseini's book such wide appeal (and helped his debut novel become a *New York Times* bestseller).

EMBRACE UNCERTAINTY

Uncertainty raises stakes. Create story questions and don't immediately resolve them. If all our questions and uncertainties are immediately addressed, or readers can easily predict the protag's path, stakes (and reader involvement) are low.

In **Taylor Jenkins Reid's** *One True Loves,* on the verge of remarrying after coping with the heartbreak of losing her beloved husband, Emma learns he's still alive. Reid could have made the protagonist's husband or her fiancé Emma's clear choice, but she doesn't—it's Emma's complicated feelings for both men and her difficulty determining the right path forward that raise stakes and make readers compulsively flip pages to find out which man she chooses.

BE IMMEDIATE AND VISCERAL

Regardless of how high the stakes you've created, if we aren't "seeing" your characters' interactions, actions, reactions, and inner life, the stakes feel low. Remember our vacation metaphor: Would you rather flip through the pictures of someone's trip to Hawaii while they dryly narrate their exciting events, or be on that zip line with them as they sail across the mouth of a volcano? Don't leave your reader on the outside looking in, or hearing about the meat of a story that happened "offstage" or in the past. Put us right there, deeply inside your protag's head as she or he lives through the excruciating, exhilarating, affecting key moments of the story.

Ruta Sepetys's powerful *The Fountains of Silence* is set in Franco's repressive regime in Spain in the late 1950s, an era and place Sepetys brings vividly to life with immediate, visceral scenes that plant the reader directly in the middle of her characters' struggles to thrive—and survive—amid the constant threats of starvation, homelessness, and loss of freedom and even life at the hands of the brutal Guardia Civil. Even those events that happen prior to the events of the story—the murder and torture of the siblings' parents, for instance—are brought to life on the page with visceral, immediate detail. In her scenes of characters' everyday lives and relationships, hopes, disappointments, triumphs, agonies, etc., we are a direct and intimate part of it all through the strong, imediate POV of her main characters as we live each painful moment along with them.

MAKE IT URGENT

Even if you have solid high-stakes elements in play, without some sense of urgency—why whatever is at stake is essential *right now*—stakes may fall flat. If a protagonist fails to attain some honor or position he covets, for instance, nothing really changes except he doesn't get the admiration or remuneration or prestige he hoped for. If your protagonist loses her job it's not great, but a lot of people face that challenge and are okay—what makes her situation so dire? Even if you have developed strong, clear consequences for losing the job—perhaps around taking care of a sick child or holding on to the family farm, etc.—what makes it urgent? Why is this disastrous (read: high-stakes) *now*? This sense of urgency will often take the form of the proverbial (or literal) ticking clock: a concrete deadline by which disaster ensues.

Effective suspense, thriller, and mystery writers put this tool to excellent use to amp up stakes. Whether it's Steven James's Patrick Bowers rushing to save his fiancée and her daughter while stopping an international terrorism conspiracy in *The King*, or the new mother in Emily Bleeker's *The Waiting Room* trying to track down her abducted baby girl before the police arrest her as the prime suspect, or Leila Meacham's multiple-protagonist epic novel *Dragonfly*, where each of her five embedded U.S. spies in World War II Europe faces the ever-growing life-or-death danger of discovery—there's always an imminent threat that creates a sense of urgency.

But the technique can be used very effectively in all genres, for instance in Katherine Center's compelling women's fiction *How to Walk Away*, in which Center incorporates urgency (among layers of other high-stakes devices) to keep raising story stakes: When Center's pro-tagonist suffers life-changing injuries in an accident that necessitates a lengthy hospital stay, she battles to regain mobility and reclaim her life against the ticking clock of the window of full rehabilitation (and the limits of her insurance coverage).

.. # ..

You may have heard the phrase "torture your characters"—raising the stakes is generally what it means. In life most of us want things to go as smoothly as possible, but in fiction (and nonfiction) readers thrive on the complications that amp up the stakes. Make sure you have created strong, meaningful, urgent stakes and you'll compel your readers to keep turning pages.

chapter three

PLOT

In the holy trinity of story, plot may be the third leg, but the tripod can't stand without all three. Plot is not action, and action isn't story, or we'd all love reading synopses. It's not only *what* happens, but the hows, the whys—the connective tissue—that keeps us reading.

Even if you have created living, breathing characters with compelling stakes that make us deeply invest in them, without something for them to *do* in service to those goals the story falls flat. (Boy loves girl, and… *yawn.*) If your characters are the vehicle through which we experience the story, and the stakes are the engine, plot is the journey itself, the road they travel. If you don't take us somewhere, we have no reason to read.

This seems self-explanatory and almost comically basic, but it's surprisingly common to see stories with well-crafted characters with riveting backstories and situations who go nowhere, resulting in a static story. It's equally common to see exciting events that happen for no intrinsic reason, lending a staccato, episodic feel to a story. Or to have an abundance of riches—too much plot that complicates the story and diffuses its focus, giving the reader no clear through line to hold on to and guide us through the story.

Your job as a writer—and as you're editing—is to find that perfect balance where the plot furthers the story (rather than vice versa)…to walk the line between underserving and overwhelming it.

✓ How to Find It

Examining your manuscript and asking yourself some essential questions can help ascertain whether your plot is working as well for your story as it can.

- What happens?
- Does one event flow organically from the preceding event and lead logically to the next?
- Is every plot development essential to move the protag(s) along her arc? And does every single development serve to move the story forward?
- Is there too much plot? Not enough?
- Is it surprising? If readers can predict where the story is going, especially if we outsmart the characters in doing so, it's less satisfying.
- Are there loose ends?
- Does it hold together? Are there plot holes?
- Why does each plot event happen? Is each one realistic? Believable?
- Is there any easier or better way out of the mess? (The answer must be no.)
- Are there loose ends? Unanswered questions? Anything unresolved?
- Any unmotivated actions (*deus ex machina*)?
- Does your story start in the right place?
- Does the time line work?

It can be overwhelming to try to answer these questions by working with the full manuscript, so one helpful exercise in fine-tuning your plot is to reduce the story down to its essential structure and see what you're working with—what's actually on the page—in a manageable way.

✓ How to Fix It

One of my favorite tools I frequently suggest to authors is what I call an X-ray for the story—essentially an outline. You may have seen similar ideas referred to as a road map or blueprint; basically it's a bulleted or numbered list of the main plot developments. This isn't meant to be in-depth or ornate; for each point you will have just a line or two at most. If you're a "plotter," a writer who outlines the story before you write it, you may have something like this already—just make sure it actually adheres to the finished manuscript if you diverged from it at any point, and that it includes every single development in the story. If you're a "pantser" (someone who writes by the seat of her pants) think of it as an outline you make after the fact.

Like an actual X-ray, this technique reduces your story down to the bones, the supporting structure, so you can see it more clearly without the flesh of the whole narrative covering it. Some X-rays may be more complicated than others if you have multiple protags and/or a complex story or time line, so it can take a little time, but it will be invaluable to you as you embark on revisions. Almost every author I suggest this to initially resists doing this seemingly reductive exercise; every single author who actually did it has told me that it clarified their story for them in ways they never imagined and served as an indispensable tool at every subsequent stage of revisions. If you're doing it right it shouldn't take more than a couple of hours to create.

The X-ray should list every main occurrence that moves the story forward, including, when needed, backstory that doesn't necessarily take place within this story's framework but impacts the overall plot of it. Here's an example using the opening chapters of Dan Brown's blockbuster *The Da Vinci Code*, since the plot is readily familiar to many:

- A curator of the Louvre is shot by what appears to be a monk who is unable to extract from the man a secret about the location of a mysterious object.

- After the monk flees, the curator is determined to find a way to pass the secret on before he dies.
- Cryptologist Robert Langdon is visited in his hotel by a lieutenant of France's version of the FBI summoning him to the crime scene of the man Langdon was supposed to meet with that evening—the curator—who desecrated his own body before he died to leave a message for Langdon, an expert in religious symbolism.
- The albino who murdered the curator reports to "the Teacher," the man who instructed him to confront the curator, that he has confirmed the existence of "the keystone."
- The Teacher instructs him to retrieve it; before he can, the albino knows he must purify his soul and flagellates himself.
- The lieutenant brings Langdon through Paris to the Louvre and past La Pyramide; inside he meets a captain with the law enforcement agency investigating the murder of the curator, who tells him there is more to the crime scene.
- The captain leads Langdon through the deserted museum and to the scene of the murder. Langdon notices an unusual religious pin on the captain's tie.
- A bishop who is the head of Opus Dei, a religious order currently under fire as a cult and besieged by a yet-unnamed threat, receives a call that the albino has discovered the keystone and asking the bishop to grant access to a church so he can retrieve it.
- As the albino prepares to retrieve the keystone, he is beset by memories of his violent past.
- Langdon arrives at the murder scene and begins to decipher for the captain the codes the curator left for him.
- A nun who guards the church where the albino is headed receives a call from her boss instructing her to admit him, despite her reservations.
- Langdon sees the message the curator left specifically for him.

Notice that these aren't lengthy descriptions, and there may be one bullet point per chapter or scene, or several; it depends how many plot-driving events you have within each one. Your X-ray may be even simpler—you won't need to describe certain story elements (like what Opus Dei is) for yourself; all you need is the basic scaffolding of the story you already know.

Let's use this mini X-ray to answer the questions above in the "How to Find It" section.

WHAT HAPPENS?

This is basically the totality of your X-ray showing the action, events, and developments that make up your story. But on a bigger-picture level, do you know what your story is actually *about*? ("About eighty thousand words…" *Ba-dum-bump.*) You can think of this as the (dreaded) elevator pitch or log line many authors develop when describing a project to agents and publishers: a one- or two-line summary that encapsulates the "nut" of the story you're telling. For instance (and if you have been living under a rock for the last decade, SPOILER ALERT), *The Da Vinci Code* is about a cryptographer who, in solving a murder, uncovers a conspiracy of Christianity that leads all the way to the secret descendants of Jesus Christ.

What is the heart of the story you're telling? If you can't sum it up this pithily, if you can't define it in terms this clear and specific, don't go any further in revising until you can clearly define the central idea of your story on which everything else is built. Everything that follows should serve this heart, so it's counterproductive to tackle the rest of the questions till you've defined it.

DOES THE STORY TAKE THE READER SOMEWHERE?

This question will lead you to the arc of your story, which is different from your character arcs. Story arc comprises that, but also includes the journey itself—your protagonists' point A, point B, and the road between them. It can be helpful to map out this story arc—literally plot your course, meaning write it down and/or draw it if you're visual—and the first step is to define a clear beginning, middle, and end. Let's go back to Mr. Brown's blockbuster (spoilers):

- **Beginning:** Langdon must solve the murder of an art curator to clear his own name.
- **Middle:** The clues he (and Sophie) discover steadily reveal a much bigger mystery, uncovering a vast and ancient conspiracy that encompasses the entire foundation of Christianity.
- **End:** Langdon and Sophie crack the codes that defeat the modern-day keepers of the conspiracy and reveal her as a descendant of Jesus and Mary Magdalene.

You should be able to sum up the journey of your whole story in a few succinct, clear sentences like this. If you can't chances are you don't have a clear story arc. This will be the story's "spine"—and this backbone is the support for the entire narrative.

Keeping in mind the central idea you defined above, do we see in the X-ray (or the manuscript itself, if you are working from that) your protagonist(s) actually traveling the journey you described? I don't just mean do you get him from point A to point B, but does every story development in between move him farther down the road you mapped out in the first question? Looking at *The Da Vinci Code*, damn skippy it does. Here's what follows in the story after the above partial X-ray leaves off:

- Langdon shows up at the scene and learns he is the prime suspect of the investigating officer.
- Sophie Neveu, another police officer who specializes in cryptography, arrives and reveals that Langdon is being railroaded.
- Sophie turns out to be the curator's granddaughter, and he left explicit instructions for her to find Langdon, whom she helps escape.
- She and Langdon find a key by following the clues the curator left specifically for them.
- They decipher the code it reveals, which takes them to a bank, where they must crack another code to get into a safe-deposit box.
- That reveals a cryptex that Sophie knows the workings of.

And amid all of this the story also develops the subplot with the albino, the Teacher, and the members of Opus Dei. He may not do much in the way of character development, but Dan Brown knows how to plot; nearly every scene lays another essential bread crumb leading us along the path he's laid out as the story unfolds, constantly pushing the story forward.

The story's plot, as mapped out in your X-ray and in the manuscript itself, should arise directly from the character arc (point A to point B, from the Character chapter). That means that each of the events in the plot should serve to move the protagonist further along the journey she travels over the course of the story—which creates the story arc. Note how Brown's plot steadily advances us along a path that is tied intrinsically into the story arc we determined above; there are few extraneous detours. That doesn't mean your story has to be all business all the time, relentlessly pushing the action forward. It does mean that it should be cohesive and elegant, by which I mean every part integrally serves the whole, whether directly or indirectly. When Brown slows the pace in one chapter to show La Pyramide en route to the crime scene, it's not just taking in the scenery; the plot will circle back to it later for a key story point, and Brown is subtly drawing focus on it now to cement the landmark in the reader's mind.

If you have multiple storylines, you'll check in the same way to make sure that each one has a cohesive story arc—and that together all of the subplot story arcs contribute to the overall story arc. For example in *The Princess Bride*, the main plot is about Westley and Buttercup and their defeating evil Prince Humperdinck, but we also have the Inigo Montoya subplot as he seeks the six-fingered man to avenge the death of his father. Inigo's story arc is equally developed and resolved, and it is essential to the main story arc: The heroes couldn't have defeated Humperdinck without him.

This same concept applies to a series: Each individual story should have a discrete and self-contained arc of its own, but each title will ideally be a point on the story arc of the overarching big-picture story of the series. *Hunger Games* is a great example of this; each title has its own unique plot, but together they create the series arc of Katniss moving from fighting for survival for her family and herself to fighting for the survival of her district, the rebels, and ultimately the entire society of the story.

IS EVERY PLOT DEVELOPMENT ESSENTIAL TO MOVE THE PROTAG(S) ALONG HER ARC?

This is a biggie, and the one that may cause you the most angst as you revise. *Every single thing* that happens must serve the story arc, meaning it must directly develop and further the spine of the story—not over and over with the same dynamic, but in a steady progression of the arc. I'll say this again, because it's the holy grail of story: *Every single development must move the story forward.*

That doesn't mean you have to strip your story of all color and interest, though. If you want a beautifully elegant example of this, again look at *The Princess Bride.* There's a reason it's such an enduring classic: There's not an ounce of flab in that screenplay. Every scene accomplishes something essential for moving the story constantly forward—and yet that doesn't mean it's dry or lacks color. Screenwriter William Goldman peppers the story with memorable, quotable exchanges and delightful scenes and characters—but watch it again analytically and note how each and every one is intrinsic to the story's momentum and forward motion.

With this idea in mind, using your X-ray get really granular and brutally honest about material that isn't essential to telling your story. (Be brave: It may be a lot.) Take a look at each plot development—i.e., each bullet point or number in your outline. Does *each and every development* accomplish something—develop character, further plot, add essential information, or raise stakes—in a way that is directly tied into the story arc you defined above? If not, chances are strong that it doesn't belong in the story. The same goes for characters—you may find that that hilarious comic-relief character you created or the protagonist's beautifully crafted encounter with a minor character doesn't actually move the protagonist or the story along their arcs. This is where you must gird yourself to kill some darlings. Notice in the *Da Vinci Code* X-ray snippet how every single action follows from the previous one and leads us inevitably to the next. Notice how every single character is also essential to moving that plot forward.

Knowing what to keep and what to cut is some of the hardest work of editing. I've broken my own heart suggesting to authors that they cut certain scenes—because often they comprise lovely moments, or are meticulously crafted, or contain beautiful prose, etc. But if they don't serve the story then they are detracting from it. Just as in a functioning society the good of the many outweighs the good of the few, in a functioning story, if a scene doesn't contribute intrinsically to the whole of the story, consider whether you may be clinging to it as a darling. It's easy to fall in love with our own writing, especially when it's especially well written or moving or painstakingly crafted. But *does it serve the story?*

I always suggest authors sit with these knee-jerk defenses of a darling for a few days. Sometimes you may decide the scene does indeed belong in the manuscript—in a creative business all critique, even on a professional level, is opinion. But often with a little distance from the first stinging suggestion (if you've ever been critiqued, you know that initial sharp slap of "some idiot who doesn't get it at *all*" daring to criticize your baby), you may find the objectivity to see whether your darling serves the story or not.

In either case, NEVER DELETE! If you decide to revise and/or excise scenes or characters, save the current scene or the material in question to another file labeled "harvest file" or "discards" or similar. There's something unbelievably comforting about knowing the words still exist—that you could change your mind at any time—that makes it easier to try a revision. It's a safety net that frees you to take a risk—if you hate the new version and feel it falls flat, the old one is right there waiting for you. But I'm willing to bank on your not going back to the old version 99 percent of the time; it's extraordinary how clear inessential material becomes once you let it go and can see how the story is improved without it. Plus you may realize you can mine some of the material you had—that's why I call it a harvest file. If nothing is truly lost, it can make it much more palatable to noodle around with a scene you may have been fervently invested in.

Here are some other areas to consider in evaluating whether every scene is essential:

Action isn't plot.

Just because there may be a lot of exciting things happening, action doesn't further the plot if the events don't directly signify in the central spine of the story. Everything that happens should intrinsically and essentially *move the story forward.*

Cover less ground more deeply.

Writers may think that "more is more" in raising stakes and tension, but having multiple scenes showing the same dynamic defuses tension and story momentum because it feels like a retread to readers of ground we've already covered.

This is especially true with scenes of violence or aggression, which can feel gratuitous and often put readers off if similar dynamics are repeated. The movie *Red Sparrow* shows no fewer than five instances of some kind of sexual assault/coercion against poor Jennifer Lawrence's character. Repeatedly hammering the same idea lessens the impact, stalls momentum, and can lose the reader. In this case showing just two violent scenes might have been more effective in conveying the writer's point if the second time showed a new dynamic: for instance, that Lawrence's character is no longer a victim as she was in the first instance, but fights back. The dynamic has shifted, so it may be a similar event but it's a new story development. Establish things once and then move the story forward—and check that each scene is intrinsic to the "nut" of the story you're telling.

Vary the levels.

Tied in with the above point, keep in mind the literal *arc* of story, meaning the shape that begins at a low point, rises to a peak, and then descends to a resolution: As your protagonist works from her point A toward her point B, we should see a change in intensity, motivation, stakes, etc. As the story and the character progress along her arc toward the climax, each of those elements should increase.

For instance, let's say you've written story about an abused wife. Initially we may see a scene of abuse where the character backs down, recoils, retreats in fear, etc. As the story progresses, in subsequent altercations with her husband we must see a change: Perhaps the protag starts asserting herself and he raises his hand as if to hit her and she doesn't flinch…that's a new level.

As the protagonist begins to stand up to her husband's bullying tactics, perhaps we see growing anger percolating inside her, or she speaks up where once she didn't. Once she attains this new level, then you add yet another layer—perhaps he accelerates his abuse, but this time maybe she reacts differently—maybe she calls the police, or fights back. So as we see stakes go up in subsequent scenes, tension builds till we get to another change in level that indicates another turning-point moment— perhaps he threatens her life or we see some other climax, the apex of her arc: Finally she stands up to him once and for all, whatever that means in the story. This development will come fairly late in the story, so if we do see another similar scene—perhaps we see her encounter her husband in divorce court, for instance, in the final chapter—the new level becomes the embodiment of her point B: In the protag's new relations with her former abuser, we see where her arc has taken her. Perhaps he tries to verbally abuse her and she simply turns away, for instance, unruffled now in her newfound strength and confidence.

Avoid entertaining filler.

Be careful that you don't include scenes that are just vignettes or anecdotes—occasions for interesting happenings or dialogue that may be entertaining, but don't further the story. Every scene needs to tie directly into the character arc(s) and into the story arc. You can pull the laces snug while still maintaining some of your favorite bits if you find organic ways to combine these moments into scenes that *are* intrinsic (see the Dread Pirate Roberts example below). Otherwise, take a hard look at these "darlings" and determine whether you're indulging these diverting moments or anecdotes at the expense of the overall story.

Don't get lost in minutiae or logistics.

I have an editor friend who calls this "GPSing"—using a lot of ink on scenes that move a character around but don't directly further the plot and story momentum. Often these involve travel—whether actual or temporal—where authors are showing a character getting from one place to another, or how they spend inconsequential time between scenes that *are* essential to move the story forward. You can leave out scenes where nothing directly germane to the central story (the spine) happens, or that don't move the story forward, show new character information, raise stakes, or further the plot.

But you can make the scene intrinsic by ensuring it *does* show something essential to the spine—like something about a character that we need to know. For instance, maybe a woman's unflappability in a minor traffic skirmish shows she's cool under pressure—foreshadowing her being levelheaded when the antagonist pulls a gun on her later. Or perhaps a quiet family scene establishes an unlikable character's softer side so we have some sympathy for him and stay invested even in the face of some unkindness or betrayal.

Verisimilitude isn't always good fiction.

I sometimes hear authors justify a scene or section of story that I've suggested may be hampering pace and momentum by saying, "But that really happened!" or, "But that's the way it would actually happen." Maybe so, but fiction is real life on steroids. What may be exactly true to life doesn't always play well in a narrative and can lack the stakes to keep a reader turning the pages: Lin-Manuel Miranda's smash show *Hamilton* conveys the spirit of the Founding Father's life even if it takes a bit of artistic leeway with the actual facts for the sake of story (there's no record that Hamilton and Aaron Burr had a lifelong rivalry, for instance). An author's job is to instill storytelling concepts onto the basis of realism to make it effective and satisfying for readers.

Show the right things and sum up the right things.

I'll talk about this in more depth in the Showing and Telling chapter, but for now, check where you have summed up story or action and where you have dramatized it on the page. In general, show is far stronger than tell *for key moments*—but tell can serve the story better than show for inessential or minor ones. Think of *Princess Bride*: Rather than showing Westley's adventures on the Dread Pirate Roberts's ship, the screenplay has him telling Buttercup about them in a dynamic scene as they navigate the fearsome Fire Swamp. The action germane to the story is the two of them surviving this challenge; Westley's experience is backstory, necessary but incidental to the central storyline, so Goldman wastes no valuable screen time on it, instead introducing it in organic "tell" amid the propulsive "show" of the Fire Swamp and Humperdinck's pursuit. Too much tell will keep your reader at a remove and make your manuscript feel like a dry chronicle instead of a vivid, visceral story. But too much show can bog a story down in inessentials and drag pace. Balance is key.

Now that you've evaluated every single scene for whether it's intrinsic and essential to move the story forward, take another look at your manuscript or X-ray and ask yourself a few more crucial questions:

WHY DOES EACH PLOT EVENT HAPPEN?

Check to see whether your story flows organically and fluidly along its arc toward the climax and resolution. Does each discrete event of the story follow from what preceded it? Does it logically lead us to the next?

The *South Park* creators, Matt Stone and Trey Parker, have a storytelling theory I find brilliant in its simplicity and applicability. They say that when they are writing they check each scene to see how it is connected to the one before it and after it based on what words would logically connect the scenes. According to them, each scene must follow the one preceding it based on the word "but" or "therefore"—meaning that each scene must be either an obstacle to whatever was laid out in the scene before it or a direct result. If the words that connect the scenes are "and then," they say, then you have nothing but a series of loosely related scenes that simply pile up one after the other—episodic vignettes, rather than a cohesive, forward-moving, tight story.

With multiple storylines you can still use this tool; separate out the events of the individual storylines and apply the but/therefore test to the scenes within each one.

IS EACH DEVELOPMENT REALISTIC? BELIEVABLE?

Ask yourself some hard questions about each of your plot developments: Is it logical, realistic? Does it strain reader credibility? A college professor can't suddenly expertly rope a steer unless you have set up a reason he would have that skill (e.g., he grew up on a ranch). A ditzy character with little education doesn't know the formula for glue (unless it's a dream about her high school reunion ☺). You must lay the groundwork earlier for any unexpected skills, actions, or developments by planting a seed that makes them believable to readers. If your petite female kidnap victim suddenly wrangles a gun from her captor as she runs away, then turns and fires a kill shot, you must either have offered a foundation for that earlier in the story (she studied marital arts, had an ex who took her to target practice, used to run track, etc.), or clearly show what extenuating circumstances allowed her to overpower, outmaneuver, and outrun her kidnapper, then accurately fire an unfamiliar weapon on the run. The moment readers begin to doubt the veracity of story developments, you've lost them.

ARE THERE ANY UNMOTIVATED ACTIONS (DEUS EX MACHINA)?

The same idea applies to justifying a character's course of action, especially extreme ones. A woman whose husband leaves her can't just decide to kill him without the author creating a realistic, believable, inevitable motivation for her to do it—otherwise it feels like a device, a shape the author has determined to contort the characters into artificially. Readers sense that manipulation and we disengage. Your job is to allow your story to flow into that shape organically. In other words, what in this woman's past began to set the stage for her to react in such an extreme way? Was she abused as a child? Abandoned? Did she experience a horrible betrayal that her husband's betrayal hits on? That's part of the shape—but most of us have experienced some trauma and don't react murderously, so if you want readers to be on board you must continue to set the stage: Did she have a history of mental instability or violence? Alcoholic fugues? Anger-management issues? Did he leave her for her sister? Or after their fourth miscarriage? The climactic development of her shooting him can't spring out of nowhere—as an author your job is to have created, step by step, every brick in the path that leads her to this inevitable action.

This same concept applies to what is often called a *"deus ex machina"*—literally "god from the machine"—when a plot element is introduced seemingly out of nowhere to neatly tie up or resolve some situation. The term is derived from the eleventh-hour magical appearance in Greek plays of a god to resolve the plot (actually an actor lowered from a crane—the machine). This kind of device leaves readers feeling cheated, as it's an inorganic, contrived way of pushing a story where the author wants it to go. The reason the series finales of *Dallas* or *Lost* or the reboot of *Roseanne* infuriated viewers so much was that they presented a contrived reveal that came utterly out of nowhere. If you spring a shock on readers, make sure that in hindsight we can spot the signs that were there for us to see—as in *Sixth Sense* (SPOILERS!), with M. Night Shamalayan's clever clues all along about Bruce Willis's character that, in retrospect, we realize indicate he's one of the ghosts haunting the boy he believes he's been counseling for seeing spirits.

IS EVERY PICKLE INEVITABLE?

It's not enough to "chase your protagonist up a tree and throw rocks at him," as the saying goes. You must make the tree the character's only viable option—because if there is any other way out of the mess, he would take it. Human nature is such that we choose the path of least resistance. It's like that old melodrama with the bow that we looked at in the Character chapter: "I can't pay the rent!" "You *must* pay the rent!" "*I'll* pay the rent!" The moment Our Hero offers to pay the rent, the story is over because the heroine has an out. The rent will be paid. The villain no longer has anything on her. No danger, no tension, no stakes…no story. But if the hero never shows, now you have forced her up that tree—she'd better figure out how to solve this crucible herself before the villain lashes her to the railroad tracks. (And pro tip: Modern readers tend to want to see stories where the heroine takes the reins on her own without needing a man to swoop in all white-knight and rescue her.)

IS IT SURPRISING?

As bestselling author Steven James says in his craft book *Story Trumps Structure*, "Readers want to predict how the story will end (or how it will get to the end), but they want to be wrong." If readers can correctly guess where the story is going, especially if we outsmart the protagonist in doing so, it's infinitely less satisfying. Be original, unexpected, even shocking—that's what makes for the "unputdownable" stories. Remember your reaction the first time you saw *Sixth Sense?* Or *The Crying Game?* Or *Fight Club?* Or the end of *The Avengers, Infinity Wars,* or season one of *Game of Thrones?*

But you don't need a big reveal or ending shocker to keep readers on the edge of their seats; just keep them guessing what's going to happen—that's what makes us stay up into the night reading just one more page. Humans are by nature curious; if we can't figure out what may happen next, we cannot resist the lure of finding out. And you delight us when you're able to offer organic, believable plot twists we could never have predicted—there's a reason *Gone Girl* seized the imagination of such a huge chunk of the reading public.

If you fear your story may be predictable, sit and brainstorm alternative developments you could sub for what you currently have in the manuscript. Keep writing even when you think you've exhausted all the ideas you can come up with. Often you have to keep pushing your own creative powers to continually surprise your reader. I like the way Pixar storyboard artist Emma Coates puts the imperative to keep digging for the story in her marvelous, must-read list of storytelling basics (https://laughingsquid.com/22-rules-of-storytelling/): "Discount the first thing that comes to mind. And the second, third, fourth, fifth—get the obvious out of the way. Surprise yourself."

ARE THERE LOOSE ENDS? UNANSWERED QUESTIONS? ANYTHING UNRESOLVED?

Readers are sharp—especially if they are invested in your characters and story—and they can be unforgiving if you leave them hanging with unresolved plot developments. (Again, reference the *Lost* series finale.) *The Princess Bride* offers a great example of this too: By the film's end every major storyline has been resolved: Westley has rescued Buttercup; Humperdinck has suffered his comeuppance; Inigo has killed the six-fingered man; and even beleaguered Fezzik has finally done something right. (Interestingly, in Goldman's book on which the movie is based, he leaves readers with a maddening uncertainty about everyone's fate, like Frank R. Stockton's classic short story "The Lady, or the Tiger?" where readers are left to wonder which of the two titular outcomes the hero blindly chooses—marriage or death. No surprise that Hollywood—where marketing is king—opted for the neatly wrapped up loose ends.)

Using your X-ray or working in the manuscript itself, can you identify every storyline or unresolved issue you've created, every thread you've woven into the plot? Now check to see whether it's wrapped up by story's end—and where, and how. You don't want to tie up loose ends too early in the story (unless you create new ones), and you'll leave readers feeling cheated if your resolution isn't organic, believable, and well thought out.

DOES YOUR STORY START IN THE RIGHT PLACE?

Can you identify the story's "inciting event"—the happening that inexorably sets this entire journey in motion, or the moment that unavoidably changes the course of the protagonist's life? If not, before you move forward with revisions stop and figure out what that development is: What is the one event that kicks off what happens to the protagonist and results, like the first tipped domino in a line of them, in everything that happens throughout the manuscript? For instance, in *Gone Girl* it's Amy's disappearance. In *Harry Potter*, it's Harry's invitation to Hogwarts. In *Hunger Games*, it's the selection of Katniss's sister, Prim, as the tribute from their district for the deadly games. Your story should start as close to that inciting event as possible—it's what draws the reader onto the ride. If that event appears well into the outline (or the manuscript itself), you might want to consider how to begin the story closer to that point.

Sometimes, mistakenly believing that readers need a lot of background before they can invest, authors start their stories too soon. Don't make the common mistake of thinking readers must be brought up to speed before they can understand or care about what's going on. The opposite is almost always true—frontloading your story with backstory keeps us feeling like we're stuck in neutral, never getting off the starting line.

What we do need from the beginning is a sense of who your character is and a reason to invest in and embark on this journey with him or her—ground we covered in the Character chapter. But it's the first major turning point—that inciting event—that draws us into your world and plants our feet in what the story is about. Beginning with backstory is like opening a play performance with the actors trying out, then rehearsing, then getting dressed in the green room before the play actually begins. Start with the action; you will weave in the backstory as you move the story forward, building real, three-dimensional characters and stories.

You may have heard this called starting "in medias res"—you don't need to show all the ingredients of a character's life to orient us; you start right in the thick of the soup, where the complications begin. Then you weave in, little by little, context as we need it to fill in the blanks—but all as you move the story forward. The story is what happens just as the status quo for your protagonist begins to change and he begins moving toward his point B.

DOES THE STORY END IN THE RIGHT PLACE?

Endings can be trickier than you think—not only must the author bring to a satisfying close the protagonist(s)' journey, but you must know where to stop. An otherwise enjoyable story can weary readers at the end by dragging on and on, trickling to a halt instead of offering us a clear final destination for the journey we've traveled with your characters. In general, your story should end fairly soon after the main climax and the protagonist's completion of her arc. A great ending resolves all loose ends, offers a glimpse of the protag(s)' new reality subsequent to how she may have changed or grown from the story events—and, in a series, also teases the reader on to the next title. If the story keeps going after that, it feels as if it trails along to a stop, reduces the impact of the climax, and lessens reader satisfaction with its resolution.

DOES THE TIME LINE WORK?

Another reason I love the X-ray is that it allows an author to more easily address technical issues like the story's time line. With each development clearly spelled out in your bulleted list, it's so much easier to examine the chronology of events and make sure it holds together. If you've created a bulleted list in Word, for instance, you can use New Comment (in the Review panel) to note each event's chronology. Then it's simple to look at those comment bubbles and make sure the time line works, and moving events around is infinitely more manageable in this reduced outline form, and will serve as a blueprint for revising the chronology in the manuscript itself.

IF YOU HAVE MULTIPLE POVS, ARE THEY DISPERSED IN A WAY THAT IS LOGICAL, MOVES THE STORY FORWARD, AND MAINTAINS TENSION IN EACH STORYLINE?

The X-ray is also a great, visual way to track multiple POVs; you can use a different color for each character's sections or scenes. When you're finished you have a visual representation of how the POV sections are dispersed—it's a simple matter then to see whether you have too many scenes with that storyline absent, or too much concentration of any one storyline. You can also then easily separate out each character's individual story and character arc in sub-X-rays, and evaluate each one using the questions in this chapter to make sure every individual storyline is fully developed and resolved.

> *Finally, it's worth saying again:*
>
> **Every single scene, every single line, must move the story forward.** Otherwise the reader feels we're treading water or drifting rudderless.

If you've been working from the X-ray, once you've honed the outline using the above assessment questions and rearranged, cut, or fine-tuned all the individual story elements that make up the overall story in that bulleted list, it becomes a crystal-clear road map you can use as you embark on your revisions in the actual manuscript.

For instance, if you discovered in the outline that you have a few characters whose stories are not intrinsic to the main story arc, you may have decided to cut or combine them. Do it first in the X-ray, rearranging and rewriting the bullet-pointed story developments as needed; then when you turn to the manuscript you can use the revised X-ray as a guide to go in and cut (or move) the scenes that correspond to those changes. If you have holes in the plot line—perhaps you see you need to show how C leads to D, or X leads to Y, etc.—you can fill in those gaps at the X-ray stage by inserting (maybe in a different font or a new color, so you can easily keep track of new material) the new or revised developments delineating what needs to be added to provide whatever connective tissue is missing.

While it's not the only way to approach revisions, the story X-ray is an invaluable tool you can use for so many purposes. In addition to making editing and revisions infinitely easier, it will help you in writing your synopsis, query letters, and cover copy, and can even serve as a fabulous marketing tool later, offering agents, publishers, marketing departments, and publicists a complete overview of the story to help them know how best to represent it.

But its highest calling is to help an author assess and revise his story with the minimum of heartache and frustration. Work from the bare bones of your X-ray before you dive into the fully fleshed meat of the story and you will find editing your plot feels more manageable, goes much more smoothly, and results in far less sanity being lost in the process.

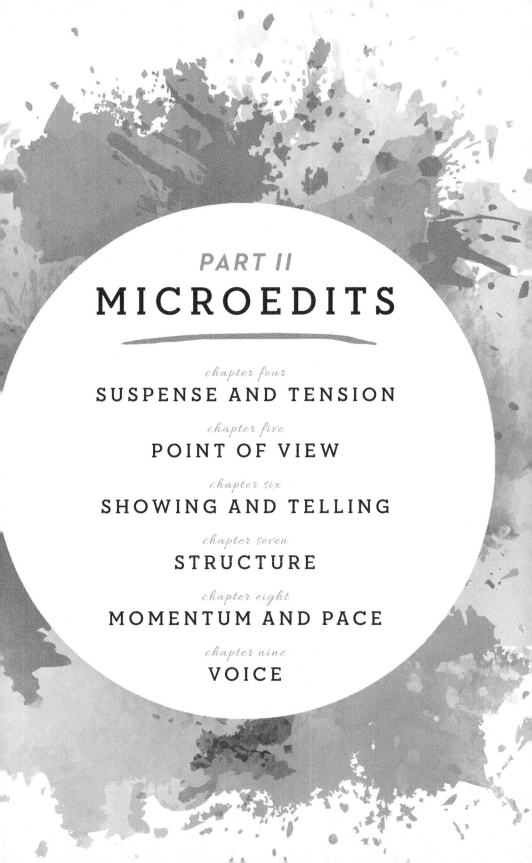

PART II
MICROEDITS

chapter four

suspense
AND TENSION

O utside the holy trinity of character, plot, and stakes, if there's a
single element of storytelling that makes the difference in how
well your story succeeds, it's how well you create and sustain suspense
and tension.

The terms are often used interchangeably, but they aren't quite the
same thing. Webster's dictionary calls suspense "Pleasant excitement as to
a decision or outcome." Brittanica defines tension as "A balance maintained
in an artistic work between opposing forces or elements." In oversimplified
terms, **suspense often equates to uncertainty**, the thrilling, unsettling
feeling of "what happens next?" whereas **tension often equals conflict**,
whether subtle or overt, internal or external, direct or indirect. I think of
suspense as a macroelement of story and tension as a microelement of style,
but we'll talk about both in this chapter because they're closely related and
often used in tandem. And the reason both are so crucial to the effectiveness of your story is because they keep the reader turning pages. Tension
and suspense are the heart of fiction, no matter your genre.

Suspense

Even if you aren't a fan of the Marvel universe (and I have to confess I
am), you may have heard about the furor over the penultimate Avengers

movie. Without laying down any spoilers, the last ten minutes or so hit most viewers like a plank in the face. Why? *Because it didn't end the way we expected it to.*

Most stories offer an inherent promise of resolution: We can go back to the classic trope of boy meets girl, boy loses girl, boy gets girl. That's why we watch (or read): for a happy ending, or to see the good guys win, or at least to find some meaning or enlightenment.

Now, like the last pair of Harry Potter films, *Avengers: Infinity War* was the first in a two-part finale, so we could bank on the end of part two delivering on that inherent story promise (as it did). But if, in most cases, we already know how a story is going to end, why do we still want to experience it?

The answer lies in uncertainty.

The appeal of story is the same reason we do a lot of things we enjoy: baking or gardening or bungee jumping. It's not just to achieve the end product, or we'd go buy a box of doughnuts or an eggplant or just stay down there on the ground. The *journey* is the point—those moments flailing through the air on the end of a glorified rubber band. For a few breathless moments you get to experience the thrill of uncertainty—will the soufflé rise…how big will my watermelon get…is that thing going to snap in midair? *That's* why we read (or watch) stories. And the crucial tool a writer uses to create that delicious uncertainty is suspense.

✓ How to Find It

Here's a handy little shortcut for determining whether and where you're using suspense in your story to draw the reader in and keep her hooked: **Suspense creates a question**:

- Why did he do that?
- What does that mean?
- What is she thinking?
- How will he react to this?
- What will become of her?
- How will he overcome this obstacle?

- How will she achieve her goal?
- Will she escape/survive/win, etc.?

And an infinite number of others. Human nature is to seek out answers, to satisfy our curiosity—so as an author you must create questions, mysteries, unknowns, uncertainties that arouse it. And all these questions are in service to the larger, through-line question of any story: **What will happen next?**

Most of us have had the experience of reading a book or watching a movie or TV show and predicting the plot resolution. If our prediction is borne out we may still be entertained, but it's less engaging, less thrilling, less satisfying than those stories that keep us solidly guessing. There's a reason movies like *The Crying Game* or *Sixth Sense* or *Fight Club* captivate such a wide audience: Most of us never saw the twist coming. There's a reason tightly and cleverly plotted stories like *Rebecca* or *The Martian* or *Gone Girl* gain such a broad readership—we read on to be surprised, because we can't figure out the plot and resolution on our own. If we can't see a way out for the characters, then the author owns us—we rely completely on her to show us the answers we can't quite puzzle out—and we are delighted to be surprised.

Generally speaking, it's no fun for readers to outsmart the protagonist, beat her to a solution, or easily figure out what she can't. That doesn't mean that we can't have an idea how things are going to turn out—in the Harry Potter books, for instance, we may assume Harry is probably going to survive any dangers, at least till the end of the series, or there probably wouldn't be a series named after him. In a romance, chances are pretty solid that the hero and heroine will wind up together. But the way skilled authors keep suspense high is with one of the most useful questions in creating suspenseful writing: *how.* It's not always the endpoint of a story that is the unknown that keeps us reading, but gradually discovering the winding and unexpected path the protagonist travels to it.

Sometimes the question that keeps us hooked is *who*—in murder mysteries, for instance, when we read to discover whodunit. It can also be *why*: In *Big Little Lies*, we know someone has died and there's suspicion of a crime, and though the story eventually reveals who has been killed and who did it, the main thrust of the plot is developing all the reasons *why*. It can even be *when*, if a character is working against a ticking clock—as in many thrillers.

Say what you like about Dan Brown as a writer stylistically, but the man is a master at creating suspense that keeps readers frantically turning pages, using an array of techniques for *making us need to know something* that compels us to read on for the answers—especially at chapter ends, one of the most important places to keep the reader hooked. (How many times have you put down a mediocre book after finishing a chapter and then just sort of forgotten about it?) Questions and uncertainty abound in *The Da Vinci Code*:

- **Prologue:** A freshly assaulted art curator realizes that he must summon every last bit of his waning strength to accomplish some "desperate" unnamed task before he dies. [What for? What task? Why is it desperate? Who is the man who killed him, and why?]

- **Chapter 1:** Robert Langdon, a code expert named in the man's dying gesture, regards a photo of the curator's bloody corpse in horror, unable to imagine who could have done such violence to the old man—only to be informed by the investigator that the victim did it to himself. [How could he have done this to himself—and why? (This is also an upended expectation, another tool of suspense we'll talk about shortly.) Why did the victim summon Langdon? What is the message, and what is it for? Will Langdon be able to decipher it? Is he a suspect?]

- **Chapter 2:** The killer calls the Teacher to tell him the murder is complete, and the Teacher tells him to retrieve the keystone. The killer then flogs himself with a barbed whip. [Who is the Teacher? Why did he instruct this man to kill the curator? Why does the killer take orders from him? What is the keystone? What does the Teacher mean to do with it? Why is the killer self-harming after succeeding at his task?]

Brown—and any good author—uses a variety of techniques for creating suspense, but all of them have this in common: **They raise questions in the reader's mind**—and they do not answer those questions immediately.

You can dissect techniques for creating suspense by analyzing your favorite books, movies, or TV shows using this idea: See if you can pinpoint the questions the writers create throughout the story or show. And pay extra attention to places where you're especially hooked. I once watched my laid-back husband literally scoot to the edge of his seat during an episode of *The Big Bang Theory* about a letter found in the closet of one of the main characters, Howard. Howard hadn't read the letter—from his estranged father—but during the course of the show every single other main character did, and only Howard—and viewers—had no idea what was in it. My husband (and I, to be honest) were practically frothing at the mouth to know what it said.

✓ How to Fix It

Your central story question is the "meta suspense" overarching the entire manuscript: What was the crime and who committed it (*Big Little Lies*); will the Avengers save the world; can Anastasia and Christian be together (*Fifty Shades of Grey*); why did Izzy set the family house on fire (*Little Fires Everywhere*). Again, this applies to any story in any genre. There's a reason that old romance trope doesn't go: Boy meets girl, boy gets girl. That's a nice bit of luck for boy and girl (if they mutually choose each other, of course), but the part that makes it *story* is missing: *boy loses girl*. That's where the suspense lies, with the uncertainty of whether boy will get girl back, and how.

So as you're reviewing your own story, see if you can define your meta suspense question: What is the reason we're reading? What big-picture outcome is in question? With *To Kill a Mockingbird*, for instance, it's whether Atticus Finch will exonerate Tom Robinson for a crime he didn't commit, despite false witness and the town's racism. In the James Bond novels/movies, it's whether Bond will defeat each story's central villain. In the first eponymous book of the Hunger Games series, it's whether

Katniss will survive—and similarly, across the series it's whether the rebels will defeat the evil President Snow, yet each book has its own main suspense arc.

But in all effective stories there are also smaller suspense arcs: in Harper Lee's classic, for instance, they include what will happen with Scout's friend Dill; who Boo Radley is and what he might do; the threat of Bob Ewell, who falsely accused Robinson, exacting revenge for what he feels was Atticus's shaming of him. In *The Hunger Games* (book one), Suzanne Collins relentlessly layers in suspense elements: whether Haymitch can train Katniss and Peeta adequately; whether they'll get useful weapons in the first moments of the game; whether Katniss will get out of the tree alive; whether she can save Rue; whether she and Peeta really have feelings for each other (and what that means for her childhood love, Gale); whether she and Peeta will both be allowed to live when they outfox the rules; what will happen when they get back to their district, and so on.

Does your story have one overarching suspense arc you can easily convey in a sentence, as we did above? Does each scene carry some question, raise some uncertainty in the reader's mind?

Once you've spotted places in your manuscript that may lack suspense, look for ways you could **introduce uncertainty**:

- Unanswered questions
- Unresolved issues, an unsettled conflict, leaving things in the air
- An unknown—withheld information, secrets
- Bread crumbs/puzzle pieces
- Misdirection or upended expectations
- Foreshadowing

Let's look at some examples of using suspense to hook your reader from the beginning.

With a screech of metal, the car went over the bridge.

This is a common mistake or shortcut authors make—assuming that starting a story or scene or chapter on an exciting event generates suspense in and of itself. The problem is that readers don't have enough information here to feel engaged—we're distant bystanders witnessing an accident, perhaps concerned but not intimately involved.

> Julia didn't even have time to scream as her car went over
> the bridge.

This is a little better—we have a character now, and as we saw earlier readers hook into a story on the backs of your characters, not your plot. This sentence raises a little bit of curiosity because of that, and because we may want to know why the car went off the bridge, but we don't know anything about Julia yet, so her accident, while unfortunate, is still of limited interest to us.

> On the way to the trial on the morning of her anniversary,
> Julia's car went over the bridge.

Now we're beginning to feel our curiosity rouse with the addition of a couple of details that provide context for Julia, and raise a question: Why is she going to trial on the day of her anniversary? What sort of trial? Is the accident connected? You're layering in context that creates more uncertainty and curiosity.

> Julia had woken up dreading the day—not least because of
> the irony: Today would have been her and Ben's anniversary.
> Instead of celebrating together, though, they would be locked
> in conflict. Not so different from most of their marriage, she
> reflected as she turned onto the bridge.
> The steering wheel juddered slightly in her hands—out of
> alignment, one more thing to have to take care of. She'd get
> that looked at today—if she could. If Ben didn't manage to get
> her arrested. If the judge didn't fall for his lawyer's "evidence..."
> She couldn't even think about the possibility he'd actually win
> custody of the girls—her job was to protect them, and if that
> meant perjuring herself in court she'd do it.

Something jolted her body violently, like limp prey shaken in the teeth of a predator, as the screech of metal assaulted her ears. There was no time, let alone air, to scream as her car yanked to the side and went off the bridge.

This raises a lot more questions in the reader's mind. What happened after the first year of Julia's marriage that turned it from "glorious" to endless conflict? What is Ben's evidence—and evidence of what? Why would it get her arrested? What is she protecting her girls from? What would she have to lie about—and why? What happened with the accident—did someone tamper with the car? Hit her? Who, and why? Did she hit someone? Lose control without realizing (perhaps distracted)? Will she survive? If Ben presents a danger to her daughters, what will happen to them if she's killed/seriously wounded?

Let's look at one last example:

Julia had woken up that day dreading the trial for custody of her two daughters—not least because of the irony: Today would have been her and Ben's anniversary. Instead of celebrating together, though, they would be locked in bitter conflict. Not so different from most of their marriage, she reflected as she turned onto the bridge. Except for that glorious first year. Before. It was how she always thought of it—that magical honeymoon period before she'd found out that everything was based on a lie and her husband was actually a sociopath.

Hmm—her car had been acting funny all morning. She'd meant to take it in for servicing last week but had been too busy with the girls—it was hard being a single parent, but still better than having Ben around. She knew he loved them, but she couldn't stand the idea of them being around his lies—and that woman. She'd get the car looked at today—if there was time after the court appearance before she had to pick the girls up at school. Her mind wandered to the call from the principal that morning: We need to talk about your daughters. What could it mean?

Suddenly her car yanked to the side and went off
the bridge.

This passage has too many baited hooks dangling—layering in a
series of mysteries can feel heavy-handed, or deliberately coy, like the
author is manipulating the reader's response. (Think of the cryptic Facebook posts that drive everyone crazy: "Desperately trying to hang on…"
or "Wow, I can't believe I did that. Not sure I can bounce back from this.")
These types of little mysteries frustrate rather than titillate—we see the
hook plainly and we may bite, but it creates a subtle feeling of resentment.

The passage also "front-loads" too much information. We have all
the answers we need about the backstory, and so we have no need to keep
reading. Give your reader a trail of bread crumbs to follow, rather than
shoving a whole loaf down our throats all at once. Readers love piecing
together a puzzle—it makes us an active part of the story, instead of a
passive recipient. There's a delicate balance between giving us context so
that we're invested in an outcome or event, and overloading us in a way
that removes all suspense.

Finally, placement matters—the second example above would contain
plenty of suspense if it were at the end of a chapter in which we'd already
"met" Julia and become invested in her, or if the accident blindsided us in
the middle of what we thought was the through line of the scene.

SUSPENSE TIPS

- Suspense is all about delayed gratification. Anticipation is its
  major element; avoid resolution as long as possible to maintain
  it. There's a reason writers kept Sam and Diane apart as long as
  possible in the show *Cheers*, or Ross and Rachel in *Friends*. Once
  the suspense of whether they will be together is resolved, the air
  goes out of the balloon. Notice that Ross and Rachel didn't wind
  up together until the very last episode of *Friends*, and Sam and
  Diane had more breakups than Taylor Swift before finally—in
  the series finale, again—realizing once and for all that they
  were never meant to be together. In both cases the suspense is
  resolved…and the show is over.

- If you do satisfy the reader's curiosity about one suspense element, you must immediately introduce another—as in superhero movies, for instance: no sooner has Tony Stark defeated Ivan Vanko and his electricity whip in *Ironman II* than a fresh villain—Stark's rival Justin Hammer—sets in motion an even bigger threat to Stark. In *Gone Girl*, over and over and over author Gillian Flynn builds suspense and plays it out; no sooner does she resolve one element of it than she introduces another—bringing in a new threat or an obstacle, upping the stakes, introducing another question, upending our expectations. That's fiction that keeps readers turning pages.

- Compound suspense elements. With some areas of craft, more is less, as with defusing the impact of a story development by showing the same dynamic more than once (see the Plot chapter). But with suspense, *more* can often improve your story. Look at the description of *To Kill a Mockingbird*'s suspense elements, above—Lee deftly balances several different unknowns, threats, secrets, mysteries, obstacles to create a rich tapestry of story that engages readers on multiple levels. Build layers of suspense throughout your story, and incorporate different *types* of suspense as well—bread crumbs, foreshadowing, misdirection, secrets, unknowns, cliffhangers. There are many ways to keep readers guessing, wondering, or uneasy; find a mix of different ways to build stakes and keep readers deeply invested.

- You can also incorporate multiple threads of suspense in stories with more than one protagonist—in each POV, build separate suspense elements for each character's storyline, as well as overarching ones that pertain to the overall story. *Gone Girl* is a great example of this technique; so is *Big Little Lies*. And for added suspense that compels readers to keep turning pages, make sure to leave each character in medias res from scene to scene—smack in the middle of some unresolved issue or unknown mystery or uncertain threat or obstacle. It's an utterly delicious seesaw for readers to be voraciously invested in one storyline, and then equally deeply pulled into another, each POV section leaving us craving more and refusing to immediately satisfy that desire. Suspense, if you will, is all about frustration.

• Tied in with the above, remember that chapter ends—even in single-protagonist/POV stories—are an essential place for suspense if you want readers to pick your book back up after they put it down.

Tension

Suspense is the question on the journey from "boy meets girl" to whether "boy gets girl," but tension is that tasty "boy loses girl" filling—everything that presents an obstacle or conflict for your characters in pursuit of their objectives.

As I suggested in the above section, both these style elements overlap, but whereas suspense is uncertainty as to an outcome, tension is everything that happens to create that uncertainty: everything that jeopardizes the desired outcome, as well as all the obstacles on the path. Suspense is whether the boy will manage to win the girl; tension is the ex-boyfriend, the sudden illness, the lost phone number, the terrible fight—in other words, every specific thing that throws into question the ultimate outcome. **Tension arises from conflict or an obstacle.**

Elements of tension belong in every single genre, and on every single page of your story—almost in every single moment. You are a storyteller spinning your thread; without tension it droops straight to the ground. Tension is what keeps it taut.

That's not to say you should have a damsel-on-the-train-tracks melodramatic approach to every moment of your story—but some element of tension is essential for keeping it consistently engaging. As we'll explore shortly, that can be external or internal, overt or subtle, evinced in action or dialogue (both verbal and internal). In fact, dialogue can be the most efficient and effective way to create tension.

Tension is the heart of fiction. No tension = no story.

✓ How to Find It

To check whether you have tension in every scene—on every single page—look for whether and where you have **opposing forces or obstacles keeping your protagonist from what she wants.**

Gillian Flynn's *Gone Girl* is rife with tension that keeps readers' hearts in their mouths throughout. Here's a summary of a single scene on pages 74–76 of the hardcover edition:

> Nick walks into his "coffin of an office" with the officer investigating him as a suspect in his wife's disappearance, and on Nick's desk is an envelope marked "Second Clue." He's obliged to open it with the officer watching—it contains both a clue to her disappearance and a folded piece of paper marked with a heart. He has no idea what either might contain. The heart note turns out to say how brilliant Amy thinks Nick is—belying Nick's having told the officer they'd been having marital problems. The cop reads over his shoulder, comments on the sweet note, then points out the pair of women's underwear flung in a corner of Nick's office. He waits for an explanation—Nick lies and says the panties are his wife's and tries to take them, but the officer slides them into an evidence bag. The cop asks Nick what the clue means, and Nick says he has no idea, even though he does.

This short scene is just dripping with tension, from the first line where Flynn uses a word that evokes death—*coffin*—to the last: "I lied."

The forces keeping Nick from what he wants—which is ultimately to be exonerated for his wife's disappearance—are:

- the investigating cop's presence
- the possibly incriminating clue
- the unexpected love note
- the exposing of what seems to be Nick's lie about their marriage
- the underwear from Nick's affair

- the cop taking them into evidence
- the import of the clue, which Nick knows and cannot reveal to the cop.

Even the seemingly casual dialogue in this scene helps create tension—Nick references Freddy Krueger and the cop says he never saw the movies (negating Nick's effort to create the simplest of connections); the officer comments that Amy is a "sweet lady" after reading her note (though Nick has painted her as anything but); he waits in a loaded silence for Nick to explain the panties (the dilemma of revealing the incriminating truth); and then he offers overly jovial assurances that taking them into evidence is "just procedure" (when Nick knows it's much more than that).

The main *suspense* in this scene—the overarching uncertainty—is whether Nick will be arrested as a suspect, whether he can prove his innocence, and even—brilliantly—whether he actually *is* innocent or guilty, as Flynn keeps the reader uncertain throughout, and there is also the smaller suspense question of what's in the letter. But Flynn additionally layers in a variety of techniques in this scene to create strong *tension*: a pending threat (the clue, the letter, whether the cop will notice another woman's panties in his office); opposition (Amy's letter belying Nick's story, the officer taking the panties Nick tries to hold on to); a lie; mood (the "coffin of an office"); and the dialogue itself, a disingenuous cat-and-mouse game the officer plays with Nick.

TENSION RESULTS FROM AN OBSTACLE OR CONFLICT

Check every scene and page to see whether you have some kind of frictional, antagonistic forces. For instance:

- a problem, challenge, or impediment (person or thing)
- a looming deadline (ticking clock)
- a danger
- a disagreement, friction
- a thwarted desire or goal

- an unmet or upended expectation
- a lack of response
- a false front or lie
- an inability to react/respond (restrained, constrained, trapped, etc.)
- a mood or atmosphere.

TENSION CAN BE EXTERNAL OR INTERNAL

External tension comes from forces outside the protagonist—an antagonist, an obstacle, an impediment. Internal tension originates within your character—a substance abuse problem, for instance; mixed or conflicted feelings; opposing goals. A hurricane endangering the protagonist is external tension; her childhood phobia of storms is an internal one. The most compelling fiction incorporates both—like Adrian Monk outwitting and catching the criminals he investigates (external), and the challenges of his obsessive-compulsive disorder and phobias (both internal and external). In the Monk books and TV show, those tensions are compounded still further by Monk's frustration at his inability to catch his wife's killer (internal and external); the initial resistance of Captain Stottlemeyer toward Monk's work with the department and his frequent frustration with Monk (external); Monk's dependence on his assistant, and his occasional chafing under it (external and internal).

TENSION CAN BE OVERT OR SUBTLE, DIRECT OR INDIRECT

Think of overt, direct tension as a slap in the face, and subtle or indirect as an ignored hand offered for a handshake. A man screaming at his wife when he gets home from work is overt and direct; his silence and lack of eye contact when she tries to greet him is subtle and indirect. A fleeting sneer on a lover's face is subtle but direct; answering an "I love you" with "Thank you" is overt but indirect. Two people bickering about something picayune can take on powerful tension if we know that the minor argument is sprouting from a much deeper unspoken one, like a disagreement over which way to put the toilet paper on the roll that really stems from the characters' impasse over whether or not to have children.

TENSION CAN BE EVINCED THROUGH ACTION, DIALOGUE, OR EVEN TOTAL SILENCE

The howling of a blizzard that shakes a rickety front door in an isolated cabin where a killer lurks outside is tense action. Dialogue can be fraught with tension even when it seems pedestrian:

> "I have an expense account."
> "So do I. I said I'll get it."

There's clearly a power struggle of some kind going on between the two characters speaking in the above exchange.

Silence can create some of the most powerful tension. Think of the silent sexual tension of two illicit lovers in an elevator heading up to a hotel room. The freighted silence as an unhappy couple eddies around each other at home. The terrifying silence after a car accident when a mother calls to her child in the backseat.

✓ How to Fix It

If you find you don't have some kind of tension in every single scene in your story, look to **add opposition and conflict** using any of the above techniques. Layer in various types of tension—a secret and a lie and a threat, for instance—as well as varying techniques: external/internal, overt/subtle, direct/indirect. Weave in tension using action, dialogue, and powerful silence.

In the Stakes chapter I referenced the Vladimir Nabokov quote, "The writer's job is to get the main character up a tree, and then once they are up there, throw rocks at them." Do worse than that: Put the tree in the middle of a hurricane…with a rotted root system…and a lion at the base of it…at the edge of a precipitous dropoff into a canyon…with a snake pit at the bottom.

Whenever possible, take the path of most resistance—and stay on it. Avoid making things easy on your characters, and don't resolve these tensions too quickly. Wring out all the juice by exploring your characters' visceral responses and showing knee-jerk reactions rather than intellectualizations (more on this in the Showing and Telling chapter). Want to see visceral, minute, real-time tension played to nerve-fritzing perfection? Watch the gritty, heart-fibrillating opening scene of 2008 war film *The Hurt Locker.*

TENSION TIPS

- Tension relies on stakes: Low stakes will rarely yield high tension.
- Tension almost always happens in "real time" and in tiny moments, not in summation or broad generalizations.
- Tension is almost always specific and granular, not broad and general.
- Tension is visceral, not intellectual. I call this "lizard-brain writing"—that gut-level amygdala reaction that kicks in long before your higher-reasoning cerebellum interprets it. "The creak of the door filled him with fear" packs little punch of tension. "As the low, moaning creak of hinges sliced through the silence, her stomach hollowed out and a chill raised the hairs at the back of her neck" does. The difference is more than verbiage (though that's part of it that we'll talk about in the Line Edits section); in the first example the protagonist's evolved cerebellum *interprets* the stimulus (the creak is a door; the feelings he's experiencing equal fear); in the second, the reader *experiences* the stimulus firsthand through the protagonist's primitive amygdala—the "feeling brain" that reacts rather than analyzes. The second statement is direct to the character's experience, rather than one step removed. In actuality the first, gut-level thing we register is not the logical conclusion we reach, but the effect on us of whatever is happening. The author must act as the reader's amygdala; it's the reader's own higher-reasoning interpretation of what the stimulus means that makes her a direct, immediate, visceral part of the story.
- Let the pressure build and draw it out—don't defuse tension too quickly. As with suspense (and foreplay), delayed gratification is key to building delicious tension.

- As suspense is crucial in chapter and scene ends, tension is especially important in scene and chapter beginnings. A chapter or section that starts with no conflict, no opposition, nothing endangered or at stake or under threat is inert and doesn't hook your reader. Begin looking to lace in tension elements from the very first sentence and setup. Read the American Book Review's list of 100 "Best First Lines from Novels," or open to the first page of books on your shelf and see which ones draw you in from the beginning—I remember reading *Gone Girl* for the first time and being utterly transfixed by that chilling opening line: "When I think of my wife, I always think of her head."

Don't stop there, though—thumb through and read the first few lines of chapters, sections. See which ones make you want to read on and which don't compel you—and notice how many of the former introduce at least one element of unresolved tension.

·· *#* ··

Tension keeps readers compulsively turning your pages—no matter your genre. Bait the hook and then don't let them off of it. No matter your genre, when tension flags, so will your reader's interest.

point of VIEW

M ost writers, hearing the term "point of view," take it to refer to which narrative voice the story is told in: first person, third person, etc. Point of view is literally the voice your story is told in, yes, but also much more than that—it's the way your reader orients and relates to it, a story's perspective and its personality. Your narrative voice is the first engagement a reader has with your story, an indication of our host and guide for what is to come, and as an author it's your chance to show us who your characters are and assure us that we are in capable hands. Strong, consistent POV lets the reader relax and lose herself in your story, trusting you to take us on a journey. Problems with point of view can detract from the story's effectiveness and keep readers from investing deeply in your story and characters.

✓ How to Find It

Before you can spot POV issues you have to have a solid understanding of the various narrative points of view, so let's first briefly define them:

FIRST PERSON

This is the "I" voice, directly narrated as if by a character—most often the (or a) protagonist (think Helen Fielding's *Bridget Jones's Diary*, Ta-Nehisi

Coates's *The Water Dancer*, or Margaret Atwood's *The Handmaid's Tale*) or a closely related character, as with *The Great Gatsby*, though it can also feature a first-person narrator who is a distinct character, but not one directly involved in the story, as in *Don Quixote*, John Steinbeck's *East of Eden*, and Melville's *Moby Dick*. The TV show *Jane the Virgin* uses a first-person narrator who is (we ultimately learn) tangentially related to the story. First person offers deep intimacy and a direct window into your character's inner life and experience, but it limits you to whatever the POV character directly sees, hears, or knows.

SECOND PERSON

This is the "you" voice, for example in choose-your-own-adventure books ("You find yourself at a crossroads. You look left…") or Dungeons and Dragons. ☺ It's unusual to see this POV choice in a novel, as it can feel awkward or gimmicky and draw attention to itself, making readers uncomfortably aware of themselves as they read, as if the actors on a stage suddenly broke the fourth wall to stare at or directly address the audience. This is a hard voice to pull off well, but a handful of successful books have used this POV with critical success: Jay McInerny's *Bright Lights, Big City*; *The Night Circus* by Erin Morganstern; *Booked* by Kwame Alexander. Neil Patrick Harris even used it—to hilarious effect—in his *Choose Your Own Autobiography*.

THIRD PERSON

This is the "he"/"she" voice common to many classic works, like Dickens and Dostoyevsky, but still much in use. This POV allows an author to explore outside a narrative character's direct experience, but can also be used to allow readers intimately into a character's direct perspective, depending on which type of third-person voice is used:

- **Limited** point of view (which may be called "deep," "close," "internal," or "subjective" POV) is colored by the direct viewpoint of a single character, as if we're actually in their head, part of their immediate experience, as in first person. This narrative voice is that of the focal character of each scene; we are directly privy to their inner lives, behind their eyes. The reader can know only what the character knows and perceives, as in first person, but the voice is the "he/she" of third person. A lot of modern novels use this POV, from Laila Ibrahim's *Yellow Crocus* to Jennifer Weiner's *Mrs. Everything* to Rachel Caine's Stillhouse Lake series.

- In **objective** POV, which you can think of as "narrator voice," the story isn't told from the direct perspective of any one character, but from an often undefined outside point of view, as if you're watching a movie. It can shift from character to character across or even within scenes, but is not *connected* to a character in the story, simply a detached observer voice. We're generally not inside the characters' heads and are confined to witnessing what they see and hear, with no access to their inner life. It allows a wider lens for storytelling, but if executed poorly can also distance readers from the direct experience of the story and can risk feeling a bit dated. Shirley Jackson's famous short story "The Lottery" is a classic example of this voice, as is Hemingway's *Hills Like White Elephants.*

- In **omniscient** POV the story has access to all characters' points of view. The narrative voice of omniscient POV is not a character in the story and can know anything—character names that the protagonist hasn't yet met, translations of languages she doesn't speak, obscure historical or technical details that may be out of her purview. This POV allows the author to reveal what characters are thinking and feeling, how they're reacting, but it can feel a bit jarring and, if handled inexpertly, leave readers feeling as if their footing in the scene (or the author's or narrator's footing) is uncertain, like a scene in a movie where the camera whirls crazily from face to face. Kevin Kwan's *Crazy Rich Asians* is told in this voice, Celeste Ng's *Little Fires Everywhere*, and Tolkein's *The Fellowship of the Rings.*

Point of view is a big topic and a complex one, and there are wonderful craft books and posts that go into much more detail—two of my favorites are the chapters on POV in Ursula K. Le Guin's *Steering the*

Craft and Sol Stein's *Stein on Writing*. For our purposes in this book I'll talk only about the first- and third-person points of view, by far the most common in modern literature (and arguably the most effective). Here's a little cheat sheet for how to think of each one that might help you keep them straight as you're evaluating whether you've used POV consistently and strongly in your manuscript:

- **First person**: The reader essentially *is* the character, living behind his eyes, seeing what he sees, thinking his thoughts.
- **Third-person limited**: The reader is the character's most intimate friend, close enough to practically read her mind as he walks in lockstep with her.
- **Third-person objective**: The reader is standing outside a window looking in at all the characters.
- **Third-person omniscient**: The reader is an invisible attendee of events, able to flit anywhere, including inside characters' heads, but only as a psychic observer, not directly sharing their thoughts or feelings.

Before you start checking for POV problems in your story, make sure you know which point(s) of view you're using, from the descriptions above.

Now let's look at some examples. Can you identify what POV this passage is in?

> Juan followed O'Shaughnessy out to the motorcar, the
> man suffering from cold feet despite the wool socks. Good,
> dammit. For the time being he wanted the Irishman a little
> uncomfortable.

If you said third-person, you're right—but you may have been less certain which third-person voice it's written in because the author has used POV inconsistently: If this is omniscient, then the jump into Juan's direct thought slips out of that voice—remember, omniscient POV sees and knows all, but the narrator is a discrete presence, and so not directly privy to a character's thoughts. You could fix this slip by instead saying something like, *The thought pleased him.*

If this is limited third-person, it's still a POV slip: Juan can't know whether O'Shaughnessy's feet are cold. He can anticipate or assume so— but you have to say that: *He hoped the man was suffering from cold feet.…*

Here's another example. What POV is the author using?

> Sarah stared up at Clay with big blue eyes, emotion washing over her like a landslide and drawing a shiver. She tossed her shoulder-length blond hair over her shoulder, her resolve stiffening. How could she live without him? Clay was absolutely everything to her. Everything.

This is mainly written as third-person limited—we're part of Sarah's direct perceptions—and yet twice the author slides out of her head in a bit of a clunky omniscient or objective attempt to describe her appearance. As you're reading this right now, are you conscious of doing it with your warm brown eyes? If your hair slips into your vision do you notice the curly red lock you flick over your shoulder? That isn't how we think of our own physicality or actions—these types of descriptions are an external point of view plopped into Sarah's subjective experience.

If this is third-person limited POV, you might have Sarah instead stare up at Clay and deliberately widen her eyes because she knows that men can never resist her big baby blues, for example—note that the difference is that we're firmly in Sarah's head and coloring the description with her conscious awareness of using her blue eyes to effect, rather than slipping suddenly into an external description of her. If this story is meant to be omniscient, you have to pull back the "camera" from her direct perception:

> The blonde stared up at Clay, blue eyes filled with emotion. He met her gaze, unsure what he saw there, and Sarah drew herself up, wanting to convey without words how important he was to her, that she couldn't live without him.

Notice that we can "see" more in this point of view, insofar as being able to also dip into Clay's perspective, but also notice that the omniscient voice significantly changes the feel of this moment, removes some direct intimacy. Omniscient voice can be effective and offer an author freedom to tell a story from more angles, a wider perspective, but it's among the hardest POVs to execute well and has ceded popularity in the current publishing market to first-person and limited third. It's also very easy to misuse and thus come across as inconsistent or filled with distracting head-hopping, and to result in a distancing feel for the reader. If you feel your story demands an omniscient viewpoint and want to try it, go forth! But make sure it offers something essential for your story (in other words, is it the strongest choice for telling this story?) and still allows you to deeply engage your reader. Then take a microscope to every line to make sure you use it consistently.

Uncertain POV can be an issue in first-person voice as well. Take a look at this sentence:

My face went pale at his words, my forehead ridging as I tried to understand.

Unless the narrator is staring into a mirror (please don't have your narrator stare into a mirror; it's one of the publishing world's most carped-about clichés), she can't know whether she's gone pale or her forehead ridges. She might assume or conclude as much, but you have to say that: *I imagined my face went white as paper, knowing my confusion must be carving ridges into my forehead.* That can be awkward, though, and not as powerful as putting the reader directly and viscerally into what a character is experiencing, so instead, try thinking about what the physical reaction or effect might *feel* like to that character: *My face went icy cold at his words* or *feeling my forehead tighten.* A POV character can't see herself blush, but she can feel the fire on her cheeks; she probably wouldn't necessarily imagine smiling at someone with her "straight white teeth," but she might relish the salubrious effect on the recipient of her painstaking dental history.

Now that you've defined what POV you're using, let's look at ways to address these and other common point-of-view pitfalls.

✓ *How to Fix It*

Three key areas of point of view can either enhance or hamper effective storytelling: **consistency**, **clarity**, and **strength**.

IS IT CONSISTENT?

Consistency is the lodestar of point of view—nothing undermines an author's authority in the reader's mind more quickly than an uncertain or shifting perspective. As we saw in the How to Find It section, the reader must feel firmly oriented in who's "talking" to us, who is telling us the story, what our frame of reference is, or he may feel adrift in the story, as if he can't quite get firm footing.

It's perfectly okay to use varying POVs within a *story*, as long as you don't arbitrarily switch within a *scene* (unless you indicate the switch with a space break). For instance, your story might be told in limited third person throughout, but have a handful of different POV characters. Or maybe you use first person for one character's sections and third for others', as Isobel Allende does in *The House of Spirits*. This is common in historicals, for instance, where the framing device is a present-day story that leads back to the sections of the story that take place in the past. Many thrillers/suspense novels do this as well, where one character is first-person, like a detective, and the killer is third-person, or vice versa. William Goldman brilliantly uses both third-person omniscient and first person—as himself—in *The Princess Bride*. You could even mix third-person limited and third-person objective—perhaps the story's antagonist speaks directly to the reader in a sort of intrinsic omniscient-narrator voice where he knows everything and is retelling this story from some future point (maybe from his jail cell, for instance), and the protagonist's sections are in limited third-person point of view as she lives the story in "real time" as it happened.

If you're using multiple POVs in a story, how do you decide which scene to tell from which character's perspective? A general rule of thumb is whichever one is most affected by the action of that scene, though depending on your intentions it can be equally effective to let another character observe the character most directly involved in the action: If a pulse-pounding escape scene is more about how the rescuee reacts to the rescuer, for instance, or the rescuee's fear or despair or hope, etc., then the scene might be much more impactful—depending on the story you're telling—if we see it through the eyes of the bound man simply observing and reacting to the whirling fists and feet of the masked woman taking on his three kidnappers. If the scene is about her facing the first test of her fighting skills amid life-or-death stakes higher than she's ever faced, then you might instead tell it from her POV.

But within each storyline and character, point of view must be used consistently: If you begin with one character in first person, for example, stay in that POV for all scenes from that character's perspective. You're not confined to showing an entire scene from a single character's POV, though. If you want to switch, simply use a space break within the scene and then resume the action from the new character's POV. (Space breaks are also used within a chapter to indicate a time lapse or location change.) But if a section (meaning part of a scene set off by space breaks) is in a particular point of view, don't switch midstream to another POV.

This shift from one character's POV to another within the same section or scene is what you may have heard referred to as "head hopping." It's different from omniscient voice, which can observe characters' thoughts and feelings but is not directly part of them; in head hopping the author flits into the direct perspective of different characters, which can evoke a dizzy or disorienting feeling, as if the camera is spinning around and the story has gotten away from the author, and you may lose the reader's trust. Shifting POV within a scene risks leaving the reader feeling ungrounded and uncertain, making him puzzle out whose perspective he's experiencing, which stalls pace and momentum—and anytime the reader comes out of the world of the story you risk losing him altogether.

As master editor (and bestselling author) Sol Stein says in *Stein on Writing*, one of the most articulate and useful books I know of about the nuts and bolts of writing: "[Switching points of view within a scene] is unsettling to the reader. If you mix points of view, the author's authority seems to dissolve. The writer seems arbitrary rather than controlled. Sticking to a point of view intensifies the experience of a

story. A wavering or uncertain point of view will diminish the experience for the reader."

Let's look at more POV slips and mistakes and see how to address
them.

IS IT CLEAR?

It's not enough for the *author* to know what point of view she's using; as
you saw with a couple of the above examples, if *readers* aren't certain of
the story's voice they can feel lost or adrift, even if they can't pinpoint
why. Very early into the story—and, if you use multiple POVs, early into
each chapter and scene—you must orient your reader to whose perspective they're in.

For example, take a look at this sentence:

> Jeff couldn't help smiling at Fred, pleased—that would teach
> the troublemaker to entertain job offers from their clients. Fred
> made no move from his chair; he wanted to ask about his sev-
> erance package. No, that would be inappropriate, under the
> circumstances. Fred took in the verdict with mounting fury as
> Jeff held in the urge to laugh.

Could you pin down who was the POV character here? At first it
seems to be Jeff in limited third person—we're in his direct perspective.
But Jeff can't know that Fred means to ask about his severance package,
and Fred can't know what Jeff is thinking. And who is perceiving or saying that severance would be inappropriate? The last sentences might be
omniscient POV, but we already saw an indication in the first sentence
that it's limited POV. The reader won't know why she feels lost—that
the author is slipping POVs—she just knows she has to stop and try to
orient herself in the scene. And now you've pulled her out of the story
and risked losing her.

Depending on what or whose story you're telling (is this Fred's
story/scene or Jeff's?) and what POV you've chosen, you could fix this
issue in any number of different ways:

Third-person limited, Jeff's POV:

Jeff couldn't help smiling at Fred, pleased—that would teach the troublemaker to entertain job offers from their clients. The traitor sat as if glued to his chair—did the presumptuous fool think he was getting a severance package? He had to know that would be inappropriate, under the circumstances, and Jeff said as much, watching with the barely held urge to laugh as the other man's face turned a delightful shade of red.

Third-person limited, Fred's POV:

That ass couldn't even make a pretense of not being pleased—the smug curl of Jeff's lips told Fred how much he was enjoying firing him for the job offer from EviCorp. It wasn't because Fred broke company policy against working for a client, either—it was his boss's jealousy.

Fred made no move from his chair; Jeff had better damn well be offering a severance package. He asked about it.

"No, that would be inappropriate, under the circumstances."

Fred's fury mounted as he watched Jeff hold in the urge to laugh.

Third-person omniscient:

Jeff smiled at Fred with a smug curl of his lips—Fred had entertained a job offer from one of their clients despite the express company policy against it, and now Jeff could finally fire him for it.

Fred didn't move from his chair. "What's my exit package?"

Jeff frowned, but the expression didn't mask the rapacious light in his eyes. "I think severance would be inappropriate, under the circumstances—don't you?"

Fred's face reddened, his fists tightening.

Third-person objective:

Jeff smiled across the desk at Fred, who fidgeted in his seat but didn't get up.

"What about severance?" Fred asked.

"That would be inappropriate, under the circumstances."

Fred's face tightened at the answer, but Jeff's smile never budged.

Here's another example:

Ariel was yanked down the stairs and into a dark stone hallway, at the end of which a barred door sealed off what could only be a prison cell. Three nuns in black habits were inside when she was thrown in—was someone looking out for her after all? "What's happening out there?" Sister Mary asked as soon as the doors slammed shut.

This one's subtle: The second sentence indicates that Ariel doesn't know these women—yet in the next sentence one of their names is used. Ariel has no way of knowing that yet, so we're not sure what point of view this story or scene is told in.

As with the previous example, depending on which point of view the author is using there are a variety of ways to orient the reader: If it's first person or limited third, planting us more deeply in Ariel's perspective as far as revealing what she's seeing, feeling, experiencing, etc., will send that clear signal, as well as clarifying whether she knows these nuns already—and in the process bringing this scene much more vividly to life.

If this is third-person omniscient, strip away or rephrase the direct perspectives of the POV character:

Ariel was yanked down the stairs and into a dark stone hallway, at the end of which a barred door sealed off what she assumed was a prison cell. Three nuns in black habits were inside when she was thrown in, making her wonder whether a higher power was in her corner. "What's happening out there?" one of them, Sister Mary, asked as soon as the doors slammed shut.

If it's third-person objective, we can know only what we actually see—no intentions, thoughts, motivations, etc.:

> Ariel was yanked down the stairs and into a dark stone hallway, at the end of which was a barred door. Three nuns in black habits were inside when she was thrown in. "What's happening out there?" one asked as soon as the doors slammed shut.

With practice you'll get good at spotting inconsistent, unclear, or shifting point of view. But even a rock-solid adherence to POV principles can leave your readers at arm's length from the story and your characters if you don't offer a strong perspective as their window into the story.

IS IT STRONG?

One of the most powerful elements of using a direct POV—first person or subjective third—is that it offers the author the ability to make the reader a firsthand, immediate part of the story. We're not simply taking in what happens to the protagonists—we're living it right along with them, along for the ride in their heads, behind their eyes. This is one of the reasons these points of view are so prevalent in today's literature, with readers trained by first-person video games, virtual reality, and more immersive film and TV show styles.

Even in objective and omniscient third person, though, the author can dig below the surface of a scene and reveal depth and nuance that heightens the reader's experience. But if POV is weak in any narrative voice then we're robbed of that opportunity, held at arm's length, on the outside looking in. The result is usually a less effective, less affecting character journey and diminished reader investment.

Let's look at a few examples:

> "Will you marry me, Chase?"
> I looked at Rick, down on one knee. "Of course I will."

"Where were you last night between ten p.m. and midnight?"
the detective asked.

Reginald chewed the inside of his cheek. "Asleep, I guess."

The footsteps grew closer now, along with the sound of something metal dragging along the concrete floor. Sissy waited, her pocketknife gripped in her hand and feeling swamped by a welter of emotions, for the intruder to round the corner. She'd have to strike fast, before he saw her—his weapon, whatever it was, sounded a lot heavier than hers.

All three of these examples definitely have action—something is happening. And all three use POV consistently: first, omniscient third, and limited third, respectively. But they lack a strong point of view—a direct window into the protagonist's visceral experience and inner life. And notice how much is missing or uncertain because of it. We don't know what the characters are feeling, experiencing; we don't have a vivid, visceral picture of the scene and the action; we don't know anything about the other characters and their behavior. And in all three we don't directly experience the scene—we're on the outside looking in, and we miss so much potential juicy nuance.

Yet these are all wonderfully potentially tense moments—it's just that readers don't really feel that because we aren't viscerally experiencing them with the protagonists. Tension can be vastly heightened by strong point of view. Watch the scene in the movie *Get Out* where fish-out-of-water protagonist Chris is led into a terrifying hypnosis experience by his girlfriend's mother. What makes this scene heart-stutteringly tense for viewers isn't what he's seeing—the Sunken Place itself—or what's actually happening to Chris. It's his reaction to it—the camera lingering unswervingly on his face as we see his terror consume him: wide eyes, trembling, helpless tears—that makes us feel this scene's drum-tight tension. That's the kind of power and impact we're looking for.

In the first example, for instance, is Rick an earnest, ardent suitor as he proposes to Chase, or is this an expected proposal, one he felt forced into? Is Chase excited, touched, surprised, even irritated by his beau's proposal? We don't know. All those evocative details come out when you dive deep into POV. You have the opportunity to create richly layered subtexts, meanings, impact.

Notice how much fuller the above scene becomes if we're allowed into Chase's perspective a bit more:

> "Will you marry me, Chase?"
>
> It was barely noticeable, but looking at Rick, down on one knee, I saw the ring in his outstretched hand tremble, and his eyes were suspiciously shiny.
>
> "Of course I will."

Here we've added simply what Chase sees in this scene, with a bit more detail, and thus Rick's physiological reactions add a new layer of meaning to the scene. This would work equally well in objective or omniscient third: *the ring in Rick's outstretched hand trembled and his eyes shone.* In all cases we see that Rick is nervous, most likely, and emotionally affected. This is already better, more visceral and visual, but notice that we're only halfway there—we now know what Chase is seeing, but we aren't yet privy to his reactions to it. Let's add that in:

> "Will you marry me, Chase?"
>
> It was barely noticeable, but I saw the ring in Rick's outstretched hand tremble, and his eyes were suspiciously shiny.
>
> The words that had leaped to my throat the moment he'd dropped to one knee froze there. I didn't want to get married—Rick knew that—but his unexpected earnestness melted loose an answer I never imagined myself giving him:
>
> "Of course I will."

Look how much more we understand about this scene now, about Chase and Rick individually, and about their relationship dynamic. We layered all that in simply by showing the reader more of what our POV character experiences and allowing her into his inner life, making her a direct, firsthand part of the character's perceptions and responses: seeing what Chase sees, reacting as he does, feeling his feelings, thinking his thoughts. Even in the less intimate third-person POVs, objective and omniscient, you can reveal what's beneath the simple action and dialogue by showing reactions, demeanor, affect—in all characters. Another of the great truisms I learned as an actor was, "Acting is reacting." In many ways so is story. What actually *happens* is only part of the story; much of its meaning and impact on the reader stems from showing its meaning and impact for the characters.

Before, this scene could have meant anything—it was neutral, flat, "just the facts, ma'am," and we had no sense of subtexts, of what was swirling underneath the words and events. Now we've added shading, color, dimension, depth. This is no longer just action—now there's *story* there. The author is like an artist creating a painting: first she roughs out the general shapes, the overall idea of the subject, but the picture doesn't really come to life until she begins shading it in, each brushstroke adding more and more nuance, layers, depth, texture.

In the second and third POV example scenes above, these are wonderfully potentially tense moments, but readers don't really feel that because we aren't viscerally experiencing them with the protagonists.

Let's look again at the second of the examples I offered at the beginning of this section:

> "Where were you last night between ten p.m. and midnight?" the detective asked.
> Reginald chewed the inside of his cheek. "Asleep, I guess."

Here's how deeper POV might improve this exchange:

> "Where were you last night between ten p.m. and midnight?" the detective asked, his mouth relaxed but his eyes hard and cold.
> Reginald nervously chewed the inside of his cheek. His explanation was no alibi at all, but the truth would be worse.

"Asleep, I guess."

We're showing the detective's demeanor now—his intimidating presence conveys his suspicion of Reginald, which amps up stakes for the character. We see that in Reginald's fear reaction—his nervousness. And we're more privy to his thoughts now, so that we understand why he's reacting this way: Reginald clearly feels he has something to hide. That also builds the moment's tension and adds layers of meaning and nuance to the story.

Here's the third example:

The footsteps grew closer now, along with the sound of something metal dragging along the concrete floor. Sissy waited, her pocketknife gripped in her hand and feeling swamped by a welter of emotions, for the intruder to round the corner. She'd have to strike fast, before he saw her—his weapon, whatever it was, sounded a lot heavier than hers.

Here's how you could bring us into closer POV:

The footsteps grew closer now, along with the ragged scrape of something metal dragging along the concrete floor. Sissy's heart thunked against her ribs—could he hear it? Hear her fast-panting breaths that tried to keep up? She waited—hot helpless tears pricking her eyes, her pocketknife ridiculously insubstantial in her trembling grip—for the intruder to round the corner. She'd have to strike fast, before he saw her; his weapon, whatever it was, sounded a lot heavier than hers—a metal pipe, a baseball bat. An ax.

This scene is much more chilling now because we're in Sissy's head and direct experience, feeling her fearful reactions viscerally (thunking heart, panting, trembling hand), our apprehension and imaginations racing along with hers about what will happen, fearing the terrible unknown along with her about what dreadful weapon the man might be wielding against her wholly inadequate pocketknife. This version uses specifics as well to deepen POV: a "sound" becomes the more evocative "ragged scrape"; the vague "welter of emotions" becomes concrete details to let readers infer what she's feeling: racing heart, panting, trembling, tears. Notice that besides drawing us more deeply and directly into this scene, diving deeper into the POV character's head also amps up tension considerably—it makes these moments visceral and immediate, rather than removed, dry.

What makes scenes like this affecting isn't the action itself, but the *effect* of the action on our POV character. It's Stamp Paid's mute horror at seeing what Sethe has done to her children in *Beloved*, or Paul D's vomiting into the dirt at the forcibly sodomized slave in chains directly beside him. It's Marianne Dashwood's shattered heartbreak at John Willoughby's cruel rejection in *Sense and Sensibility*, Bridget Jones's embarrassment and plucky recovery when she shows up in a risqué costume for the tarts-and vicars party and realizes she misunderstood.

The only way we can understand and experience those emotions is through the characters' reactions. Character is the soul of fiction, and POV is a powerful way we relate to character. If you want readers to deeply invest in your characters, their journey, and the story, *let us into* their direct perception and inner lives.

Strengthening point of view, particularly in close third-person and first-person, as we discussed in the Character chapter, also means orienting readers firmly in the worldview and perspective of your POV character. In this type of third-person POV, where you allow us into the character's direct experience even though you're using the one-step-removed voice of he/she, you're still telling the story from the character's direct perspective. That means, for instance, that the POV character can use only words he knows, references she would have. A blue-collar mineworker whose narrative—not just his dialogue—features academic or pedagogic allusions would be a POV slip, unless that's a deliberate character choice, for instance that he was a thwarted scholar forced to work in a mine, or that he spends every evening reading philosophy classics. You could deepen a birdwatcher's POV narrative by using frames of reference she might naturally make in both her dialogue and narrative sections:

she might observe someone flitting like a sparrow, or a Milwaukee town emptying out every winter as residents flee south like a mass migration. This fleshes out your characters even more deeply, brings them more vividly and fully to life in a way that likely will fly under the radar of most readers: the technique is subtle and smooth, but the effect is to intimately and completely plunge us into that character's perspective.

Similarly, you can intentionally use the vernacular and speech patterns and mannerisms of the POV character to deepen that characterization and instill the narrative with a powerful sense of voice. Consider this example:

> Jack looked at the woman; he didn't need another crazy girlfriend like his ex, Melinda. He clenched his jaw, not wanting to think about her.

By letting the narrative voice more closely reflect Jack's character, perhaps you'd write something more like this:

> Jesus. Jack eyeballed the woman; last thing he needed was another damn crazy like Melinda. The ache in his jaw told him he was clenching it again. Not going there.

A close third-person POV character also wouldn't think of herself in external ways in references: *the redhead,* or *Ms. Fredericks.* This immediately pulls the reader out of the immersive experience of subjective POV and into a removed narrator voice—you've slipped into omniscient or objective POV. Instead you can frame thoughts like this in that character's direct POV. If we need to know the color of her hair, let us "see" it through her direct perspective: "sunlight slashed into her eyes, filtered by the hair hanging over them into an almost aggressive orange" or "she always liked herself in green because it was supposed to be the most flattering color for redheads," or similar. Notice how each of those examples not only makes the perception of her red hair organic to her direct point of view, but it also layers in more meaning: in the first case it sets a mood with verbiage like "slashed" and "aggressive"; in the second it might suggest to us that she's vain or at least conscious of looking her best. Good writing multitasks.

Subjective third-person POV characters also don't need to label or describe other characters they are familiar with: "Manuel's older sister, Juanita, came into the room. As usual, she entered talking." Manuel has no need to identify that Juanita is his sister as she comes in—doing so yanks us out of his head, into that external POV again. It's not how he would think of her. Imagine your partner coming into the room where you're reading this. Would you think, "Ah, there's my husband, Phil." Unless someone is sitting in the room who has no idea who Phil is and you need to actually tell her, this is unnatural. In close third-person POV the character isn't "telling" anyone what's happening—he's simply living it, and we're living it with him, along for the ride inside his head. Instead make the explanation a seamless part of his narrative: "Juanita came into the room—as usual his older sister entered talking."

In the same vein, in this voice there's no need for descriptors like "he thought," "she knew," "he decided," "she felt," "he saw," and so on. If we're deeply in a character's POV, we assume that these are his thoughts, knowledge, decisions, feelings, perspective. These are unnecessary filters because your character is the lens we're experiencing the story through directly—the reader understands that. So instead of, "It was raining; he supposed he wouldn't go to the store after all," you can simply say: "It was raining; he wouldn't go to the store after all." Rather than, "Brad saw her flinch," you can simply say, "She flinched." The observer is Brad by default.

In fact in close third-person point of view we assume everything in the narrative is the POV character's perspective; therefore we don't need lots of pointed direct thought:

I can't do this in front of her, he thought. Her seeing his cruelty would destroy them. *I need her gone—now.*

Notice how this is a bit distancing—the thoughts are being described to us. Dropping "he thought" brings us more intimately and directly into his head. Or you can avoid direct thought altogether, since everything we read that describes his inner life in his direct POV is, by definition, his thought: "He couldn't do this in front of her. Her seeing his cruelty would destroy them. He needed her gone." Or you could make this even deeper POV with his direct silent plea to her:

> *Not with you here.* Her seeing his cruelty would destroy them. *Go...please.*

Most of us don't painstakingly delineate our thoughts in nice descriptive complete sentences—we think in shorthand, flashes rather than full scenes. Conveying a character's inner life that way makes it even more intimate and visceral, making us a part of it. Also, avoid too much direct thought for characters—big chunks of italicized direct thought feel clunky and weary readers.

Finally, consider how many direct-POV characters you're presenting in your story. Too many viewpoints can spread your net wide but too shallow—we don't get a chance to feel we know any character well—and it can lend an unfocused or chaotic feel to the story, as if the camera is jumping from character to character to character. Consider your central story, as we defined it in the Plot chapter: What is this story actually about? Which characters are essential to furthering that particular story, as we discussed in the Character chapter? And of those, whose direct viewpoint adds something intrinsic to moving the story along its arc? A well-killed darling or two can offer you the narrative space to instead flesh out more fully and strongly the points of view you do decide to retain.

WHICH POV IS BEST?

As with so many topics in writing, the answer to this question is an annoyingly nonspecific, "That depends"—on you, on the story you're telling, sometimes even on your genre. Basically, choose the POV that helps you tell the story most effectively. That's one of those "squishy" definitions, like the Supreme Court justice who famously defined what porn is by saying he knew it when he saw it, but there are a few guidelines that might help you decide:

First-person:
- Allows for maximum intimacy between reader and character
- Very popular in the modern publishing market
- Requires strongly developed character and voice
- Limits you to what the POV character directly experiences or knows
- Can feel manipulative if author keeps "secrets" from reader despite the transparent nature of this POV

Third-person limited:
- Allows intimacy between reader and character, but less casual than first-person
- Very popular in modern literature
- Requires deep dive into character and voice
- Reader can't know more than POV character (but in multiple-POV books you can reveal more facets of the story)
- Can slip into head-hopping

Third-person objective:
- Provides a broad, uncolored overview of the story
- Allows the author to withhold information from the reader
- Can strip your writing of voice
- Keeps us on the outside looking in—readers are passive witnesses to the story
- Lacks intimacy and a strong connection between reader and character
- Author can only show behavior, not reveal thoughts or motivations
- Can feel dated

Third-person omniscient:
- Narrator—and thus reader—can know and "see" things the characters do not; gives the author broad license to present information
- Requires a strong, consistent narrator voice

- Allows glimpses into characters' heads, but not in the direct visceral experience or voice of the characters—the narrator is a separate entity
- Can lend itself to head-hopping
- Can feel distancing or dizzying for readers
- Can leave readers uncertain what or whose story is being told

In addition, different genres have different POV norms: You're more likely to see first-person stories in YA, women's fiction, and domestic suspense, for instance; third-person is common to genres like fantasy/science fiction, thriller, and espionage. That doesn't mean you can't write in those genres in different POVs, though.

Consider which point of view feels most comfortable to you. Some authors swear by a certain POV for all their writing; others vary it from story to story. Writing in a voice that doesn't feel natural to you just makes the challenge of writing greater.

If you feel your chosen POV is not working for the story or a particular scene, or you're undecided which is best for your story, try changing it. Rewrite an existing scene from a totally different POV—whether that means trying third-person from first, for instance, or even choosing another POV character entirely. Sometimes this exercise can pull back the curtain on a whole new perspective that brings a scene to life. Sometimes it can simply shed light on the scene in a way that allows you to see additional dimension and depth you were blind to before, so while you may go back to the original POV, it's now informed by that insight, richer and fuller.

Experiment. Alice Sebold's *The Lovely Bones* is told in an unusual first-person omniscient by a narrator who's been murdered. Marcus Zuzak's *The Book Thief* is narrated by omniscient Death.

One rigid literary school of thought holds that first person is "lesser" than third person. I see this now and then in blog posts, articles, panels, and workshops from people who righteously claim that third person is the voice of Great Literature and first person is basically for populist pap. As with most blanket statements about writing—like "avoid adverbs," "prologues are bad," and "never use semicolons"—this is useless advice. First person is indeed the voice of a lot of popular modern "genre" fiction, but it also has a venerable history with respected classics: *Jane Eyre, The Catcher in the Rye, The Great Gatsby, To Kill a Mockingbird, Lolita*—as well as plenty of lauded literary works, like Jeffrey Euginedes' *Middlesex*, or Donna Tartt's *The Goldfinch*, both Pulitzer winners, and Booker Prize–winning *The Remains of the Day* by Kazuo Ishiguro, who is a Nobel prize winner. POV doesn't determine a book's merit any more than the type font does. Choose the one that serves your story best, and tune out the purveyors of ridiculously limiting advice meant to judge or stratify artists.

chapter six

showing and
TELLING

"Don't tell me the moon is shining;
show me the glint of light on broken glass."
—Attributed to Anton Chekhov

The quote above, likely a paraphrasing of writing advice Chekhov offered his brother in a letter, is often used to convey the difference between show and tell.[1] Usually you see this story element written as "show *versus* tell," like an Ultimate Cage Match, but I think your kindergarten teacher had it right: show *and* tell. The two ideally work in tandem; the trick is to understand the difference, and know which will serve your story best, where.

Just so we're talking in the same terms, some thumbnail definitions. *Show* generally means presenting elements of a story in immediate, "real-time" dramatization on the page. *Tell* is used to convey exposition, a description of the thing (whatever that is), rather than the thing itself. If show is the on-screen version of your story, then tell is the voice-over narration. And as with film, sometimes one is more effective than the other, and sometimes you need both. (For a hilarious exaggeration of this

---

1. Here's the original quote, for fellow word nerds: "In descriptions of Nature one *must seize on small details, grouping them* so that when the reader closes his eyes *he gets a picture.* For instance, you'll have a moonlit night if you write that on the mill dam a piece of glass from a broken bottle glittered like a bright little star." The italics are mine—I love this description of vivid writing.

idea, watch the Will Ferrell movie *Stranger Than Fiction*, where Ferrell's character discovers that he's actually the protagonist in a story being written by the woman who is the voice in his head.)

Show is most effective when you want to draw the reader in viscerally to the character's direct, immediate experience in key areas of the story. It's why the heart-wrenching scene in *Sophie's Choice* when Meryl Streep's character must choose between her children is still one of the most memorable, viscerally affecting scenes in film for many people. In both the film and William Styron's original novel, that pivotal scene switches from the "tell" format used frequently throughout the story—of Sophie recounting her experiences to young novelist Stingo—to direct, powerful firsthand show.

Tell is most effective when presenting supporting story components, or factual information readers need to know, or things that aren't directly germane to the story you're telling in *this* manuscript. In these cases show might slow pace or defuse tension or suspense or pull focus. Inigo Montoya had it right in *Princess Bride*—when he and Fezzik and the Man in Black are preparing to storm the castle to rescue Buttercup, there's no narrative use in re-creating every step that got them there (and which viewers already know). He wisely makes the most effective use of their limited time and *tells* Westley only what he needs to know: "Let me explain. No, there is too much—let me sum up."

Show and tell often work best together to heighten a reader's emotional engagement. There is a scene in the movie *Crazy, Stupid, Love* that wrings my heart out every time I see it. Childhood sweethearts and longtime spouses played by Steve Carrell and Julianne Moore are separated after the wife's infidelity. Carrell's character can't stop sneaking back over to his house, though, to take care of his lawn under cover of night, and one evening he's startled when his cell phone rings and it's his wife, whom he can see through a dining room window. Unaware that he's watching her, she pretends to have called for help relighting their pilot light, and although he can clearly see she is nowhere near the furnace, he proceeds to talk her through it step by step. That's the "tell."

But the scene isn't actually about that. It's the "show" of it that conveys the real story: that Carrell's character is still in love with his wife in the way he watches her and the tenderness in his voice. That she misses him but is afraid to say so. That there is hope for the two of them to reconcile. Even the ostensible reason for the call carries metaphorical weight—she needs his help *relighting the pilot light*. Hitting those beats directly in a scene about those motivations wouldn't fit the story or characters at that point in their arcs; screenwriter Dan Fogelman knows that the "show" subtext of their reactions, expressions, demeanors, and tones is far more powerful humming beneath the "tell" of the trivial fix.

You can dissect how skilled writers effectively use show and tell by analyzing scenes in books or movies that are particularly affecting or impactful to you. List out everything you know about the characters and plot in the scene based on what you read or saw—and see if you can pinpoint exactly what let you know it, as with the scene I describe above. (Try the final scene in that same film, or the opening montage in *Up*. Or the first chapter—or page—in Elizabeth Berg's *Say When* or Lottie Moggach's *Kiss Me First* or Laurie Frankel's *Goodbye for Now*.) Then identify which are tell and which are show.

Let's talk about each one separately.

Show

Remember that vacation metaphor about watching a slide show versus being on the trip yourself—feeling the sand between your toes, the sun on your shoulders, the smell of seaweed and brine filling your sinuses? The latter is what "show" brings to a story—puts us *there* with the characters; lets us live a scene through their eyes, in their heads.

Show also lets you multitask—"the moon on broken glass" doesn't just convey that it's nighttime and the moon is out; it also implies a setting (outside or near a window), a mood (broken glass creates a feeling of unease), and a character (one who notices details, perhaps, or looks at the ground rather than the sky). Without overstating, you can examine every scene, every page, and nearly every single sentence to see whether it's working as hard as it can for your story, and make it do double (or triple or more) duty. You can make show multitask for you at the overarching macro level and all the way down to the most granular of choices.

Even the smallest moments and details can reveal fathoms about a plot, a scene, and all the characters in it (watch how much screenwriter Martin McDonagh does with a glass of orange juice in *Three Billboards Outside of Ebbing, Missouri*).

For instance, say you have a scene where a stay-at-home mom is invited to a party of corporate wives when her husband is being considered for a huge promotion, and she winds up making a huge gaffe and costing her spouse the job.

You can look for ways to set this situation up with "show" from the moment she walks in. Perhaps she stammers her thanks for inviting her to the woman who answers the door, only to have the hostess come up behind and greet her, as the housekeeper who answered the door takes her coat. "There's coffee in the kitchen—help yourself," the hostess instructs, and when the woman finally finds the huge kitchen she freezes at the sight of a fancy espresso machine on a counter, all chrome and gleaming and industrial. She gamely walks over and tries to use it, blushing furiously when she can't figure it out. Then one of the other wives walks over to point her toward the silver urn of brewed coffee on the island, and the woman glances around to see whether anyone noticed before fleeing to the powder room to splash water on her flaming face.

These are just a few seemingly minor moments, but notice how much they accomplish. The intimidation the character feels shows us that she's uncomfortable/unfamiliar with these upscale surroundings (which are in turn shown by the housekeeper, the high-end appliance, the huge kitchen), suggesting to the reader that she has a humbler background. Her trying to fit in anyway shows pluck and courage, traits that strengthen her and reveal character. Her blush and looking around when another guest has to help her with the espresso machine shows her embarrassment or shame—and additionally suggests that her flash of courage was fragile, thus showing us an Achilles' heel for her character and giving her arc somewhere to go. That's a lot of meaning and facets in a few simple beats of blocking.

✓ *How to Find It, How to Fix It*

As you get more proficient at spotting the techniques authors and film-makers use to convey this depth of information using show, you'll become more adept at seeing it (or the lack of it) in your own work, too. But there are also some tools you can employ to weed out areas of tell where show might be more effective.

FOLLOW THE DESCRIPTOR WORDS

Comb your manuscript for adjectives and adverbs. These descriptor words are sometimes indicators of author shortcuts for conveying a sense of character or place or action. See if you can substitute more effective and visceral show. Instead of "She was skinny," for instance, you might say something like, "There she stood, just a rack of ribs and cheekbones." Notice how using show in this kind of situation also allows you to reveal more about the character making the observation: The first is a dry statement of fact; the second implies a certain personality in the observer.

Think of showing *behaviors* that indicate the descriptors you want to convey, rather than simply summarizing those traits. See if you can find representative scenes and moments to dramatize that can show what you are trying to establish, rather than simply reporting these actions and interactions secondhand.

Here's a brief example:

> Amelia was standing with her arms crossed, surveying the room. She walked to the sofa, gazing down her surgically straightened nose at it before extending two fingers like forceps and removing an invisible hair from a back cushion.
>
> "Charming, Joyce," she said without inflection.
>
> "How about a cup of coffee?" I blurted. "I made it strong, like you like."
>
> "I'd prefer tea."

This is a direct, visceral way of showing a lot about both characters: We see firsthand Amelia acting judgmental, nitpicky, contrary in asking for tea though the coffee is made, rather than the author labeling her with those adjectives. The action of her picking something off a cushion with just two fingers shows her attitude more viscerally than would labeling it with an adverb like "disdainfully" or "primly" or similar. Her "surgically straightened nose" might imply something about her vanity or concern with appearances or perfectionism—or something about Joyce's cattiness or views on cosmetic procedures. We get a sense that Joyce wants Amelia's approval—she made the coffee already "like you like"—without having to label the way she offers it (e.g., "eagerly" or "obsequiously," etc.). These behaviors may or may not say something more globally about the characters—perhaps Amelia is usually a lovely person but Joyce has spent her life needling her and she's on guard or on the offensive. We don't know—but you have shown us something about them and in doing so raised those questions, so the reader keeps reading to find out more.

A Word about Descriptors

There is a lot of antipathy out there for adjectives and adverbs—some writing teachers and professionals actually give the advice to avoid using them. I beg you not to impoverish your writing or decimate your writer's toolbox by removing any gorgeous part of language or storytelling from it (I'm also speaking up for the maligned semicolon and prologue here). Used well, every single delicious part of speech, punctuation, storytelling device, etc., can enrich your writing and your story. As with any absolutes or dogmatic "rules," I advocate taking this kind of blanket advice with a big grain of salt. Adjectives and adverbs aren't detractors in and of themselves, but overreliance on them can strip your writing of impact, immediacy, and voice. It's great to examine where you've used descriptors to see whether they are the most effective or efficient choice—but sometimes they absolutely are.

EXAMINE THE PHYSICAL DETAILS

Look at where you've presented setting and surroundings in your manuscript. Is it a rainy night? That's tell—perhaps let us see the character straining to make out the road even with her windshield wipers on high, or feel the mist sprinkling her skin even underneath her umbrella. Is it springtime? Instead of telling us, why not let us smell the gardenia and see the tightly gathered buds just beginning to emerge on tender green branches?

Let your descriptions pull double duty—marvelous multitasking— to reveal character or backstory or action. What does this excerpt say about your characters?

> I followed Jill's tailored silhouette silently to the "formal living room" she used to call the den. Gone was the comfortable sprung futon whose cushions were practically imprinted in the shapes of our sprawled bodies from countless confabs; in its place was a backless white leather couch with a new-car smell. Jill lowered herself to an upholstered chair as if doing it a favor and I almost laughed, but the expression on her face told me she wasn't goofing around. She gestured to the odd sofa— "Please take the divan"—and I found myself perching upright at its edge, finally settling my aimless hands on my lap like an obedient schoolgirl.

Jill and the narrator clearly used to be close, and something has happened. Jill also seems to have perhaps newly come into money or success, which has evidently changed her—perhaps she's become a bit pretentious. We infer all these things from the behaviors and setting we see through the protagonist's eyes, which tells us something about that character too: that she feels uncomfortable with the changes in her friend, or left behind, or that she's awkward in these surroundings. Note that showing these details this way instead of flat-out telling them raises questions in the reader's mind—and remember from the Suspense and Tension chapter that that's one of the best ways to keep them turning pages. If the author simply told us those facts—"I walked into Jill's house, feeling uncomfortable in her newly swank surroundings"—we already have all the answers, so we're less intrigued, and the scene is less visual and visceral...thus less directly engaging.

You can bring this same technique to blocking and stage direction too—turn action into *story* by layering in color and meaning. A character stalks or lumbers or glides—all say something very different about him and his state of mind. One who orders a scotch, neat, and tosses it back is very distinct from the character who asks for a frozen daiquiri with a straw.

LET US IN

Look for places where you sum up potentially important or telling developments with narrative verbiage ("Nan was by Arturo's bedside when he came out of the coma, and she held his hand, crying, as his eyes cracked open"), rather than showing us the actual scene, or when you skim over or ignore details that might add richness and color. In any human interaction what we say and do is only a fraction of the picture; like an iceberg, most of what's actually happening lies beneath the surface. Let us in—meaning let us into the characters' inner life, direct experience, perceptions, motivations, thoughts, beliefs, reactions, emotions.

I don't mean you have to painstakingly delineate every minuscule moment with internal monologue, but scratch below the surface of dialogue, action, and dry fact to reveal a sense of who your characters are, how events strike them, why they do what they do, how they react. Let us see the dynamics between characters, their interactions—all the subverbals of a scene that happen underneath the surface events and action and create a deep, textured tapestry: the expressions, glances, pauses, tones, body language, the things the characters say—and don't say—and all that it means.

For example, here's one way you could present a closeted gay man's first kiss with a man:

> Fredo moved closer and Amir waited as he leaned in, his lips finally touching Amir's. Wow. His first kiss—first real one, anyway, with another man. The few pallid, obligatory pecks he'd

exchanged with the women his mother foisted on him didn't count—and they certainly didn't compare.

This adequately conveys the information and the action, but it doesn't put readers *into* the scene, into Amir's direct *perception*. Let yourself slow down; excavate a bit more beneath the surface. Let us see and feel and hear and taste and touch. This is a huge moment, for instance, for a man who has lived in the closet denying who he is for so long. Is Amir's heart slamming into his rib cage as if it might burst free? His hands shaking, sweaty, awkward as he suddenly doesn't know where to put them? What is that first touch of Fredo's lips like—softer than he expected? Firm and demanding? How does that accelerate Amir's reactions? How does Fredo smell? Taste? What's it like to rub against stubble? Does Amir worry he might hyperventilate from his racing heart and short breath as they kiss? You don't have to be this detailed or dramatize every scene or exchange quite this granularly—but especially with important, telling moments like this, let us live them with your protagonist directly, viscerally, powerfully. Put us inside their immediate experience so that we essentially *are* the character.

Similarly, let us into your characters' inner lives in *reaction* to what's happening. In this example you might reveal more of how Amir reacts to acting on these long-suppressed impulses. Does his brain seem to shut off? Or is he panicking? Or totally unconscious of the world outside this room, this man? Does shame rise up but get smothered under desire? Does he inexplicably tear up?

Dramatizing rather than summarizing important action brings the story to life more fully and richly, amping up our involvement, the stakes, and our investment. Let us live the scenes through your characters' eyes, in their heads. Let us witness directly how they talk to each other, what they say (and don't say), the undercurrents and nonverbals. The sinking stomach and uncomfortable drop of a gaze from one half of a couple in therapy can convey volumes about both characters' feelings—and their chances.

This is what I mean by "lizard-brain writing"—those instantaneous, unconscious physical reactions that precede the brain's intellectual conclusion of what they mean. In some ways it's like the author slows down time—you stretch out that microsecond of lizard-brain reaction on the page so that the reader can experience the scene along with the character, rather than being told about it by the higher-reasoning cerebrum that draws conclusions, which is one step removed from the visceral reactions that make fiction compelling and draw the reader in.

For example, most of us don't react by thinking, "I am scared!" First we feel our heart race, our stomach hollow out, our mouth go dry. Our cerebrum might almost instantaneously put all that together and conclude, "I am scared," but the first gut-level, lizard-brain thing we register is the *effect* of whatever is happening on us, not the intellectualized logical *conclusion* we then reach.

Show is the former, tell the latter. Let us come to the conclusions you want us to reach by leading us there, instead of stating them directly for us. We get the intention for ourselves from the picture you have painted, rather than being told the same thing and having to "take the author's word for it."

USE SPECIFIC BUT ECONOMICAL DETAIL

You don't have to painstakingly describe every element of a room or a character's surroundings to give us a clear, vivid image of it. One of the beautiful things about books is that unlike film or TV, they are a collaborative medium: The author begins to paint the picture, but the reader fills in the details for herself. Look for areas where you may have taken a lot of ink to describe a setting and—unless its exact layout is of narrative importance—see if you can instead simply show a sense of it that will create a vivid image in readers' minds:

> The gleaming-white kitchen was immaculate, but the reek of rot suggested garbage that hadn't been taken out in weeks, a disposal that hadn't been run.

> Streetlights reflected off oil spills streaking the asphalt, no doubt from the plethora of cars in various states of disrepair parked in overgrown driveways.

She felt dwarfed by the Louis Quatorze chair, clutching her hands in her lap in case her silver-plated watch scratched the pristine mahogany of the arms, and praying the dust clinging to her skirts from her long walk here left no imprint on its white upholstery.

In each case, the details given are relatively sparse, but did you get a full image in your head of the setting? You need to offer only a few evocative details and readers will fill in the rest for you.

Notice also how these examples multitask for the story. All three not only use show to describe a setting visually, but to create a mood, raise a question, or imply character or background or stakes.

VET YOUR VERBIAGE

As we touched on in the Character and Point of View chapters, take a look at your descriptive prose and see if you can fine-tune and streamline areas of telling to give it more visceral impact.

You can reveal more depth in your characters' inner lives, for instance, with POV references specific to who they are. Perhaps a pilot feels that trouble follows him like sparrows in the slipstream, or a Vietnam vet thinks of distance in klicks instead of miles.

Look at the words you use and consider shades of meaning, connotation, even sound. If you think "sparkle" and "glitter" are interchangeable, compare the warmth and joy of the sparkle in a new lover's eye to the sharp, tawdry glitter of a peep show. Even the phonetics create distinct impressions, the sibilant, breathy fricative of the former and the sharp, hard plosives of the latter.

Watch for areas of superfluous tell—phrases like "he felt," "she thought," "he decided, "she believed," etc., often spoon-feed the reader; they are telling, not showing. If you've successfully put us in the character's POV, then readers will infer that all thoughts, emotions, reactions, etc., are those of that point-of-view character; there's no need to underscore it.

. . # . .

It may help to think of show as giving the reader more *scene*, less *summary*—meaning let us "see" on the page right in front of us these important story developments spooling out directly, as if you are filming them. The idea is that you're putting us directly in the scene, giving the reader a "you are there" feeling. Dramatize, rather than summing up—slow down and squeeze all the juice from key scenes.

As you're revising, look for the places where adding this kind of immediate impact and depth brings the story more vividly and viscerally to life for the reader. "Show, don't tell" is a general rule of thumb for key scenes intrinsic to character, plot, or stakes: This is where it usually matters most to be specific and detailed, rather than defaulting to generalizations or summation.

Tell

As powerful a tool as "show" can be, a story that's all show and no tell will quickly grow wearying for the reader. Imagine living every single painstaking moment with your characters—the mundane, tedious minutiae of their lives. Not only would books be unmanageably long, but readers would glaze over and give up. Stories are enhanced reality—they cherry-pick the highest highs and lowest lows, the salient parts of events that are most germane, most engaging—or, as in Elmore Leonard's simple, pithy secret to his success: "Try to leave out the parts people skip." This is where tell can be show's helpful handmaiden.

✓ How to Find It, How to Fix It

Here are the most common areas in your manuscript where tell might offer a more efficient, effective way to convey parts of your story than show.

WEAVING IN CONTEXT

As powerful as the visceral nonverbals of show can be, physical reactions without context can leave readers guessing (and not in the good way). It's usually not enough to know a character is upset, for instance; we need a clue why—show *and* tell. Consider this example:

> "Richard said he's bringing Carolyn with him for dinner."
> My hand flew to my mouth.

This passage does show us the POV character is shocked or disturbed by this news, but without a bit of context readers flounder as to why—we're held outside the scene, the characters privy to something we are not.

An easy enough fix: You might add a bit of tell conveying that Carolyn and Richard have been in the middle of a bitter divorce, or that the protagonist used to date Richard and still has feelings for him, or that Carolyn died last year. Now we understand the reaction more fully—we're part of the story, rather than watching two "insiders" discuss something we're excluded from. Further, with judiciously used tell like this you propel the story—multitasking again. Reread the first sentence of this paragraph and notice that each possibility suggests a nuance of story that the show alone does not: raises a question, introduces a possible conflict or tension, adds suspense. Trying to *show* this information—unless the background is a key part of events in *this* story—would result in tedious paragraphs or pages of verbiage expended on a flashback or memory that yanks readers out of the present-day story we're actually in, stopping pace and momentum cold and unnecessarily complicating the story. Sometimes it's more effective to just convey the information.

Here's another example:

> "John, I'm afraid we have to let you go."
> I stared. "Really, Alexis? You, of all people?"

There's obviously some context here between these two that we may need to know, but unless it's an essential part of the central story you're telling, there's no need to stop to create a vivid flashback or memory of how Alexis hired our protag twenty years ago, or has been his mentor and champion until John fell out of favor and she abruptly distanced herself, or how Alexis has been his nemesis at the company for years and gunning for his job. Just state that background as succinctly as possible to convey the info we need to orient us, and then continue to move the story forward.

Achieving balance between show and tell in cases like this, rather than all heavy-handed tell, can help an author avoid "As you know, Bob" syndrome, where characters offer information that everyone in the scene is already cognizant of—so named for a common construction of this pitfall: "As you know, Bob, last year we were divorced and you've been living in a hotel nearby so you can see the kids." Not only is this clunky prose, but it pulls readers out of the reality of the story—no humans on earth talk like this to each other—and draws attention to the author's efforts to convey information.

When context like this is needed, look for ways you can thread it in organically, the way we actually think and speak. Depending on what mood and emotions and background you want to convey (multitasking!), you could weave in this information naturally with a combination of show and tell: for instance: "You look like crap, Bob—all that room service you're paying for with my delinquent alimony money keeping you up at night?" And then perhaps Bob defends his luxury lifestyle to fill in the rest of the blanks: "It's the only hotel anywhere close to the kids, Jackie—and it's hard to pay alimony to a woman who was screwing your brother." Notice how much more *story* is contained in the show-and-tell version: not just the added info of the unpaid alimony and the infidelity, but the emotions between these two, the tension and conflict. We're getting all this information through the characters' direct perspectives and behaviors—even the tell portions—rather than having it vomited on us presentationally, and that makes us part of the story instead of a passive bystander.

The "As you know, Bob" principle applies to narrative too, not just dialogue, as we saw in the Point of View chapter. Consider this sentence:

My fourteen-year-old brother Enrique, tall and thin with a mop
of brown hair, came into the room.

This is presentational, as if the POV character is stepping outside his own direct perceptions to turn to the reader and explain. If we're in the protag's head in direct point of view, he wouldn't think of his brother this way. Imagine your spouse coming into a room and you think, *Ah, here's Rogelio, thirty-nine years old, a little out of shape, with brown hair and hazel eyes.* That's not how we think and perceive, at least with those already familiar to us (one might assess a stranger or newcomer this way, though). In our direct perception we shorthand observations, and as an author your job is to find ways of *showing* that realistically to avoid yanking us from the world of the story, while still *telling* us the info we need as outsiders. You might say something like:

> Enrique shambled in, my little brother either tripping over his own gawky limbs in the full throes of puberty, or maybe just unable to see past the mop of brown hair nearly covering his eyes.

There's still tell here, but in conjunction with show in a way that reflects the protagonist's direct, natural observations as if we're in his head with him, rather than his metaphorically turning away from the scene to narrate his observations to us.

BUILD BACKSTORY

You can apply this same principle to presenting backstory: key background info readers need to fully understand a character's arc or the story setup. Here again show and tell work beautifully hand in hand.

Just as we shorthand observations in our own perceptions, we do the same with memories. The way we remember isn't in full scenes, but rather in snippets, flashes of images/words that are representative of the whole.

Think of a meaningful event in your life—for example, I was chosen for a summer language-study program in high school that I was really excited about (word nerds aren't made—we're born). But the memory of that event that pops into my mind doesn't begin chronologically with me applying, testing and interviewing for the program; then finding out I was going; then getting ready to go; then going; then studying my chosen field and meeting the people who had such a profound effect on me, etc. Instead a few vivid images flash through my mind in a nanosecond:

my thudding heart when I opened our mailbox and finally saw the letter from the organization; the extra sixty dollars my single mother miraculously scraped up to send with me for spending money; walking in the rain with my new friends on the college campus where we stayed, heady with my first sense of independence and a newfound feeling of camaraderie and joy.

Every detail of that experience isn't germane to the effect that summer had on me and my life—if you asked me about it and I told you the whole plodding thing, or even stopped to re-create for you that full evening in the rain juiced on our own adolescence, you'd quickly get bored and check out (trust me). But those moments I mention above convey the salient parts of what that summer meant to me: the excitement of it, the achievement, the poignancy of my mom's mad money, the freedom, the acceptance and companionship. Those are the relevant details—the rest is extraneous (to anyone but me).

Look for places in your manuscript where, in the interest of creating backstory for your characters, you stop to dramatize a memory in the form of a flashback, or unload an info dump. See if instead you can find key highlights like this to more elegantly and efficiently represent just the parts of that memory we need to understand the main story you're actually telling. For poor divorced Bob and Jackie above, for instance, rather than stopping the story's forward momentum to give us a full flashback scene of how they met, you might pick out a few salient, vivid moments that give us a sense of their history:

> For a moment, as Bob smiled at their daughter, Jackie saw the eager boy who tripped over her table that day in the coffee shop twenty years ago, spilling her coffee into her lap and flushing crimson as he nonetheless proceeded to ask her out.

We don't need to stop the story's momentum in the current scene and see that whole coffee-shop flashback to understand that at the beginning Bob was the pursuer, that he was ardent and determined, gawky and sweet. You can give all that background to us in a sentence while you keep the story moving forward. In cases like this, less really is more.

That's not to say that flashbacks are never effective. As with the *Sophie's Choice* scene I mentioned earlier, sometimes they serve the story best. But try to be ruthless in assessing whether one does. If its purpose is simply to fill in backstory you want readers to have, then often weaving a more streamlined mix of show and tell to convey the information directly into the "real-time" action of the main story you're telling is a better narrative choice to keep the story moving forward and keep readers invested.

Flashback Etiquette

If you do use a flashback, don't fall into the trap of announcing it to readers. Leading into a flashback with a heavy-handed segue like, "The memory came rushing back" or "It felt like it happened yesterday" or "She relived it as if watching a movie" is the narrative equivalent of the cheesy intro that old films and TV shows used to use to transition to flashback or dream sequences. (You know the one: "Hmmm, I wonder what that would have been like...?" Cue magical chimes and dissolve...) Hanging a neon sign on an upcoming flashback that way is clumsy and draws attention to the author's voice, pulling readers from the story.

We enter memory similarly to the way we experience it: abruptly and piecemeal. Quick—tell me where you were when the Twin Towers fell. Most likely what just popped into your head wasn't how you got up that morning, like any other day, went about your routine, got in your car and drove, or walked into work and settled in, and then heard the reports. It was probably a flash of that moment you first heard. For me, it was walking by a television at the hotel in Colorado where I was staying, en route to my first appointment, and seeing a clump of people watching in bizarre silence, and the sinking of my stomach before I even stepped close...the horror of watching it unfold...the strange and immediate sense of companionship and comfort from strangers. Those images are the entrée to the memory—and *then*, perhaps, once my lizard brain has automatically flashed on those visceral, imprinted moments, I might remember the rest of the day. But the first gut flash of memory is that power moment that takes me back.

So imagine you have a character being reminded, in the present-moment story, about the day her best friend died. Rather than leading in with that cheesy-movie intro and spooling it out in chronological order, think about what part of that memory haunts her most. Maybe it's the look on her friend's face right before she got into the car before she wrecked—a silly, cross-eyed tongue-out look of teasing. Maybe it's the last thing she ever said to your protagonist as her new date picked her up at the door: "Don't wait up!" with an exaggerated wink. Start your memory with that. Then you can decide whether your story is best served with a full flashback or you more organically weave the backstory into the real-time story with the show-and-tell technique above.

Also, I beg you not to set flashbacks (or dreams) off in italics. They are distracting to readers, as another type of neon sign, and publishers will likely remove them anyway. A well-paved-in flashback or dream doesn't need to be announced this way: If you've segued us in organically readers will understand this is a memory/dream, and verb tense will do the rest (i.e., past tense if the real-time scene is told in present, past perfect if it's told in past tense).

Don't overdo the past perfect, though—it can quickly result in unwieldy narrative ("She hadn't intended to get in the car, but she had wanted to please her new date, so she had climbed in..."). The occasional well-placed usage amid regular past tense, even if your main story is told in past tense, will keep readers firmly placed in the memory—in the previous example you could delete all but the first instance, for example ("she hadn't intended") and then revert to regular past tense and readers will be with you.

Finally, use backstory judiciously with secondary or supporting characters so it doesn't overtake the main story or lend an episodic feel to the manuscript. If the info doesn't directly serve the plot or central character arcs it may feel like a detour to the reader, stalling pace and stopping momentum. We can't keep track of that many characters and backstories, and you don't need to give us the whole backstory on every character to invest us—in fact, just the opposite. Develop the secondary characters, show their relationship to your protagonist's journey and how that is affecting his arc, and layer in brushstrokes of context on their individual backstories little by little as you move the story forward—and only as much as needed for that purpose. The secondary characters are part of the scenery but not the main subject of the picture.

Look for places where you have a lot of exposition about a character's past or psyche or backstory and see whether we need the complete, exhaustive picture for the purposes of the story you're telling in this manuscript, or whether just a few salient details will more effectively accomplish your purposes and keep the story moving forward.

Series: A Special Case

Writers of series books (think Harry Potter or Hunger Games or the Game of Thrones series, for example) face particular backstory challenges with each novel: how to bring new (or forgetful) readers up to speed on info they need to know from previous books to fully engage in *this* book without endless swaths of recap.

Think of this as an expanded version of the context building we discussed above, where the characters' backstories will be encapsulated in previous books, rather than in the exhaustive character development you no doubt do as an author before writing your standalone story. ☺ The principle is the same: Weave in, using judicious show *and* tell, just enough context to allow readers to understand the backstory that's essential to orienting to your world and characters.

Just as you wouldn't begin a standalone with giant info dumps of backstory to "bring the reader up to speed," don't do it in your successive series titles either. Start the story of *this* manuscript and keep propelling it forward, organically threading in context and background from previous stories in the series only where we need it. Readers don't require the complete background to fully enjoy a title midway through the series if it's written skillfully—pick up any book in Jim Butcher's Harry Dresden series or Camilla Monk's Spotless series to see what I mean. And as always, the best way to learn how to do this effectively in your writing is to analyze the work of other authors who already do.

SETTING UP A SCENE

A bit of tell at the beginning of a scene can provide a quick orientation for readers, to "place" us. Consider the following opening sentences:

Her scowl didn't bode well as my wife barreled into our room.

The day went so much worse than I expected.

She'd gotten her suitcases unpacked and everything tidied away in drawers and closets, but Ananya still didn't feel settled, prowling the house restlessly as she waited for Ravi to come home.

All three cases are flat-out tell—but this can be a useful narrative device to allow readers to get their bearings before you bring us more directly into the scene with show, which can sometimes be a bit disorienting on its own. And in the first two cases the setup serves as a bit of foreshadowing of what's to come, creating some suspense where there may be none if you started from the chronological beginning of the scene.

Children's/YA book editor Cheryl B. Klein calls this a "topic sentence"—similar to the thesis statement of an essay—in her enlightening talk about how J. K. Rowling uses this tell technique in *Harry Potter* (a brilliant speech chock-full of valuable writing analysis, if you want to read the whole thing here: http://bit.ly/2UaxAW1), but it can also work effectively at the end of scenes to either help readers process what they've just seen, or as a sort of cliffhanger for what's to come.

CREATING CONNECTIVE TISSUE

Related to the above idea, tell is often the most efficient way to lead readers from one scene to the next. I often read manuscripts where authors dive right into show in each and every scene. This can work if each scene is directly contiguous with the one that preceded it, but if not—if time has passed or a location has changed, for instance—it can be confusing to readers and lend the story a jerky feel, as if we're being yanked around corners on a particularly aggressive roller coaster. Offer us a bit of tell to connect the dots for us from one scene to the next. For instance, say you have a thrilling revelation at the end of a chapter—a character learns his mother was married before and had a child the protag never knew about. If you begin the next chapter with the character at work, hanging around the watercooler with his buds and sussing out Sunday's game, readers feel as if we've missed something. We don't know how the protagonist got from there to here, as if a key scene were dropped somehow.

Even if you're trying to show that the character is ignoring or feigning indifference to the bombshell (or actually *is* indifferent), we still need to see some indication early in the next scene of what happened between the revelation and this moment, though it doesn't necessarily have to be the very first sentence. You might say something like, "Giorgio left his mother crying at the table, the other coffee shop patrons staring at him as if he were a monster as he calmly paid the bill and walked out. He hadn't heard from his mom the rest of the night, and that was just fine with him—this wasn't his sordid secret, was it?" And then you can let us join him in the watercooler scene, which might show more keenly his efforts to avoid the disturbing topic, or illustrate his superficiality in some way, etc. But first you plant our feet, offer some indication of the aftermath of the previous scene and segue us fluidly to this one with a little bit of germane tell.

Even just transitioning us from one setting to the next often requires a bit of tell: "After she finished her interview with the first witness, Freya headed back to the station to compare notes with her partner." Not only does this orient us to where we are, but it leaves out Elmore Leonard's "parts people tend to skip" insofar as the travel logistics.

Getting the character where she needs to go and letting readers in on it is as simple as the above example sentence; don't waste ink and squander reader attention with tedious details of Freya getting in her car, pulling onto the highway, being cut off in traffic and angrily giving a guy the finger, finding a parking space, walking into the station, etc.—unless for some reason that trip is important to the plot or character.

But even in the latter case—say you want to show her quick temper or impatience—make sure you're showing those traits in scenes that are germane and essential. A GPSing scene usually isn't—but it sounds like that witness interview was, so why not let Freya's impatience seep into her questioning, or show a flare of anger despite her efforts to maintain a neutral façade? Use your resources (in this case, words—and your reader's attention) wisely and efficiently.

AVOIDING MELODRAMA

Tell can be valuable for conveying a scene of exceptionally high emotion that might detract from the main story, or to allow the bare potent fact of an event to impact the reader without the filter of the characters' reactions.

Author Kelly Harms has a chapter in her novel *The Bright Side of Going Dark* about the death of the protagonist's beloved dog, and it's written as mostly straightforward, factual description—yet it packs a wallop. And it's a key part of the character's backstory and arc—if it weren't the scene might feel gratuitous or maudlin.

> **Pro tip:**
>
> In most cases pet death or suffering scenes in a manuscript are commonly regarded in the industry as off-putting to agents and publishers, not only for the obvious reasons, but because they're seen as a cliché or a "cheap trick" for manipulating readers' emotions. If you use them—or scenes of torture or violence, particularly of a child—I suggest using the coldest of "tell" and only sparingly and without graphic detail—and make sure they are absolutely essential to your story.

In events of extreme drama or emotion, unless they are central to the story—as with the *Sophie's Choice* scene—see if writing predominantly in more objective tell rather than show allows you to elicit the response you want in the reader without melodrama or an accidental telenovela feel (unless that's what you're writing). But even in that case, watch for "purple prose"—sometimes tell can offer just as much melodrama as show if it's written in an overly lurid style. The old saw is often true that the hotter a scene, the colder you write it.

.. # ..

"Show, don't tell" might be some of the most familiar advice in all of literature—even among nonauthors. But as with so many other "rules" and often-demonized story devices, tell has a valuable place in good writing (after all, it's called story*telling*). Adept authors use both to create juicy, engaging stories and draw readers into their world.

chapter seven

STRUCTURE

S tructure is both a macro- and a microlevel element of story: Big-picture it refers to the gestalt of the story arc, as we discussed in the Plot chapter, but on a more nuts-and-bolts level it's specifically how you arrange your scenes to most effectively tell your story. The two are inextricably connected, but structure is a function of story— not the other way around. Don't get stuck on following the "rules" of a particular writing system and rigidly impose that prescribed structure onto your story, or write to try to force it to conform. Imagine taking a trip cross-country where your driver has mapped out not only the route, but every single stop you'll make, how long you can stay, and exactly what you must do there—and if something comes up unexpectedly there's no deviation allowed. That kind of regimentation and inflexibility would kill any chance of you enjoying your trip very much, and in storytelling it can stultify an author's voice and creativity and make for neutered writing and a joyless reading experience.

There's no one right way to structure your story, and no universal "rules" for what structure it should adhere to. There are, however, some fairly unshakable guidelines for making sure you draw readers in and take us on a journey we invest in and stay invested in, common to almost all schools of thought on structure:

The protagonist moves steadily along an arc, and winds up different at the end than at the beginning (whether that's a changed situation, outlook, internal growth, etc.). Along the way toward a goal or destination she faces challenges and setbacks that steadily increase in difficulty, followed by renewed pushes toward that goal until she achieves a satisfying realization of character arc—not necessarily a happy ending, but at least one that ties up most of the loose ends.

Despite a seeming wide variety in approaches to structure—the Hero's Journey, Save the Cat, the Six-stage Plot Structure, the W plot structure—they all have these basic mileposts in common. The biggest differences in these schools of thought, to me, lie more in which approach makes the most sense to you as an author and for the particular story you're telling rather than in any inherent superiority of any of them. As with all writing advice—including editorial feedback—I advocate that you take what works for you and toss what doesn't. But make sure you are hitting these universal beats of story in whatever way you decide to structure yours if you want to engage human readers. Lisa Cron, in her enlightening book *Wired for Story*, talks about the neuroscience that shows our brains have specific hardwired expectations for story—we evolved that way to quite literally guarantee our survival—and the most basic of those is that we expect to go on a journey where the main characters are somehow changed by the end as a direct result of what we experienced with them along the way.

I find it useful to think about story structure visually, and I often use the W story structure idea as a concrete image for writers struggling with structure. You can immediately understand from looking at a W that your protagonist(s) should experience challenges that lead to some downward trajectory to a low point, then begin to overcome them in an upward trajectory toward his goal, then face another setback followed by another downward trajectory and low point, and then a final renewed push upward till the goal is attained.

But that's not the gospel of story structure. Stories might look like this:

W

Or like this:

M

Or this:

Or even this:

WW

But good story *doesn't* look like this:

—

Or this:

And certainly not this:

Silly as these drawings might seem, they can actually be a really useful, concrete way of visualizing story structure.

In the first what-not-to-do case above, the straight line, nothing really happens. The character goes along at the same basic level throughout until he stops—but you haven't taken him (or the reader) anywhere. This is the novel version of basic normal life, where we generally tend to get up, go about our routines, go to sleep, and do it all over again the next day. We don't read to hear about ordinary, uneventful, rote life—we're usually living it. We read to experience something greater.

In story we crave the anomalies—those extreme highs and lows interspersed in every life that are out of the ordinary and intense: the great love, the seemingly insurmountable challenge, the existential crisis, heroic action, etc. The peaks and valleys are where story lies—not in a flat line.

The second image may have levels and hit highs and lows, but they're not intrinsically connected. This is the visual representation of a story that feels episodic: *this happened, and then this, and then this.* It may include ups and downs, but it's not a cohesive journey, just a series of vignettes, so it doesn't take the reader anywhere either.

The third image suggests a meandering story that has little coherent structure, doesn't follow the cognitive expectations for story that humans have, and thus feels aimless, unengaging, and unsatisfying. We're lost in the woods with no clear destination, so we quickly lose interest in trying to follow such an aimless path.

So how do you use all this to figure out what structure your story has, and whether it's working as effectively as possible on both the macro and micro structure levels?

✓ *How to Find It*

It's generally most helpful to start this exercise without going back into your manuscript—just work from the story in your mind. First, jot down where your protagonist is in his journey when we initially meet him. Let's use *Romeo and Juliet* as a fairly universal story reference, and I'll include where in the play each of these events falls. At the "point A" in each character's journey, mercurial Romeo is moping over a love interest who isn't interested; underage Juliet is resisting an arranged marriage to an older relative of the prince [beginning of act one].

Now write down what kick-starts your character(s) on the journey of the story: In this case, Romeo and Juliet—members respectively of two feuding families—meet and are instantly smitten [end of act one].

Next, write down the main high and low points—the successes and triumphs, and the challenges and setbacks—of your protagonist(s)' journey.

- **High point**: Romeo and Juliet ardently court in secret and declare their love [beginning of act two]; they get married [end of act two].
- **Low point**: Juliet's cousin Tybalt kills newlywed Romeo's best friend, and in his rage Romeo kills Tybalt and is banished [beginning of act three]. Juliet, whose marriage to Romeo is still secret, is told she will be forced to marry the prince's relative [end of act three].
- **High point**: Juliet devises a plan to sneak away to be with Romeo [beginning of act four] which seems to succeed [end of act four].
- **Low point**: Romeo, unaware of the plan, kills himself. Juliet, discovering him dead, kills herself as well [end of act five].

Now write down the endpoint of your protag(s)' journey when we finish the story. In *Romeo and Juliet*, the lovers are tragically dead (point B), but their families vow to end their generations-long feud because of it.

This story structure most closely resembles a modified W, above—more like an M in this case, since it starts and ends at low points. It's useful to read (or watch a staging) of *Romeo and Juliet* to see how meticulously and classically structured it is—notice how each high or low point corresponds with the beginning or end of an act, and how every other scene of each act—and the entire play—comprises an intrinsic step toward each peak or valley.

If Shakespeare isn't quite your bag, you can see an equally tightly structured story in the film *The Princess Bride* (of course!). This story also has clear high and low points, with each scene an essential step toward the next obstacle or victory, propelling us steadily from point A to point B.

Even if your story is more complicated than these relatively straightforward ones—with many POV characters, or time shifts, or multiple storylines, etc.—you can parse out the structure using this same exercise. Use separate lists if you have to, breaking down each storyline or time period into the above major points. Even subplots can (and should) follow some variation of the essential elements of story structure given at the beginning of this chapter. We'll talk more about weaving it all together below.

To sum up, ask yourself:

- Do we clearly see a challenge or issue facing your protagonist(s) from very early into the story?
- Is there a defined goal or finish line for your protag(s)—whether external/tangible (Romeo and Juliet succeed in fleeing Verona together) or internal (they find true love) or both?
- Are there clear high points and low points (triumphs and obstacles) on the path to that final goal?
- Is every step on the path essential to carry your protag to her final destination?

If any of the answers are no, it's time to dive into the manuscript and address those issues.

✓ *How to Fix It*

You're probably noticing that story structure has a lot to do with plot, but remember plot is not story. Structure is also intrinsically, but not exclusively, tied to character. As we saw earlier, story is a combination of both character arc and plot—specifically how the latter helps bring about the former—so you can use many of the tools from the Character and Plot chapters in evaluating and strengthening your story structure, particularly your character arc exercise in the Character chapter, and the X-ray exercise from the Plot chapter.

As you continue to examine your story structure after making your list above from memory, now refer directly to the manuscript itself. Start by looking at the first point you wrote down—the challenge or issue your character faces. Where in the manuscript does that become apparent? It should be pretty close to the beginning—a rough rule of thumb is the first chapter or two, or around 10 percent. (Are there successful exceptions to this guideline? As with everything in writing "rules," of course. But the longer it takes, the more you risk losing—or never gaining—reader investment.)

Similarly, where in your manuscript do we find out your protagonist's driving goal? This may not be the ultimate goal he ends up pursuing for the entire story—goals can and do shift as the character progresses along his journey. But we need to see something driving him early in, even if it's aversive: For instance, a character whose ultimate goal is to stand on her own feet for the first time and, let's say, buy a house on her own after a messy divorce for herself and her kids might initially have the goal of sabotaging her ex's new relationship. Her arc may evolve so that that goal shifts, but readers are still wired to see a character we're invested in pursuing a meaningful goal. We tend to quickly detach from one who seems rudderless or unmotivated—so make sure your protag's initial goal is evident very early in. (See the Stakes chapter for more on this idea—including how to infuse that sense of drive and goal even in characters whose point A is a lack of motivation and whose arc is that they go from being "stuck" in life to finding their focus or purpose.)

Referring back to the exercise you did above, now find where in the manuscript your high and low points fall. There are lots of "rules" and guidelines in various schools of writing thought about precise placement of these challenges and successes, like the Hero's Journey, or Michael Hauge's Six-stage Plot Structure, three-act structure, etc. Most of them are based on solid storytelling convention, so if it's helpful to use that kind of mapping or structure guide, go ahead. But you don't need to adhere to a particular set of rigid structure "rules." In general, remember my fancy structure drawings above—all the ones that work well share the common feature of alternating highs and lows: a roller coaster, not a treadmill or a hopscotch board. Are you putting your protag through those ups and downs throughout? Are they reasonably spaced through-out the story—in other words, we don't get a flat-line structure till halfway through before the first up or down, or an upward or downward trajectory all the way to the end, etc.? Does the most significant setback occur close to the end, shortly before the final triumph (or, for a tragedy, the inverse: the pinnacle of the character's journey occuring close to the final defeat at the end)? It can be helpful to actually create a line drawing for your story similar to my works of art above so you can see a physical representation of your story's development and levels, mapping out each high and low point visually.

Now check each step on the path—the scenes that propel your protag-onist from the beginning to each high and low, and all the way to the end. (If you made an X-ray in the Plot chapter, this is another excellent use for it.) Does the story propel the character(s) along the path toward each of those highs and lows—meaning does every scene offer something essen-tial to move the protag along the course of the story? Is what happens to him a direct result of the events we see, and do those events intrinsically, inevitably lead to those peaks and valleys? In *Romeo and Juliet*'s case, you can easily map out that the answer is yes—even the bare-bones sketch above shows the logical, intrinsic story progression. If you see or read the entire play (or a detailed summary), you see that every development in the story, even the minor ones, either propels these two toward their goals or derails them, to the inevitable conclusion. Be ruthless—if any scene in your WIP does not intrinsically affect the story arc, either revise to make that scene essential, or delete those inessential darlings.

Finally, does the end point of your story—your character either achieving or failing to achieve her goal—also complete her arc, taking her somewhere different at the end from who/where she was at the beginning, as a direct result of the events we have lived with her? Notice how the ending of *Romeo and Juliet* not only completes the arc for each of the young lovers, but that of the framing story as well—their feuding families, who began at odds (point A) and, as a direct result of the events of the story, end at peace (point B). And does this happen either at or very near the end? Stories that peak or "wrap up" too early and continue past their resolution seem to trickle to a halt rather than offer a definitive, satisfying ending for readers.

Here's the checklist:

- Do we see your protagonist(s)' point A clearly at or near the story's beginning?
- Does the character's initial challenge or opportunity that begins to move them away from point A along their arc occur within the first one to two chapters (around 10 percent)?
- Does the protagonist experience high and low points throughout the journey that move her closer to her goal/threaten to derail its attainment? (Another way to think of this: Is the character's arc always on either an upward or downward trajectory? Flat lines are narrative dead space.)
- Is every single scene leading to a peak or valley essential to propel the protag along that path?
- Does the protagonist achieve his goal (or, failing to achieve it, significantly change as a result from his point A) either at the end or very close to it?

WHERE SHOULD YOUR STORY START?

It's easy to say "close to the inciting event," but what does that actually mean? Often newer writers take this advice to mean starting with a high-stakes event, like a car crash or a murder or a spectacular breakup, etc. Or sometimes they will insert a "prologue" of one of the really exciting scenes later in the manuscript as a way of ostensibly baiting the hook. (This is one reason prologues get a bad rap; when they are improperly used this way it feels like an author shortcut or a cheat—i.e., "Keep reading! Eventually it's going to get good....") But remember that stakes are dependent on character: If we don't yet know or invest in your protagonist(s), even the most objectively exciting event will leave us unaffected.

And what is the "inciting event" anyway? Basically it's the moment at which the character's journey in the story becomes urgent or inevitable. *Gone Girl* doesn't begin on the deterioration of Nick and Amy's marriage or Nick's affair because those events don't make *this* story—about how Amy tries to frame Nick for murder and their subsequent cat-and-mouse game—inevitable; what does is Amy's disappearance, which happens on page 23 of 415 in the hardcover edition, in the first five percent of the story. If the book were about, say, how Amy's desperate insecurity and need for attention ate away at their relationship, or how Nick's affair betrayed his wife's trust and destroyed their marriage, it would have a different inciting event.

But if Gillian Flynn had begun with Nick rushing home from work to find that ominously gaping front door, readers likely wouldn't have been drawn in. We wouldn't know enough about Nick or Amy at that point, and this event, while objectively intriguing, wouldn't really affect us, as we learned in the Stakes chapter. Instead she paves in their point A (or so it seems), with context about each character and their marriage, and a delicious inherent conflict in how different each of their versions of it seems to be. Where to start your story is a balance between showing something intriguing and giving the reader reasons to invest in it.

For instance, let's say your story is about a woman who believes her husband was murdered and sets out to find his killer. If it opens on your protagonist trying to figure out who killed her husband during his funeral, likely the reader isn't really drawn in. We don't know these people at all—this is a faceless story to us.

But let's say the story opens on a woman clutching the edge of the casket so tightly her fingers are white, but not letting any other reaction show because her young son is distraught and needs her to comfort him over the loss of his father. The dead man's best friend comes to put an arm around her and she gratefully leans into his embrace, letting him lead her and her son to their seat for the service. And then just before he steps up to the dais to offer his best friend's eulogy, the man whispers something in her ear about the circumstances of her husband's death that he couldn't possibly have known—unless he was there.

Now you might feel quite invested in what's going on. The combination of the situation (dead husband), offering more context (suspicious circumstances), showing something about the protagonist that allows us to invest in her (she's being strong for her son), and introducing intriguing story questions (did the best friend do it? will he get away with it?) creates the hook. The inciting event is definitely the friend's inadvertent clue that points her suspicions at him, but the place to start is a bit before that, with enough information and more of her "point A" setup so that we care. This is what I think of as good uncertainty, as opposed to being cryptic—the author creates questions in the reader that keeps her turning pages, but gives enough information so that we aren't simply floundering in the dark.

The Much-maligned Prologue

Prologues aren't inherently bad any more than are snakes or sharks or bears. As with any dangerous animal, it all depends on how you encounter them. A few headline-grabbing terrible shark attacks can color people's opinions of the whole species—which is how prologues got such a negative reputation: Agents and editors see a lot of bad ones.

Here is what a prologue should *not* be used for: It's not a preview of better things to come if only the reader sticks with you through the boring setup parts. It's not a shortcut to action. It's not a summary of the character's journey you're about to read. It's not a way to cheat in a backstory dump to "bring the reader up to speed" before you begin the actual story.

I worked with an experienced, multipublished author on an art-heist mystery/thriller. The story itself was excellent, but it began with a slow build. The structure fit the story well—the reader needed to invest in the protagonist, to understand the setup of the art world, the stolen art, the stakes—but it didn't feel as effective a hook as it could be. So I suggested moving a very short anecdote from a later scene to the beginning of the story as a prologue—a fascinating true story of a very famous unsolved art theft. In context this story had appeared well into the manuscript, but it wasn't essential there and didn't significantly add anything to that scene. However, when we tried moving it to the prologue it set the tone for the entire story, drawing the reader in immediately with a mystery and suggesting a similar sort of intrigue to come. It also provided context for the story world, as well as the world of the protagonist, an art expert.

A well-executed prologue can add a lot to a reader's experience of the story. Think of it as an amuse bouche for a full-course gourmet meal: It sets up the palate for what's to come. It might serve as a frame for the story—like a character reflecting back with perspective on a past event that sets up his journey in this story, as in Rochelle Weinstein's *Where We Fall*, where one character in a painful love triangle remembers a joyful scene of the youthful friendship of the trio. It might be an element like a newspaper article or letter or fable that orients the reader to the story or suggests a theme or cautionary tale, as with Paolo Coelho's prologue in *The Alchemist* about what happened after the Narcissus myth ends. It might set up essential context for the world of the story, as with Ruta Sepetys's lead-in to *The Fountains of Silence*, which offers a brief, informative overview of the Spanish Civil War and Franco's thirty-six-year dictatorship that followed, where the story is set. It might foreshadow what's to come in a tantalizing way: Arthur C. Clarke's prologue to *2001: A Space Odyssey* beautifully poses a central story question—is there life outside of Earth?—that creates delicious anticipation in the reader of finding out the answer.

If you want to try a prologue for your story (and why not? art is experimentation), keep in mind a few guidelines:

- Keep it short—the examples I give above range from a single paragraph to two pages.

- Set up an expectation or question, or illuminate something essential for the reader to fully understand the story.

- Be ruthlessly honest about whether the prologue actually adds something significant to the story—or you're shortcutting.

The above are general guidelines for storytelling that form the basic shape of your story—within that, how you choose to arrange your scenes is partly a function of individual style and voice. But structure can also significantly impact how well you draw in readers. Your job as the author is to find the most effective way to tell the story you are telling. The crucial questions to ask yourself at every step, to paraphrase the Watergate hearings, is what do we need to know, and when do we need to know it?

Some stories unfold perfectly linearly from beginning to end—each event is presented in chronological order as it happens, as with *Romeo and Juliet*—while some leap around in chronology, like *Gone Girl*. Often the way an author chooses to present the story can become an integral part of the story itself—imagine Toni Morrison's *Beloved* unspooling strictly linearly, or the time-jumping TV show *This Is Us*. Much of what makes those stories as effective as they are is the way the writer chooses to tell them.

As long as you keep in mind the holy grail of storytelling—every single scene should move the story forward—how you do that is a matter of style. See how story arc might dictate individual scene placement. Play with structure—see if moving things around enhances the story you're telling. In Sarah Bird's *Gap Year*, the two protagonists' storylines unfold chronologically in alternating viewpoints, but a year apart. Allison Winn Scotch's *Between Me and You* tells one protagonist's POV in forward chronology and the other in backward chronology, in alternating chapters. Kate Atkinson's *Life After Life* repeatedly jumps back in time to show alternate lives for her protagonist. *Cloud Atlas* skips all over POV and time line to hell and gone. There's no "right" way to tell the story you're trying to tell, as long as you move the story forward—whether that's through advancing the plot, revealing something new and germane about the character, or divulging essential information—with every single scene.

momentum
AND PACE

As with suspense and tension, while momentum and pace are closely related they're not quite the same thing, although they're often used interchangeably. Momentum is how well the manuscript propels readers through the story; pace is the speed at which it does. Both Niagara Falls and the Mississippi River have momentum, but each is moving at a very different pace. You can think of momentum as a function of story, pace as a function of scene.

Momentum

Momentum is a story's impetus, its driving force—what propels readers through the pages—and it's the essence of the storytelling holy grail: Every single scene should move the story forward. If I did a search for that phrase in this book I'm betting it's already appeared half a dozen times, but what does it actually mean?

The most successful stories give readers a seamless experience as they travel through the story, carrying them along fluid as a flume ride. But that doesn't mean constant high-energy action—relentless "happenings" in your story can lose readers as surely as lagging momentum. Every scene should contribute to that forward propulsion by doing at least one of the following:

- Advancing the plot
- Advancing the character arc
- Raising stakes
- Providing essential information

In addition, each scene should accomplish this *in the most effective way*. For instance, if it's essential to the story to know that a character was abused by his father (but not a story *about* that), then a long flashback scene of his childhood abuse in the middle of the forward momentum of the central plot is likely to yank the reader out of the action and stall pace; it's not the most *effective* way to weave in that essential information.

If we go back to our river analogy, there may be areas of whitewater rapids as well as calmer sections, but in all cases it moves constantly toward the sea. If it doesn't—if something dams up the flow—the water may spread arbitrarily over its banks, or stagnate, and then it's not a river anymore. Story, like a river, must flow steadily toward its destination.

Techniques for making sure you've created and sustained strong story momentum overlap with every other area of story—character, plot, stakes, suspense and tension, showing and telling, structure, even line editing—and I refer to some of the techniques offered in those chapters you can use to help make sure your story flows.

✓ How to Find It

Seeing where our own stories flag or stall can be tricky, partly because of the unconscious fill-in-the-blanks every author does with his own writing—*you* know what's coming. Or the story may not feel slow to you because that detailed portrait of the political situation of Weimar Republic Germany just before the Nazis came into power that you spent three months meticulously researching is fascinating to you—but it may be a momentum-killing info dump for the lay reader.

This is an area where beta readers and crit partners can be especially helpful—when soliciting feedback you can ask specifically where their interest or focus may have lagged, or if they put the manuscript down at any point and it took a while to get back to it. For nonwriter beta readers, you can give them sticky notes and ask that they simply flag anywhere they felt less engaged with the story, or places where they put the book down between reads (often a great way to spot momentum killers).

But you can also do a gut check with yourself if you dig down a little deeper as you read, asking yourself with each scene, "Is this really necessary to move the story forward?" and if it is, "Is it the most effective way to do so?" Readers may need a sense of the political environment of your pre–World War II setting to fully understand the story, but do they really need five pages' worth?

If you made an X-ray of your story while working on plot elements, this is another great use for it. Check that every bullet-pointed story development furthers the plot or character arcs, raises stakes, and/or offers essential information. In stories with the strongest momentum—the "unputdownable" books—scenes accomplish more than one of these objectives.

✓ *How to Fix It*

As you checked your manuscript for momentum, refer to the "but/therefore" exercise from the Plot chapter: Does every event follow from previous one, and lead inexorably to the next? This doesn't always mean your protagonist(s) must be relentlessly taking action—scenes where we see him react, process, and regroup are equally important for propelling the story: When Our Hero is bashed over the head and kidnapped by the bad guy, she doesn't regain consciousness and immediately start seeking escape; people aren't robots, mechanically commencing each next task. First she has to react: Is she hurt? Disoriented? Scared? Then she has to assess her situation: where she is, what her circumstances are, what happened. Is she tied up? Is anyone in the room with her? Who is it? Then she can start formulating a plan: Can she take her captor? Are there weapons at hand? What are her escape options? Etc. And while she's doing that she might reflect on her own mistakes that got her caught, or maybe she's hatching revenge or already trying to figure out where to start tracking her bad guy again. *Now* she can act—but this scene where she's regrouping is essential for moving the story forward, meaning not simply the action but the character's pursuit of her goal. With multiple storylines and POVs, each scene in that thread should also have this same cause-and-effect forward propulsion.

Another crucial element of momentum: In addition to your protagonist(s)' overarching goal in the story, check that he has a goal within each scene as well that directly serves that main goal. In the above example it's to escape her captors (immediate goal) so that she can resume pursuit of the bad guy (longer-term goal) to, say, keep him from blowing up Manhattan and killing millions (ultimate goal). Every objective for every scene should serve the ultimate objective in some way to keep momentum strong.

Creating and maintaining forward momentum is a balancing act between what to include in the manuscript and what to take away. Imagine your story as a ladder, taking the reader to the destination you choose. If the rungs are too far apart, where the reader doesn't have enough connective tissue to fluidly follow the story arc, climbing the ladder is such hard work we might give up. In places where you give the reader extraneous info—too much description, introspection, info dumps, etc.—it's as if you've built rungs every two inches; it's cumbersome for us to try to take each tiny step, and again it wearies us. Space those rungs out so you guide your reader smoothly up the story ladder.

That means giving the reader enough info to hook us, but not so much that you spoon-feed us every exhaustive detail. Remember stories are a collaborative art between the storyteller and the reader; the author sets the stage, but the reader becomes part of the performance with what he brings to the experience.

WHAT TO ADD

Fill in the Holes

If you realized in your X-ray or from your own evaluative read or beta readers' responses that you left out crucial parts of the story, now's the time to add those in. Did you forget to include a key step in the plot?

Introduce a thread that got lost? Neglect to resolve a subplot? Fill in those gaps.

Make Sure the Meat Is on the Plate

Just as you wouldn't leave the crown roast in the oven and tell your dinner-party guests how delicious it is while they dine on the side dishes, don't let key story events happen "offstage" and sum them up for readers secondhand (it's watching that dry vacation slide show rather than being on the adventure yourself). Check to see whether you're telling essential story events that would be more effective shown directly on the page. These include:

- essential plot developments (i.e., those that are germane to moving the story forward)
- key conflicts—especially do we see the protagonists directly grapple with their antagonists, whether that's a person or thing
- turning points: character choice points, changes of heart or thinking, shifts in the character's arc
- peaks and valleys—your main characters' triumphs and setbacks, per the Structure chapter
- the black moment—the protagonist's lowest point.

These essential plot developments are the meat of your story; bring them onto the page to propel your story and keep the momentum strong. Don't skip the entrée for the side dishes.

Put the Characters in the Action

Story is a journey and the plot is the road—but remember your characters are the drivers. If your protagonists aren't driving the action—if they passively experience events that happen to them, rather than having agency and effecting change, or they are merely bystanders or witnesses to the action—the story will quickly lose momentum and stall. In addition to making sure that your characters are steadily pursuing their overarching goal, in every scene they should also have an immediate one. Make sure that readers see the momentum of the story being directly driven in pursuit of that goal by your characters' choices, actions, behavior, and even inaction (passivity is okay if it's part of the character's arc—but that passivity must still directly propel the story, as we saw in the Character and Stakes chapters).

We also experience the story's urgency and impetus through your characters' perceptions and reactions. If we're held outside their direct experience it's as if we're standing onshore watching the river go by, rather than being carried along on the current. Refer back to the chapters on Character, Point of View, and Showing and Telling and keep the action visceral and immediate to help propel momentum.

Layer in Tension and Suspense

These elements are the rocket fuel of momentum. Refer back to the Suspense and Tension chapter and make sure you've woven in suspense throughout the story, tension on every page. It's counterintuitive, but slowing down in certain scenes and adding more of these elements often creates more story momentum, pushing readers to turn pages.

Connect the Dots

Regardless of how you get us from point A to point B, the reader needs what I call connective tissue to orient us along the route. Beginning a new scene without offering the reader some idea how we got there from the last one in the same POV, for instance, can leave us floundering and a bit lost, as if the story has speeded ahead and left us behind, or we missed a step somehow.

This can be as simple as letting us know when and where we are, relative to the previous scene: "Two hours later, Mickey met the witness at the bar." It can be the character's motivation for being where she is: How does what happened in the scene before directly lead to the character's next decision or action—e.g., "She knew she had to confront Jack about his brother's secret before she lost her nerve"—so that we see it's not just a chain of unrelated sequential events, like a slide show, but a cause-and-effect progression that creates *story*.

But we also need the character-arc connective tissue—if you end a chapter on a major revelation or turn of events, readers need some indication what happened afterward before you move the character forward to a new scene.

This also applies to transition within scenes. Let's say you have a passage like this:

> She opened the door and there was John, down on one knee and a tiny square box in his shaking hand.
> They called both their parents to tell them the good news.

It feels as if we've missed something between these two beats—one second John's proposing and the next they're calling the folks. Yanking readers from one moment to the next without orienting us to how we got there, narratively speaking, feels jarring and jerky, like jump cuts in film, or a stuttering engine jerking the car down the road. This is another more-is-more area where it can actually increase momentum to add verbiage. It can be as simple as a word or phrase to orient us: "*Later* they called both their parents..." Or you can insert a space break (usually indicated by a hash mark) as a transition to another scene, so that we don't necessarily need to see the actual proposal but we understand that it did happen "offstage"—which might work or might actually be the meat that needs to be on the page; you have to assess whether it's a key event to show for the story you are telling. For instance, if this is a romance, damn skippy you'd better let us see that peak moment! But if this is about, say, Our Heroine's journey toward self-actualization in the form of reclaiming her neglected art career, John's actual proposal may not be essential to show; the *fact* of it may affect her arc, but not necessarily the details. This is part of why I call this approach "intuitive editing"—there aren't always (or often) "right" answers—just the rightest answer for *your* story, *your* vision.

> **Remember, space breaks are generally
> used to signify three things:**
>
> • Passage of time
>
> • Change of scene/setting
>
> • Change of POV

A great way to learn how to assess your transitions between and within scenes to make sure you're smoothly leading your readers through the story is by paying attention when you're reading a book that carries you seamlessly along: Go back and thumb from section to section (separated by space breaks) and from chapter to chapter to see how the author leads the reader from the end of one to the beginning of the next. Then reread some of the scenes with an analytical eye, paying attention to how the author paves in connective tissue in these transition moments within scenes to fluidly propel the reader along the river of story.

WHAT TO TAKE AWAY

Often the biggest improvement you can make for momentum is to clear away the extraneous material clogging the flow. The writer can and should know much more about the story and characters than the reader—if you've done your homework you know your characters' histories, special skills, demons, friends and enemies, dreams, and vulnerabilities; you may even know their hobbies, their favorite subject and teacher in school, the circumstances of their first crush and heartbreak. All of that can and may inform the story and their arcs, but we don't always need to know every detail exhaustively. As in sculpting, often the ultimate shape comes clear only as the artist chisels away the extraneous stone.

Just as you examined your X-ray to see whether you'd left out any essential scenes, go through and see whether every scene you have included is essential for moving the story forward (refer back to the list at the beginning of this chapter of what makes a scene essential), and whether it does so in the most effective way. Again, be as objective and ruthlessly honest as you can—just because a scene or chapter may be beautifully written, that doesn't necessarily mean it serves the story. If a scene or development or moment stalls momentum it's hampering the story. Try moving the scenes in question out of the manuscript into another file and see whether you actually need each one, and if you do, whether you need the full scene or chapter, or if a few lines would accomplish the same end more effectively. (Remember: Save those lovely darlings! You never know when they may come in handy for marketing, or for another story.)

Do the same within every scene: Does each paragraph, each line (dialogue and narrative) accomplish a purpose that helps drive the story forward? If not, take it out.

One and Done

If a scene establishes something you already established in a previous scene, it's treading water rather than moving the story downriver.

This is an area where analyzing films is especially useful; movies with strong momentum establish information *once* and then keep moving the story forward.

In *Pretty Woman*, for instance, the opening scene establishes that people are secondary to work for wealthy businessman Edward. That's a theme that runs through his character arc throughout, but this is the only scene that shows it unadulterated. In subsequent scenes when we again see Edward consumed with work after he's met Vivian, a prostitute, the dynamic changes: That first night at the hotel he gets up from what he's working on to sit next to Vivian to watch TV and they have sex, but late that night we see him presumably going back to what he left unfinished at work while she sleeps. In the morning he's on a call about work with his lawyer when she wakes up and as almost soon as he sees her he hangs up. When she offers to leave he stops her—now he isn't just passively turning his attention away from work for Vivian, as he did last night; he's actively seeking out her company instead of working. Then he invites her *into* his work life for a working dinner that evening. Later he calls her *from* work—twice—and actually dismisses a work issue to speak with Vivian. Later still he skips work altogether to go shopping with Vivian.

With each iteration of this same idea—Edward's obsession with work—we see the levels changing: Edward moves along his arc in each scene as the plot develops, stakes rise, and we are steadily given new information (all objectives that make a scene essential). If we simply saw repeated scenes of Edward totally eschewing people for work as he did in the first scene it would feel redundant and stall the flow; screenwriter J. F. Lawton already established that dynamic. If subsequent scenes showed the same level of distraction from work with Vivian, they would also be redundant. But Lawton ups the ante each time, showing Edward more and more fascinated by Vivian and quicker to abandon work for her, pushing the character steadily further along his arc (and also furthering the story arc).

Once a fact or specific character dynamic is established it stalls momentum to show a scene establishing the same thing again. Even if we see a similarly *themed* scene multiple times—as with Edward's work-aholism, or the protagonists' crumbling marriage in *Revolutionary Road,* or the multiple physical therapy scenes in Katherine Center's *How to Walk Away,* for instance—each scene must offer something new that moves the story forward with character arc, plot, stakes, or essential information.

Flashbacks

As we discussed in the last chapter, flashbacks aren't inherently bad, but a poorly placed or executed one can stop forward momentum cold. Nothing says, "Put down the book and go grab a coffee" more than one of those clunky *Wayne's World* lead-ins I mentioned, or a long chunk of text set apart in italics (banish italics from your flashback repertoire, I beg you).

If you have flashbacks in your manuscript, go through and assess each one using the questions offered above to see whether showing a whole flashback scene is really necessary. If you're simply establishing a certain fact or element of a character's past whose specifics are not a key part of the main story, see if you can cull out the germane parts instead and weave them into the main narrative for a more fluid reading experience. Refer back to the "Flashback Etiquette" box in the Showing and Telling chapter on how we remember—in snippets and flashes—and see if that might more effectively serve story momentum. Or weave a few paragraphs of the memory or flashback into the forward momentum of the present-moment scene. Or, if a flashback truly is germane and the best way to move the story forward, simply set it off in its own section or chapter. Which is *not* in italics. ☺

·· *#* ··

If something isn't propelling the story forward it's likely bogging it down, and making these hard cuts is one of the toughest but most useful skills you can develop in editing your own work.

BEGINNINGS AND ENDINGS— CRUCIAL PLACES TO CHECK MOMENTUM

There's an art to ending a scene or chapter on some sort of tension—an unresolved question, conflict, etc.—and then smoothly seguing us into the next, and it's one of the best ways to facilitate your reader's seamless propulsion along your river of story. See earlier chapters on Suspense and Tension, Structure, and Plot for ways to double-check that you begin the story, as well as every chapter and scene, with a hook that compels us onward, and leave each one with an uncertainty, question, unresolved tension, mystery, etc., to propel us forward.

It's equally important for momentum to end the story where it ends. In other words, once you have reached the climax—the moment of truth, ultimate face-off, greatest challenge—and resolved it (the denouement), the story should end very soon thereafter. Michael Hauge actually prescribes that the final, main turning point for the character's arc should occur as close as 99 percent of the way through the story. The story is over when the character has fully traveled her arc. Readers do often relish seeing the protags in their "happily ever after," enjoying the fruits of their journey and their new transformed existence as a result of it, but continuing the narrative beyond a brief glimpse of that makes the story feel as if it ends not with a bang but a whimper. Last impressions are strongest, and even if your story maintains strong momentum through-out, letting it hobble across the finish line leaves readers feeling impatient and less satisfied.

THE GREAT SWAMPY MIDDLE

I'm borrowing this heading from author Jim Butcher's glorious essay on how to address middle-of-the-book sag (https://jimbutcher.livejournal. com/1865.html), a story phenomenon especially common with early drafts. Frequently the reason a story feels as if it loses steam in the mid-dle can be traced back to momentum. Double-check your manuscript to make sure:

- your characters' goals remain clear and strong throughout, both the overarching goal and their goals for each individual scene
- their motivations remain strong and clear, both external and internal
- consequences for failure (or the reward for success) remain strong and clear throughout, both on a big-picture story level and within each scene.

More suggestions for propping up the sag:

- Introduce or develop a key subplot.
- Reveal surprise new information to the protagonist (be careful it doesn't seem like a *deus ex machina*).
- Amp up urgency—a new ticking clock or heightened stakes.
- Introduce a new conflict, or intensify an existing one.
- If you're using different POVs, make sure you're taking us away from one in the middle of a "cliffhanger"—some narrative uncertainty—right when we least want to go, and then hook us immediately in the opening of the next POV character's scene or chapter, again leaving us in medias res. As with focusing on chapter/scene endings and beginnings in the above section, this will serve as a strong push for readers at the end and beginning of each section.

Pace

Momentum, as the engine of story, should be constant—the river always moves downstream to the sea. But pace—how fast it gets there—can and usually should vary throughout the story.

Different genres have different pace expectations—readers of lyrical literary works aren't necessarily expecting pulse-pounding, page-turning action; thriller readers may grow bored if pace slows for more than a few pages. Know what you're writing (for so many reasons), and know reader expectations for your genre.

But for almost any book, varying the pace will increase reader engagement and enjoyment. I always think of it in musical terms— a steady, metronomic beat is almost soporific; it's the thrilling change of tempo—adagio to allegro, verse to bridge—that sparks our souls. As much as we love flying through the action of a story, readers also need moments to breathe.

✓ How to Find It

I'll talk more about specific prose techniques for setting pace in the Line Edits section, but here are a few general guidelines for figuring out how fast (or slow) to move a scene:

- **Suit the pace to the genre**. While within each story pace will vary, the overall feel of the story should reflect reader expectations for the type of book they're reading.
- **Suit the pace to the action.** A high-tension scene where your protagonist is fleeing her nemesis will most likely move at a fast clip. The lazy morning in bed after your hero and heroine finally get together may allow you to linger in a more relaxed pace.
- **Suit the pace to the mood**. In general, a slow pace reflects a somber or solemn tone; a tranquil or peaceful mood; deep emotion, introspection, respite. It can be effectively used for lower-urgency scenes where you want to give your reader a breather; "sequel" scenes where your character may be reacting,

reflecting, regrouping; resolution scenes (we enjoy seeing our hero relax a bit after all the hard work of achieving her goal). A faster pace is generally most effective in scenes involving a heightened sense of arousal, like fear, excitement, fury, etc. It helps drive scenes of danger, conflict, competition, suspense, pursuit, even razor-sharp banter.

- **Use pace unexpectedly.** You can also use pace to layer in depth to a scene or character, for example by contrasting it with the mood, or between different characters in the same scene. For instance, a funeral that's forced to lightning speed by the threat of rain or similar might be intentionally incongruously hilarious...or more tragic if a character feels cheated of the chance to properly honor his departed beloved. A love scene where one character leisurely revels in the intimacy while another keeps rushing it says a lot about their relationship and respective characters. A sharp shift to one slow moment in a fast-paced scene can add wonderful emphasis to that single beat.

✓ How to Fix It

Setting the pace in your story is often a function of the prose itself.

- **Sentence length and structure**: Longer, more complex sentences—those that use multiple clauses, prepositional phrases, appositive construction, and other grammatical ornamentation—often, like the slow rolling of a lazy river, create a more relaxed, leisurely, laid-back pace. Short sharp ones fly. (Notice how I used each technique in the two previous sentences describing what their pace illustrates.) You can control pace by varying sentence lengths: grouping longer ones together draws a scene or moment out, a series of short ones keeps it moving along, and varying the two can create a thrilling roller coaster of a scene. Let the rhythm and meter suggest action and mood.
- **Word choice**: Multisyllabic words tend to slow pace; single syllables speed it. Again, look at the two sentences in the first bullet

point. Connotation impacts pace as well: a *lugubrious* speaker suggests a plodding delivery not just through meaning but by feel; similarly a *curt* one suggests haste. *Lovemaking* implies taking one's sweet, sweet time; *sex* might get right down to it.

- **Paragraphing**: Long paragraphs tend to feel slower-paced; short ones increase the clip.

Pace Killers

Watch out for these common areas where a story can get bogged down:

Dialogue tags: Painstakingly attributing every piece of dialogue slows the conversation. To keep pace clipping, if the speaker is clear don't worry about attribution. (We'll visit this area in more detail in the Line Edits chapter.)

Description: Long passages of description—of a place, a person, a thing—can pull the reader out of the forward momentum of a story and stall pace.

Background: Imagine someone telling you a story about the car accident they just witnessed, but stopping periodically to fill you in on where they were coming from when they saw it, how they got to that intersection, the last time they witnessed an accident, etc. When you want to create a compelling pace, get to the damned point. ☺

Info dumps: Imagine your long-winded friend above also pausing to fill you in on the make and model of each car involved and the auto manufacturers' safety record and crash ratings. If you want to keep a scene moving, don't slow it down with extraneous detail.

· · # · ·

Sustaining forward momentum throughout a story keeps readers invested and engaged; controlling pace in every scene lets authors orchestrate the experience they want readers to have. Using both these tools effectively can ensure your book stays in their hand, not on the nightstand.

chapter nine

VOICE

W hat makes readers pick up a specific author's books even with- out knowing anything about the story? What makes you prefer one musician or band or composer over another, seek out the work of a specific actor or director (or even cinematographer, if you're a real film buff), gravitate to the paintings of a certain artist, feel mesmerized by the movements of a particular dancer or choreographer? What brings any art form fully, vividly, memorably to life?

The answer is voice.

Voice is a little hard to pin down, harder still to "teach" in writing— I think of the process less as *creating* your artistic voice and more as *revealing* it. You have a singular, distinctive voice already because we're human, each of us a unique pastiche of our makeup and experiences and perspectives. What teaches you to access and free your individual voice is partly craft, but mostly learning to tap into authenticity: to dig deep, open yourself, and let your truest self emerge onto the page. This is the magic part of writing, where the muse or your subconscious or the little writing fairies who possess authors when they get in the zone— however you like to think of it—takes the basic elements of story and elevates the whole.

Like so many elements of this book, voice applies to nonfiction authors too: One of my favorite biographers is A. Scott Berg, and I'll pick up anything he writes, whether it's about Katharine Hepburn or editor Maxwell Perkins (of course) or Woodrow Wilson or Charles Lindbergh, because I love his vivid, intimate style and voice. Norman Lear's autobiography is replete with his distinctive voice—his wit, intelligence, his conversational rhythms—and so is the nonfiction of Stephen Hawking or Roxane Gay or Yuval Noah Harari, among many others. Michael Paterniti's 370-page nonfiction book about a specific cheese (*The Telling Room*) is one of the most original, vibrant, entertaining nonfiction books I've read, largely due to his distinctive, personal voice; Melody Warnick wrote a fascinating book on relocation and building place attachment (*This Is Where You Belong*) that reads like a good friend helping you find and create community.

Voice is style. Voice is what makes art, art. Discovering how to infuse your writing with it involves first identifying what voice is in general—then practicing how to access and reveal yours.

✓ *How to Find It*

As with so many elements of storytelling, so much can be learned from analyzing how other artists reveal voice—and it's also some of the most fun work of honing your craft. My approach basically involves seeking out your favorite creators and analyzing what makes their work stand out or speak to you.

Why can I pick up a book by Pat Conroy or Toni Morrison or Kent Haruf or Rita Mae Brown and know without the author's name on the cover that it's theirs? It's because their distinctive voices infuse their writing: Conroy's languid Southern lyricism; Morrison's rhythms, sentence structure, and rich, evocative simile; the punch of Haruf's spare and unsentimental prose; Brown's distinctive phrasings and raucous irreverence. The millions of people who adored *Love, Actually* probably wouldn't be surprised to know the same writer is behind *This Is Us*, a show with an equally fervent fan following; the two share a sensibility and "feel" infused into them by writer Dan Fogelman.

Voice sets an author apart in music too—and not simply the literal tone of the singer's voice. The same song is an entirely different animal in a certain artist's treatment, like Tom Jones's cover of Prince's "Kiss," or Israel Kamakawiwo'ole's version of "Over the Rainbow," and a Carlos Santana song is a Carlos Santana song no matter who is singing. You know a Leonard Cohen tune the second you hear it because of his entirely distinctive voice—which includes his phrasings, cadence, quirks. The way a dancer moves is also her artistic voice: Gene Kelly, James Cagney, and Fred Astaire each have an instantly recognizable—and distinctive—style, and nobody dances like Beyoncé.

You can also identify authorial voice in films. When I watched *The Intern*, I kept thinking that the last time I smiled all the way through a movie that way was *It's Complicated*—my experience of this film strongly reminded me of that one. Sure enough, I found out afterward it was the same director/writer, Nancy Meyers. You see distinct voice in the films of Steven Spielberg, George Lucas, Martin Scorsese; in the shows of Marti Noxon, Phoebe Waller-Bridge, Shonda Rimes. *Big Little Lies* season two had a completely different feel—its voice—from season one; sure enough it also had a new director.

Another way to understand voice is to study the way some artists lend themselves to impressions—Christopher Walken or Robert DeNiro, with their distinctive phrasings, mannerisms, tones. Watch Jamie Foxx do his John Legend impersonation, or Matt Damon do Matthew McConnaughey, or Tina Fey do Sarah Palin—it's not so much that they re-create the exact tone of the person they're mimicking (though Foxx comes damn close), but the way they capture the essence of the person through their vocal tics, their affect, their demeanor. (This close observation and even mimicry is also a great technique to use not just in studying other artists' voice, but in creating your individual character voices.)

Whole artistic sensibilities can be conveyed through voice. One of the reasons Jonathan Van Ness's parody series *Gay of Thrones* is so rampantly popular is because he understands the voice and feel of *Game of Thrones* thoroughly enough to mock it to fiercely funny effect. When I was an actor I was part of an improv troupe for a time (feel free to groan), and one of our most popular games was "In the Style Of…" where audience members would shout out directors or singers or authors, even TV shows or films, and we had to present a scene that captured that feel—which meant understanding specifically what created it.

Most particularly helpful for your writing as you learn to identify, develop, and reveal your own voice will be seeking out the writers you love most and diving into the pages of their books to your favorite parts: the scenes that deeply affected you, the lines you had to stop and reread, the characters who came alive on the page and felt like people you knew. Analyze what stands out to you particularly—the phrasings? the rhythms? the overall style of the prose—ornate and mellifluous, strong and spare? the feel of the story? I love both Jennifer Weiner's and Emily Giffin's books, but though they both write character-driven, relationship-based stories in the same genre, I'd never mistake one for the other. Get as detailed as you can as you parse out these books, dissecting them for exactly what conveys to you the sensibility of the author.

It's almost equally instructive to analyze the works of writers you don't care for; what rubs you the wrong way about their writing? Chances are good it has at least partly to do with their voice; every reader has preferences, the same way each of us vibes to different types of music or visual art.

For a real immersion into identifying voice you can even try writing a few passages in the style of other writers, or creating a parody of certain authors' voice—you can't do parody without a deep understanding of what you are parodying. My high school AP English teacher, Connie Corley, understood this concept so well that she allowed me to turn in for our assigned paper on *Heart of Darkness* a spoof I wrote of Joseph Conrad's classic story (talk about a teacher who knew how to make learning fun...).

Once you have a solid understanding of what reveals voice in other authors' work, take that same magnifying glass to your own writing. Have you fully revealed your voice in your manuscript? Does it carry the distinctive flavor of what makes you, you as an author? Can you find places to infuse more of your most authentic sensibility in the story? Here are some likely places to look:

- **Root out the overfamiliar**: Comb your writing for clichés, aphorisms, well-trodden turns of phrase or ideas or figurative imagery.

- **Invigorate the ordinary**: Watch out for workmanlike, under-imaginative, generic writing.
- **Notice your rhythms**: What's the music of your voice: stripped-down and direct? lean and simple? fluid and melodic? a mix?
- **Tap into your perspective**: The background, cultural inheritances, societal situations, upbringing, etc., that shaped you are an enormous part of who you are, and can bring a distinct sensibility to your writing.
- **Identify your themes**: Every human being has specific struggles, challenges, demons that we wrestle with all our lives; let yours find their way into your body of work.
- **Free your personality**: While the author's hand should never be directly visible in the story, her individuality can infuse every line.

We'll look more closely at each of these areas in the next section.

✓ How to Fix It

An author can have a great story, hit all the right marks—many tell me which storytelling system they have studied and employed faithfully, like Save the Cat or Michael Hauge or the hero's journey or what have you—and yet the manuscript feels a bit flat. More often than not it's because it's become homogenized and stripped of voice; it may be a "perfect" story as far as the formula, but it's not coming alive because it's bland, generic.

Voice is an individual thing, and authors lose it by ignoring that. Writing becomes a technique they "do" with a studied, deliberate intention: crafting careful sentences, conveying specific info, devotedly following whatever "rules" of storytelling they've studied. What gets lost is unique perspective and that intuitive, intrinsic use of language that is so distinct to each of us. It's as if it's bulldozed underneath all that "craft." True creativity is a little bit indefinable, looser, free, instinctual…intuitive. But accessing it—in this case learning to excavate and release your voice—is a process and a skill you can develop and hone with practice.

You can't necessarily create author voice—it's like a fingerprint, already a part of who you are. You just have to find a way to take off the gloves and let it out. As much as analyzing other authors' work for voice can be a lot of fun, so is digging deep to discover and free your own.

LANGUAGE

Just as what much of makes a singer's voice unique is tone, phrasing, vocal mannerisms, etc., language use is a big part of what reveals an author's distinctive voice: word choice, rhythm, meter; phrasing and sentence structure; what you say and what you don't say.

I always think of an example from Jennifer Weiner's *Goodnight, Nobody*, a line where she describes another character as "Everyhipster." Not only is this an instantly evocative portrait of a character (in the most efficient way possible, with a single word), but it says so much about the author's voice: her humor, her use of language that is so identifiably Weiner. Another author with a distinctive narrative voice is J. R. Ward, in her Black Dagger Brotherhood series. She is prone to making up words to describe things: "bitchsicle," "chesticular," "classhole." She also invents descriptive compound words: "goat-fuck," "knuckle-bouncer," "low-dosers." You can tell one of her books from a single page.

You don't have to invent new words, though, or do acrobatics with language. Just let "yourself" seep into your phrasing and word choice. Every one of us has a distinctive communication style, and it's evident in our verbal communication as well as in almost all our writing, including emails, texts, and social media posts. One way to become cognizant of your unique language characteristics is to ask friends and colleagues to describe or try to demonstrate the way you express yourself.

Start by identifying your habits. For instance, I love wielding five-dollar words, frequently employ figurative language (simile and metaphor) and hyperbole, write in compound sentences with lots of clauses and appositives, really enjoy the semicolon and em-dash, etc. Understanding your communication style is a great way to begin infusing it into your writing—but don't simply default to your automatic choices; dig down a bit more. As much as the above language traits are part of my voice, relying too heavily on those automatic, easy fallbacks will quickly give my writing a repetitive, one-dimensional feel.

Don't worry too much about this in your first-draft process—remember, that's when you wear the artist hat, not the editor hat. First-drafting should be creation, not assessment. But once you've done revisions and gotten the storytelling elements in place, go back through and examine the language itself, the way you've presented the story. I'll talk more in the next section about the technical side of line editing; for now, just focus on the authenticity/originality side of it.

Look for where you may have defaulted to overfamiliar language

Did you describe something as flat as a board or a pancake, for instance—say, an ice slick on the road? That's a cliché, and readers have seen it dozens of times. Find a fresh, unique way to describe it that lets your voice shine through: Maybe it's flat as a tortilla, or flat as a bath mat, or flat as a tone-deaf soprano. Or perhaps you don't use simile at all: You could describe the hard flat glint of ice sprawled over the asphalt, or as a shining silver plate, or glazing the rough road smooth. Maybe you keep it simple—just describe it as flush or level or uniform, or as a plane of ice (and watch out for the trap of defaulting to another cliché, like "sheet of ice"). Again, there's no right answer—how do you see it in your mind? Your ice-slick image is different from mine, and from anyone else's. Let us see as you see. This is what makes your story yours.

Clichés and overfamiliar language can sneak up on you. Most of us can readily spot obvious ones like "you can't judge a book by its cover" or "ignorance is bliss." But watch out for tired clichés you may default to without even realizing it because they're so deeply embedded in our vernacular, like fresh-baked cookies, hard-packed snow, beet red, hard as nails, a pregnant pause, sparkling eyes, piece of cake. (And for the love of originality and physiology, I beg you to reconsider having a character "swallowing back bile.")

Memes and social media and other cultural commonalities yield a whole other batch of linguistic "tics" that can quickly become clichéd (and also make your writing feel dated as these vernacular fads change):

"This. So much this." "Hard pass." "All the feels." "Don't go there." Or sentences where. You. Emphasize. Each. Word. (Did you feel yourself rolling your eyes at these overworked trendy phrases?)

Popular culture—books, movies, songs, even commercials—can create a slew of other shopworn words or phrases that initially catch our attention because they're clever or creative or funny, but when everyone adopts them they join the ranks of trite clichés: recognize "singletons" or "muggles"? "Whassup" or "yippie-ki-yay" or "I'll be back"? "The long and winding road" or "if you like it then you should have put a ring on it" or "oops, I did it again"? I'm not saying don't use any of these words or phrases, just encouraging you to be more conscious and deliberate with your verbiage—a cliché can be very funny when used ironically, for instance, and in characterization it can be a great way to indicate traits, like a lack of imagination or someone who plays it safe or is hidebound.

Reimagine generic, workmanlike language

In the wild, unreined first-drafting phase, your focus should be on getting the story on the page. But often that creative, goal-oriented writing results in linguistic shortcuts or defaults to the first phrasing that pops to mind. That's fine for your early draft, but revision is where you get to elevate your story and your prose. Go through and look for where you may have taken these shortcuts—where your narrative, dialogue, and descriptions are flat or ordinary or expected. Does your protag *really* sashay into a room? If she does—if that's indeed exactly how you see it—that's fine. But if not, can you find a more genuine and authentic description, show her action in a way that's more unique to your vision and your voice? Maybe her hips sway like a boat on high seas, or she boom-booms through the doorway, or she owns the room the moment she steps inside. What are you really trying to convey with her "sashay"? Confidence? Sexiness? Attention whoring? Whatever it is, see if you can find a more unique way to show *exactly* that.

Does the sunset take a character's breath away? Don't just address that cliché; think about what he is actually seeing, and how you want to convey its effect on him. Maybe the sunset tinges the sky a red so vivid it hurts his heart; or the sun pierces the horizon, leaving a bloody smear in its wake; or it simply fades away, the crimson sky the only evidence of its passing. Each one of these tells us something much more specific about not only the sunset, but the character's reaction to it, his state of mind. Not only does it add voice to your writing, but it multitasks by layering in meaning and impact.

While it's good to take the magnifying glass to every sentence of your manuscript to make sure it's saying what you mean it to say as finely as possible, don't overdo this sort of descriptive writing or your prose may come across as too ornate or "purple." Think of it as seasoning, not the stew. These carefully drawn phrases will stand out to the reader. In moderate amounts they will bring your writing to life, free your voice; overused they can weary readers, pull their attention onto the prose itself, and then you've yanked them out of the story. Your verbiage should always enhance and serve the story you are telling—not overshadow it.

Conduct the music of your writing

Just like poetry or song, narrative writing has rhythm and meter, pattern and phrasing.

I tend to be a very aural writer—I "hear" the sound and rhythm of words and sentences as I'm writing and I'm cognizant of my prose's tempo and flow. My voice leans toward a more elaborate melody; authors like Kent Haruf or Hemingway use simpler rhythms. There's no "right" tempo or feel; it's simply how *you* convey your story. Your natural rhythm is part of who you are—it's likely how you communicate in conversation and casual writing, as well as your fiction/nonfiction writing. (I tend to be a bit maniloquent and ornate even in speech. Even, Lord help my friends, in texts.)

But experienced writers vary their rhythms—otherwise prose can start to feel metronomic, flat. Just as great painters know to give the eye somewhere to rest, great writers give readers peaks and valleys, winding roads and straightaways, sprints and marathons. And as we discussed in the Momentum and Pace and Tension chapters, varying tempo can also help contribute to the mood or feel of a certain scene or beat (more wonderful multitasking).

Meter is the way stressed and unstressed syllables flow together. You may have studied the topic, at least to some degree, in high school and college English classes—remember the iambic pentameter of Shakespeare's sonnets (stress on the second of two syllables: *da-DUM*), or the trochaic meter of Edgar Allan Poe's "The Raven" (two syllables where the first is stressed: *DA-dum*)?

Likely you already do this instinctively to a degree—that's part of your voice too. But it's worth taking a look at the types of meter in poetry to get a more specific idea of how stressed and unstressed syllables can convey a feeling or mood.

And I'm a big fan of at least a passing familiarity with rhetoric—the mechanics of language that can help you use it more deliberately and effectively—to give you a few more tools in your toolbox for playing with the use and effect of your language and taking authorship of your voice.

We'll talk more about using language most effectively and efficiently in the Line Edits chapter.

SENSIBILITY

Voice isn't just what you say or how you say it; it's who you are: your background and experiences, your thoughts, reactions, emotions, your worldview. It's what you see, how you see it, how you present it.

If one of the traps of learning craft is homogenization of your distinct, unique perspective, one of the traps of the wealth of marketing tips tsunami-ing over authors these days is the misguided attempt to please all readers. Don't try to write to a mass audience—you'll strip your work of what will make it great. Write from your most genuine, naked soul— write what is true for *you*—and you will speak to your people...they will find you.

Access your perspective

My improv comedy group played another game, Prop Montage, where we were given a random item—usually something ambiguous-looking, like a pool noodle or a P-trap section of plumbing pipe—and had to use it in a scene as anything except what it was. Watching each person in my group create something fresh and unexpected out of the object always amazed me, not just for their imagination and quick wit, but for the utterly original, unique way each of them saw the same item.

Revealing your perspective in your writing is like that. Each of us may see the exact same thing—like the ice slick I described earlier—but it will strike all of us a different way, bring up different memories, feelings, thoughts, reactions, even look different to each of us. (Don't believe me? Watch a political debate with a group of folks of differing mind-sets and see how astonishingly varied their interpretations and reactions are to the exact same statements and dynamics.) It's why some people adore *Love, Actually* and some virulently despise it; why *Fifty Shades of Grey* can be both a mega-bestseller and broadly ridiculed; why there are even different genres to begin with—start a book with a murder and some readers will immediately want to follow the clues to find the killer; some will want to see how the forensics and investigation lead to a conviction; some will want to dig into the backstory of the killer's relationship to the victim and why they did it; and some will simply be turned off by the violence from the get-go.

While there are universal commonalities almost all humans share—generally we all want to be safe, secure, happy, to love and be loved, to find personal fulfillment, etc. (check out Maslow's hierarchy of needs)—the way we define what fulfills those desires varies widely. Great writers tap into those universalities while exploring a deeply specific and personal angle on them. Look at *Chariots of Fire* or *Seabiscuit* or *Dunkirk*—each a movie with a very distinct, focused subject, slant, and feel, but sharing the common idea of desperately pursuing something you believe in and will fight for against all odds: whether it's running, horse racing, or country. Look at *The Water Dancer* or *The Fault in Our Stars* or *Pet Sematary*—all distinct genres and entirely different plots and subjects, yet each a story of dealing with loss and grief.

What drives you? What are your passionate interests? What are your core beliefs about people, the world, love, fairness, war, spirituality? I often suggest authors read a handful of psychology books among my recommendations for developing craft, not just because they are immeasurably helpful in creating fully fleshed, nuanced characters, but because the more clearly and deeply writers know themselves and human nature, the more vivid, alive, and relatable their writing is—and the more fully they can access and reveal their voice.

Find your themes

I have a theory that each of us is wrestling with just a handful of specific "big questions" we spend our lives trying to find answers for. Do you know what yours are? Likely they infuse your writing subconsciously whether you do or not, but identifying what your core issues are can often help define the themes that make up a big part of the voice of your writing.

I find, for instance, that I am constantly thinking about the meaning of family—not just of origin, but the families we make for ourselves from the people we choose to share our lives with…and not just partners and children, but also the friends we choose as family. I also wrangle a lot with forgiveness and what it means, how to find it for even egregious trespasses, whether it's always possible. And I tend to think in shades of gray—without absolute "good" or "evil," but the ways in which individual perspective defines those judgments to and about oneself and others.

What are your themes—do you know? If you aren't sure, and you've been writing long enough to have a body of work (whether published or not), see if you can identify the common threads running through your stories. Ask your crit partners and beta readers what they would define as the themes of your work. You can even ask your friends and loved ones how they see you—what they believe are the driving questions that motivate you, or the ideas that are most important to you.

Notice the kinds of stories you gravitate to reading and watching, and see if you can identify commonalities among them. I am deeply drawn to stories about relationships, about flawed but decent people, to stories about foundational struggles but with a message of hope. What are you drawn to? Try making a list of what you feel are the most important things you've learned about life, or what you still know you need to learn, or what you feel are life's highest values, the meaning or purpose of life. All these methods will begin to paint a picture of who you are, what foundationally motivates you, what makes you, you—and let you access that more deliberately in your writing to free your authentic voice.

Show your personality

Are you a funny person, always finding humor in a situation no matter how dire? Snarky? Sarcastic? Are you an idealist or a realist? An optimist or pessimist? Do you have the soul of a poet or a statistician? Do you favor hard truths or the kind white lie? Do you cut right to the chase or gently lead up to your point? Do you tend to dissect and analyze, or intuit and feel? How do you handle challenges—with gritted-teeth determination, dogged and steady perseverance, practical acceptance?

You don't necessarily have to figure out your Myers-Briggs personality type to access yourself in your writing, but great writers do tend to have a clear understanding of what makes them tick. And taking a Myers-Briggs or similar personality test can't hurt in the quest to deeply know yourself in order to access that in your writing. Therapy is useful too, as are psychology and self-help books, spiritual studies and practice, even pop-culture questionnaires you find in a magazine or online. Developing fully as a writer isn't just about your writing—it's from deeply and intimately understanding and freeing the creator of that work, you.

EXERCISES

Here are a few more specific suggestions for helping you learn to identify voice in writing and access your own:

- Try writing some short exercise passages with a variety of different setups—e.g., "A character tells his wife he's leaving her" or "A woman runs into an old flame on the street." Start with a simple, straightforward description like this and then re-create it with your distinctive voice. Treating this as an exercise independent of your actual WIP can be freeing—it releases any strictures or preconceptions you may unconsciously feel in your current story and lets you "play." No one needs to see this, so let go of the reins—see how much of "yourself" you can let seep into the writing in these few brief exercise paragraphs.
- Take an example from a book you've read of a line or passage that you feel has a clearly identifiable voice, and see if you can pick out exactly what creates it. Is it the language—the words or phrasing

the author uses? Is it some identifiable orientation toward the world or the subject that feels distinctive to you? Is it the author's personality that shines through? What made this passage stand out to you, specifically?

• Try rewriting that same passage in your own voice, or in the style of another author, or even without voice—just a straightforward description of what it conveys.

• Think about your favorite authors (or even the ones you hate the most) and write down specifically what about them makes you love or dislike their work as an oeuvre (rather than any one specific story). Is it the worldview they present? The themes this author tends to write about in her stories? The actual writing style? If so, in what way?

A Word on Voice and Character

When you write characters, their voices will supersede the author's. Your narrative shouldn't sound the same in every single POV; it should reflect the way that character thinks or phrases things, his or her lexicon, frame of reference, background, ideology.

Creating character voice involves a lot of the same techniques I suggest above for accessing your own author voice—but instead of tapping into *your* truth, you're mining down for your characters'. We talked in the Character and Point of View chapters about ways to do that. You can also look to resources like psych books, personality tests (take one in the mindset of each of your characters, inasmuch as possible), or other craft books that offer specific questions and considerations you can use to deeply explore who your characters are (a favorite of mine for this purpose is Donald Maass's *Writing the Breakout Novel Workbook*, with a wealth of provocative prompts).

Each character has his or her own way of communicating, thinking, reacting. Each has a disparate background, upbringing, cultural inheritance, societal situation, emotional makeup, intelligence level, education—all of which factor into voice. And not just in dialogue— the narrative is every bit as crucial in creating a strong sense of voice for each of your characters: how you describe things in their POV, how you "filter" their observations, reactions, thoughts, etc., through their distinct individual perspective.

· · # · ·

What makes the greatest, most memorable books stand out is how they're told—the author's voice. You can master every other element of story—spin an excellent plot, build well-developed and relatable characters, create high stakes we care about, etc.—but if you don't let us hear your authentic, original voice it's likely to fall flat on the page, and never come fully to life.

PART III
LINE EDITS

chapter ten
LINE EDITING

line EDITING

Mastering the craft of writing requires developing your skills in its two key components: storytelling plus language. The most beautifully crafted prose in the world won't hold a reader without a great story, but excellent storytelling can miss the mark with prose that's cluttered, vague, or inauthentic.

In other chapters we've spoken about deliberately using your prose to help serve various storytelling elements: creating character, building a sense of tension and suspense, showing and telling, pacing, revealing your voice, and other macro- and microedit areas. In this section we'll look at some of the other most common linguistic ways writers may undercut their story by cluttering their prose, confusing readers, or otherwise lessening the effectiveness of their story.

This type of revision is often referred to as a line edit, and that's basically exactly what it is: an examination of your prose line by line. That's different from the developmental or substantive edit we've been doing with the storytelling elements of parts I and II; line editing directly addresses the language element of good writing. It's also different from copyediting, which examines the technical side of your prose—grammar, spelling, punctuation, even fact checking—although there can be overlap in the two; for instance, a good copy editor will keep an eye out for redundancies of language, or where your word choice doesn't quite accurately convey the author's meaning. (And all of these are different from a proofread, which is a line-by-line comparison of the manuscript against the final typeset galleys prior to publication.)

Polishing your prose and using language exactly and most effectively is a big topic, and this isn't an exhaustive review of the types of issues you may encounter in making your prose most effectively and elegantly serve your story. As Stephen King advocates in his book *On Writing*, like any other craftsman a writer must thoroughly know and possess the proper tools for her trade, and in an author's case your greatest tool is language. The study of it can take a lifetime: I majored in English, started working in publishing as a copy editor in 1992, and I still learn about language every day.

Even if you memorized Merriam-Webster's Collegiate Dictionary (the industry standard) and *The Chicago Manual of Style*, English, like most languages, is constantly evolving. The reason the dictionary is updated every few years is to reflect new words, new usages: *website* used to be *Web site* in the baby days of the internet (which was itself another word that used to be capitalized, as was World Wide Web), former trademarks become common nouns and lose their original capitalization (like *aspirin*, *laundromat*, or *google* as a verb), compound words are made into new single ones, like *lightbulb* or *steampunk* or *bloodred*, and new words altogether enter the lexicon—remember *truthiness*, coined by Stephen Colbert, which was not only added to Webster's dictionary but chosen as its word of the year in 2006?

Beyond these evolutions of our lexicon, though, language use evolves as well—meanings change, slang and vernacular develop, cultural sensitivities evolve, society's level of formality varies, and even our collective human attention span has been altered by technology. As an artist whose primary tool is language, your responsibility is to wield it like an expert.

I've mentioned my love of home-makeover shows. I'm always astonished at how a coat of paint, some new light fixtures, a sassy rug and some wall art can transform an already pretty renovated house into something extraordinary. And right before the big reveal even the tiniest details of staging—the bowl of green apples or spray of hydrangea on the kitchen island, the artfully tossed blanket, the pops of color in the throw pillows—add the perfect finishing touches.

We're about to HGTV before-and-after the hell out of your writing.

✓ How to Find It

In line edits you'll literally go through and examine your prose sentence by sentence. At this point you'll worry less about story, except insofar as how well your language is serving it.

For instance, have you restated something you already clearly established, or conveyed the same information in slightly different ways? Do your metaphors and similes actually convey the idea you intend, or are they not quite an effective or evocative parallel? Have you used overfamiliar turns of phrase? Do you have extraneous verbiage cluttering the flow?

Does your language state, exactly and clearly, what you mean to convey? For instance, have you ever actually seen sparkling eyes? I'm going to go ahead and answer that for you: Nope. You haven't, because according to Webster's "to sparkle" means literally to throw off sparks, or to reflect bright light, or to glitter. These are things eyeballs physiologically cannot do. Now, can you use the word figuratively to convey shining or otherwise lively eyes in a character? Sure, you can—but so have thousands of writers before you, so now you have taken a shortcut straight to a cliché. Why not convey your meaning in a way that's fresher?

Streamlining and clarifying your verbiage is only part of a good line edit; the other part is the more ephemeral artistic side of it. Do your characters speak and—importantly—think in a way that is consistent with who they are? Does the prose fit the story, the action, the mood, the pace—the genre? What is the rhythm of your sentences, and do you vary it? Does your prose have voice, resonance, originality? Is it evocative, vivid, memorable—while not losing precision or accessibility?

These are wide-ranging, broad questions; let's look at specifics of what to look for and how to address it.

✓ *How to Fix It*

I think of line editing in the two areas I mention above, streamlining the prose and making it elegant—or trimming the fat and adding the flavor. In the first case you'll comb your words and sentences for anything superfluous; if your language isn't directly serving your story it's hampering it.

Making It Lean

There's an old word-nerd joke about streamlining prose that goes like this: The owner of a pier-side fish market hires an advertising expert to make his sign out front more effective. The ad exec takes a look at the fishmonger's sign—"Fresh Fish Sold Here!"—and starts slashing: "You can cut the word 'Here,'" he says; "that's evident because the sign is in front of your shop. 'Fresh' is unnecessary—you've got boats unloading their catch right out front. You don't need 'Sold'—this is a fish market; clearly you're in the business of selling." He turns the adjusted sign around, which reads simply, "Fish."

DECLUTTER YOUR PROSE

You don't have to be quite this brutal in your slash-and-burn, but if you clear the clutter you'll let your writing shine. Padding your prose with unnecessary words or phrases when the meaning is clear without it slows pace, draws attention to itself, and can feel clunky to readers. Here are some places to root out extraneous verbiage:

Verbs modifying inner life/reactions

If we're in a character's direct POV—whether first or third person—the reader infers that all thoughts, realizations, emotions, reactions, etc., belong to that character. There's no need to spell it out. For example:

> John picked up the knife, testing its blade with his thumb. He
> thought it seemed plenty sharp, but he realized the true test

would be when he used it. He imagined that even a dull knife would do a fair amount of damage.

We're in John's point of view here—we don't need a neon sign announcing his inner life, and doing so distances us one level from the story; we're not directly experiencing it ourselves, but being told secondhand. You can delete "he thought," "he realized," and "he imagined" and the meaning is still crystal-clear, but now we're inside John's head directly experiencing his reactions and thoughts along with him, so the story is more immediate and impactful:

> John picked up the knife, testing its blade with his thumb. It seemed plenty sharp, but the true test would be when he used it. Even a dull knife would do a fair amount of damage.

"Filler" words

These are gilding the lily, adding in extra words where none are required: like using "that" where not needed ("I believed that he was telling the truth"), or "like" ("pretend like"), or certain adverbs in a phrase that doesn't require them ("decide on"). "That," "like," and "on" are superfluous in these examples; the sentences are correct and clear without them. "Whether" all by itself implies uncertainty, so appending "or not" to the end is superfluous.

Unneeded explanation

Overexplanation of a word or phrase that's clear on its own: "nodded her head," "shrugged her shoulders offhandedly," "thought to himself." In the first two cases there's no other body part you can nod or shrug, and a shrug itself connotes offhandedness (try shrugging intensely or with great focus), so you can simply use the verb by itself: "she nodded," "he shrugged." In the third example "thinking" is by definition something one does internally (unless the author specifies "aloud"); "to himself" is extraneous padding.

Overadjectiving/overadverbing

Just what it sounds like. This is where these descriptor words get a bad rap—when authors use them egregiously:

> "No, thanks," she said softly, touching her husband on the arm affectionately.

> A slow, sexy grin inched its way along his strong, stubbled jaw.

> His kiss was everything she'd dreamed of in a kiss. Everything she hoped for: soft and sweet, tender and gentle, sexy and hot.

(This one has bonus redundancy in the first line with the repetition of "kiss." It's also a phenomenal amount of "tell" we sure would like to experience more viscerally firsthand in "show.")

Watch this in dialogue tags especially—resorting to a lot of descriptions of how a character says something may indicate lazy writing, rather than taking to the time to craft the character's words, actions, demeanor, behavior to let readers "see" the scene for ourselves.

ELIMINATE REDUNDANCY

Say what you mean—once. More is usually less in these areas:

Unnecessary modifiers

Adding adjectives or adverbs where none is called for creates redundancy that clutters your prose and implies an inexpert use of grammar, for example in phrases like:

- *complete destruction, total overhaul, mix together, repeat again* (each of these verbs already implies the modifier word—destruction is by definition complete; overhaul means a total change, etc.)
- *never before; never, ever* ("never" already comprises both these flabby phrases all on its own)
- *PIN number* ("PIN" stands for "personal identification number")
- *reasons why* ("reasons" already implies the cause—the "why")

- *fall down, lift up, kneel down* (there is no other direction in which these actions can happen)
- *overexaggerating* ("exaggerate" already means to overdescribe)
- *so therefore* (these mean essentially the same thing; pick one)

Saying the same thing a different way

We waited with the patience of cattle, a bovine acceptance in the faces around us.

"I don't think so," I said flatly, no intonation in my voice.

All of a sudden, without warning, she yelled, "Watch out!"

His attitude suggested that it was decided. There would be no wondering what course they'd choose. It was settled.

"What happened? What did he do?"

Repetition doesn't augment in this case; it diminishes effectiveness. Pick the strongest one.

Dueling descriptions

The more times you restate a description, the less effective it is. Where you see you've said essentially the same thing more than once, try varying the descriptors to add something new—or better yet, simply choose the most effective one. Here are examples where you could easily delete all but one of the descriptors (redundancies in bold):

Everything below him lay in **sharp**, **well-defined** light.

Chloe stepped into the room with a sudden sense of **déjà vu**, a strange **feeling as though she'd known this place her entire life**. There was **an odd familiarity to it**.

She felt **annoyed, irritated**.

I was **stunned into silence, too shocked to speak**.

Echoed words

These can sneak up on you in the form of repeated words or root words that lend sentences and paragraphs a redundant feel:

But once she fell **asleep**, it wasn't dreams for Jane that disturbed her **sleep**.

There were **loading** ramps to the left and right for **loading** livestock.

He stepped **back**, turning her so he saw only the **back** of her head, the delicate curve of her **back**.

When he sees **me**, he turns his head to fully face **me**. "Anita," he says. "Can you do something for **me**? Get **me** something?"

Echoed words can also be sprinkled throughout a story in the form of "pet" words or phrases that can call attention to themselves (every author has them), especially if they are relatively unusual in everyday communication, like "snatch," "astonishing," "amiable," "inestimable," "artless," "alabaster"; or distinctive phrases like "just a skosh," "inasmuch as," "riddled with," and so on.

More commonly these will be ordinary words or turns of phrase that are an author's default verbiage, like any of the filler words mentioned above ("just," "really," etc.); or verbal tics like "clearly," "oh," or "uh-huh"; or shortcut stage directions, like smiling or looking or shrugging. Try doing a find-and-replace search for some of these words—including the root of commonly used verbs that would appear in any conjugation, like "smil" or "scoff" or "laugh"; you may be shocked how many times you use them.

Showing and telling

As we discussed in the chapter of the same name, both have a useful place in good storytelling, but using both in your prose to describe the same thing is often overkill and clogs your pace. Pick one—whichever serves the story most strongly.

- "'What can we do to help?' Anita asked out of concern." (Wanting to help implies concern; her question shows more vividly what the narrative tells.)
- "He obviously thought he'd said too much, and he pressed his lips closed and stared back down at his paper." (The second half of the sentence shows what the first half tells; why not let the reader infer that he feels he's said too much by witnessing his behavior that indicates as much, making us an active part of the story?)
- "'Don't do that!' Will shouted. He was angry and it showed in his tone." (We see anger from the exclamation point and the fact that he is shouting; why underscore it with tell?)
- "'Undoubtedly. That fact isn't even in question.' He gave Sofia a look that told her he was certain." (Three ways to say the same thing—two redundant "shows" and then a "tell." You could leave either of the first two sentences and cut everything else.)
- "He headed straight to Marta's shop, turning his car south onto the main highway over to the neighboring town till he reached her exit ten miles later, then taking the surface street to the right address." (This is showing and telling in the form of GPSing—most likely showing us exactly how he gets where he's going is immaterial; the first six words of tell are more efficient.)

Telegraphing

Another version of showing and telling, where the author steals her own thunder by telling readers what is going to happen or how a situation resolves before going on to show it. This deflates tension and robs the reader of the pleasure of seeing the story unfold before us; if you already tell us what's coming, why do we need to read on?

He told her what had happened: "Ralph and Laura came over and . . ."

The unexplained delay would be followed by a stunning reversal of roles.

A mistake. Most often, when I ignore my instincts, I pay for it. That night was no exception.

STREAMLINE DIALOGUE
Dialogue tags/attributions

Dialogue tags are functional, not stylistic, and shouldn't draw attention to themselves. Check your scenes for these common missteps:

- **Don't get too fancy.** Trying to whip out a variety of dialogue tags can quickly become melodramatic or unintentionally comical, and stalls the story's flow:

  "Oh, no!" she wailed.
  "Yes!" he exclaimed.
  "Please go," she snarled angrily.
  "Gladly," he sneered.

  That doesn't mean you must confine yourself solely to "said" and "asked," as some schools of thought maintain, but if you do decide to use more colorful dialogue tags, do it sparingly, deliberately, and as powerfully as possible—meaning make sure it's the strongest way to convey what you want to convey. "Sneered" is certainly visual and vivid, but it might not be as exact or evocative or original as something like, "He looked at me like toilet paper on his shoe."

- **Don't overdo it.** Not every line of dialogue needs a tag, and inserting extraneous ones—even if it's a plain, unassuming "said"—clutters prose, slows flow, and wearies readers:

"I see you came here too," I said.
"I did," she said.
"Why?" I asked.
She said, "Where else am I going to go?"

- **Ease off of adverbs.** Chances are you don't need to append an adverb to your dialogue tag—often these are red flags for an author shortcut. The dialogue and action should generally stand on their own to convey the speaker's demeanor, affect, or mood. "You bitch!" doesn't need "she shrieked angrily" to be crystal-clear, and adding it is tell that underscores what's already clearly shown, diluting the impact. If the dialogue itself doesn't convey the nuance of the character's reaction or demeanor, you might look for stronger ways to show it instead of telling it: Maybe her face is red, a vein in her forehead distended; or maybe tears fill her eyes as she says it; or maybe her words are barely audible as she looks at the floor. Each suggests something clear and distinct about her feelings and intentions without having to spoon-feed it to us with an adverb.

- **Don't use it if you don't need it.** If the speaker and the action are clear, reiterating the obvious with a dialogue tag just slows pace:

"Hi, Mark, you old sod," I greeted my friend.
"Belinda! You're looking cheery," Mark said.

"Hi" is a greeting, so there's no need to label it that way. We see (or will as the scene goes on) the relationship between these two; no need to label Mark as Belinda's friend. And it's clearly Belinda who greets and Mark who replies, so we don't need tags here at all.

OTHER DIALOGUE TIPS

- You cannot snort, sneer, breathe, hum, chuckle, sniff, growl, purr, or chortle dialogue. These are physiological actions humans can perform, but not simultaneously with speaking (really, try it). If your characters perform these actions, just make sure it's a separate clause or sentence rather than using it as a tag: *"You fool," he said with a sneer* or *He sneered. "You fool."*
- You also can't stage-direction dialogue—you may be moving or acting as you speak, but that action isn't properly used as a dialogue tag, but rather as a separate clause or sentence: *"Don't rush me," I evaded her pushy grasp* would work if you separate these two sentences with either a semicolon (*outside* the quotes, for the love of all things grammatically holy) or a period. This kind of action beat *within* a line of dialogue must be separated with em-dashes (outside the quotes), not commas: *"I'm not"—she sniffed—"impressed."*
- Notice how rarely in real life we use one another's names in conversation. Doing so excessively in your dialogue (which is really anything more than sparingly) feels unnatural and calls attention to itself.
- Each character's dialogue, action, or thought should be in its own paragraph; it's one way the author signals to the reader who is speaking or acting. When the speaker/actor changes, start a new paragraph:

> "I never meant to—"
> She cut me off: "It doesn't matter what you meant."
> I nodded. She was right.

In this exchange, even though the initial speaker is the one being cut off, the second character is the one doing it, so the stage direction goes in a new paragraph, along with her dialogue. By that same token, the first character's reaction and thought also gets a new paragraph.

• Dialogue that is dialect is a classic area where more is much, much less. There's no quicker way to stall your story and wear your reader out than with heavy-handed dialect. (Don't believe me? Read a page of Chuck Palahniuk's book *Pygmy*, written entirely in pidgin English. Funny and original, yes—but exhausting.) Overuse of dialect can also draw attention to itself and pull the reader out of the story. Worst of all, it risks being offensive—as the backlash against books like *Gone with the Wind* or *Huckleberry Finn* attests.

  You can very effectively convey a character's speech mannerisms and background with just a few judicious uses of dialect, as Sarah Bird does in *How Perfect Is That* with a Latinx character whose dialogue features only occasional indications of his accent, but clearly conveys it: "Hey, sometimes you get the elebator. Sometimes you get the shaft."

  Good writers don't need to lean too heavily on dialect to indicate a character's speech mannerisms; they might incorporate a few common misuses of grammar, like "should of" or "you better" or "irregardless," to indicate a less educated or intelligent character, for instance. The occasional dropped final "g" in -ing words is plenty to indicate an accent: *No, darlin', I'm not going to give you my blessing* works effectively to indicate a drawl without annoyingly dropping every final "g" in the sentence. Regional words or idioms can say plenty about a character's way of speaking: phrases like "fixin' to" or "het up" or "co-cola" interspersed into a character's dialogue are more than adequate to show she's Southern without leaning hard on the accent. Think of dialect as seasoning, and salt it in judiciously.

• Finally, the same rules apply to dialogue as to narrative in line editing: watch for clutter. Characters in fiction don't speak exactly the way we do in real life, where our speech is often littered with empty filler like "um" and "uh-huh" and "like" and "so" and "okay"; where we pause and stumble and stammer, circle around our point or state it repeatedly, speak inexactly, or run on and on. Story dialogue is crystallized speech; you can still create realistic, natural-sounding dialogue without clogging the flow and exhausting your reader with all the circumlocutions we're guilty of in our everyday exchanges.

AVOID VERBAL GYMNASTICS
Check for passive voice

Using the object of a sentence as its subject often lends an inert feel to prose, as if there is no vital actor driving action but things simply happen by some vague unseen force: "Dinner is served."

Passive voice is often, but not always, signaled by "be" verbs:

- *The pie was baked by Annie.* (Active: *Annie baked the pie.*)
- *Train was her preferred method of travel.* (Active: *She preferred to travel by train.*)
- *I was attacked by my neighbor's dog.* (Active: *My neighbor's dog attacked me.*)

But not all "be" verbs signal passive voice: *He is an opera singer,* for instance, is active voice: "He" is the subject, and "is" serves here to define his profession.

Passive voice can leave the actor uncertain, lending the action a vague or distant feel. Sometimes, though, when the actor isn't directly germane to the story or character journey, or is implied, it might be cumbersome or distracting to spell it out:

I never felt safe at home anymore since I was robbed.

I disputed the unfair grade I was given.

The house is being foreclosed on.

But you might still strengthen your prose and up its impact by reworking the passive voice:

The burglary robbed me of more than my things; I never felt safe at home anymore.

I disputed my unfair grade.

I'm losing my house to foreclosure.

And make sure to watch for where passive voice can detract from the story by making readers stop to puzzle out or wonder who the actor is:

When my privacy was invaded I slammed my book down, annoyed.

A new policy was instigated at work.

Parcels of food and medicine were handed out, one per family.

Watch for convoluted verb tenses

The overuse of past perfect and pluperfect can bog the reader down in verbiage. This happens most often in flashbacks, memories, and backstory, where a character is reflecting back on something in the past. It's often red-flagged by an auxiliary—or helper—verb (usually some form of "to be") coupled with a participle (or form of another verb), and it can get pretty sticky:

She had told him she loved him and then he'd taken her face in his hands and they'd kissed.

He hadn't remembered he'd told her that.

The trouble she had had had had no effect on her determination.

(The last example is completely grammatically correct, believe it or not—but comically clunky.)

Generally if you salt in a few sparing uses of the correct verb tense for a flashback, memory, etc., it's enough to signal to readers that we're in a moment that occurred prior to the story's real-time action, and you can then default back to simple past tense:

I looked at Jim while I formulated my reply, remembering the day we met. He'd been twenty; I was seventeen. We were both studying Latin, a language that died years before we were alive, and when the professor failed to show for our first class Jim's first words to me were, "Let's carpe the hell out of this diem."

The above example is a flashback in a past-tense narrative, so technically the correct verb tenses are the past perfect and pluperfect, but that will get unwieldy in a hurry. Setting the stage for the memory with the single initial past-perfect verb tense for "He'd been" is enough to signal the reader that after this we're still in that same memory from the past. When we rejoin the "real-time" scene, the author can signal that with the setting, stage direction, or the POV character's inner life reflecting on the memory she just had—for instance, *Jim cleared his throat and I realized I still hadn't responded to his question,* or *The man standing in front of me now looked the same, except for a few more wrinkles, but I felt I barely knew him anymore,* or *The sound of the barista working the coffee grinder drew me out of the memory.*

Unnecessary compound verbs can also convolute "real-time" story action:

The box was resting in his lap, but he was staring out the car window.

My mom is shaking her head as she's running water over the vegetables in the sink.

These are easy fixes—make the verbs simple present or past tense:

The box rested in his lap, but he stared out the car window.

My mom shakes her head as she runs water over the vegetables in the sink.

Purple prose

This is overdramatic (sometimes melodramatic) writing that can come across to readers as flowery or hyperbolic or overwrought. It's a bit of a subjective description—what's "purple" in a thriller might be perfectly suited for a romance, and every reader has a different threshold for ornate or extravagant prose. But comb through and see whether you might be spoon-feeding the reader over-the-top descriptions or explanations, or exaggerated dialogue or action:

> My words left him dumbfounded. He thrust a hand to his heart, clutching his chest. "How dare you!" he shrieked.

That's an egregious example, but this kind of overstated writing is surprisingly common in early drafts amid the creative push of getting the story so vivid in your mind onto the page. In general, the more your prose works to overtly amp up tension or drama or impact, the less it succeeds—like a friend's gushing recommendation of a movie that winds up leaving you underwhelmed. Examine every sentence to see whether you are "overselling" the moment; what are you actually trying to say? Simplify, avoid commentary and hyperbole, and let the story—the characters, what's at stake, what's happening, etc.—speak for itself.

Vague or ambiguous words and phrases

Imprecise language is a hallmark of our everyday speech, but it weakens your prose. Watch for fuzzy words like "it," "something," "thing," "stuff," "this" (used on its own); or phrases like "sort of," "kind of," "and so on," or phrases like "etc." (guilty!) or "et al." What are you actually referring to? Be concrete and specific.

Dangling or misplaced modifiers

These result when modifier words are in the wrong place or too far away from what they modify, and they can be unintentionally funny:

> Exhausted, her lips pulled down in a frown.

Walking along the sidewalk, her long hair streamed behind her in the breeze.

Lying abandoned on the floor was a giant baby's rattle.

The first two examples are danglers—"exhausted" and "walking along the sidewalk" actually modify the woman implied in the sentences, but that identifier is missing, so the first sentence actually describes her lips as exhausted and her hair walking along the sidewalk. The third sentence is a misplaced modifier suggesting that somewhere a gigantic baby is missing his rattle, rather than that the rattle itself is supersized.

To fix a dangling modifier, just insert the correct subject—*Exhausted, she felt her lips pull down into a frown* or *As she walked along the sidewalk, her long hair streamed behind her in the breeze.* Fix the misplaced modifier by rearranging the descriptor words so the modifier abuts what it modifies: *a baby's giant rattle.*

Awkward, confusing, or convoluted narrative or dialogue
Basically, get to the point as efficiently and powerfully as possible. In the words of John Mayer, say what you mean to say. Let's take a sentence that winds around a bit as an example:

Rutger sat looking out of the window in the front living room at the car slowly pulling along the road past the edge of his driveway, uncertain who might have been behind the wheel and what their intentions could be.

This is a really roundabout way of conveying a simple event: Rutger sees a suspicious car driving by his house and is curious. Let's break down the flab in this sentence:

- "Sat looking" is a multipart verb that doesn't really add anything strong to the action.
- "Of" is unnecessary in the phrase "out of the window," which is a prepositional phrase followed immediately by another

prepositional phrase, "in the front living room," and then yet another one, "at the car," creating a clunky rhythm.

- "The edge of" the driveway is superfluous here—the car is driving past the driveway altogether, edge and all.
- "Slowly pulling along" is a little clunky, especially with all the alliterative "l" sounds, and butts two more prepositional phrases against each other ("along the road past the edge"); "the road" is superfluous because if the car is going past the driveway it can be assumed that it's on a road (very few driveways abut fields or prairies).
- The phrase "uncertain who might have been..." is a bit of a dangling modifier, and confusingly ambiguous—does it refer to Rutger or the car?
- "Might have been" and "could be" are multipart verbs, unnecessarily cluttering the prose, and they weaken and distance the narrative.

This kind of convoluted writing can so easily sneak up on a writer, especially in a first draft when you're in creator brain and hopefully letting the story fountain up onto the page. Line editing is your chance to make your prose work more efficiently for your story, though. In this case, you might streamline this way:

> From the living room window Rutger watched a car eke past his driveway, curious about the driver and his intentions.

This sentence isn't perfect, and it isn't necessarily elegant—there are more vivid and powerful ways to convey the same information, which will be unique to your voice. But already it's smoother and easier to read, and ready for the next step in line editing: adding the flavor.

MAKING IT ELEGANT

The word "elegant" in the context of writing doesn't mean how flowery or decorative your prose is, but rather how efficiently and well the prose serves the story. Think of it in terms of poetry, which is basically prose crystallized down to its essentials, where every word is deliberate and necessary, every line serves the whole, and the language has power, impact, and immediacy. In general we'll look at three stylistic questions to contemplate in line editing your manuscript: Is it clear? Is it effective? And is it yours?

Is It Clear?

Did you say what you mean?

We talked about word choice in the Voice chapter; take a magnifying glass to every line of your story and ask yourself, Do your descriptors say what you want to say as closely and evocatively as possible? Do someone's eyes actually twinkle, or do you mean that they are just bright, alert? Does her heart really beat in her ears—meaning she can literally hear the sound of it? Or do you mean she could feel her heart racing or the reverberations in her chest—or something else entirely?

Think about words' shades of meaning, connotation, and even their sound: Compare a *slim* woman to one who is *gristly*, a *dewy* complexion to skin that is the dreaded *moist*. Whether a stabbing victim is pierced, impaled, punctured, gashed, or something else says something different—and specific—about the wound.

Are your descriptions and imagery clear, specific, and vivid? If you describe towering trees, readers may picture the redwood forests of California or the piney woods of Georgia or a thatch of swaying palms on a tropical beach. Don't just clarify the types of trees; let us experience what your characters do, in sensory specifics: the density and texture of the trunks; the color and breadth and movement of the leaves; the scent of the foliage, the humidity or aridity of the air; the sounds of the foliage, the wildlife, the character's footsteps in the underbrush or on the bare forest floor.

This applies to your characters' actions, reactions, thoughts, and emotions as well. "She felt herself responding to the peaceful setting" doesn't really convey anything about her actual response. Does her chest seem to loosen, her shoulders relax, her breathing slow and deepen? Does a warm flush of joy suffuse her? Or maybe she's a city girl and every nerve ending stands at attention in the freakishly calm forest. Readers don't know what you mean unless you show us, and generalizations don't give us the vivid, visceral sense of immediacy clear, specific writing offers.

Is it accurate? Does each word or sentence convey what you intend it to convey, down to the nuance?

Have you used the correct word? "I lathered myself with sunscreen" implies that the lotion worked up nice frothy suds; did you mean "slathered," i.e., spread thickly? Did you describe a character as disingenuous when you really meant ingenuous? The latter means innocent or candid; the former means the exact opposite: dishonest or insincere. This is why it's the writer's prime job to know his tools—you can't get the job done right unless you have and can use the exact implement to do it.

Do your similes/metaphors hit the mark? Comparing a lover's eyes to the moon is confusing, for instance: Do you mean they are round, or some other shape of a moon phase? Or pocked with spots? Or white or light gray? Or vastly distant, or a pallid reflection of the metaphorical sun of someone else's gaze, etc.? Have you used your figurative language clearly and consistently? Mining someone's psyche to unearth the fresh sprouts of change, for instance, mixes two metaphors—mining and farming—and diminishes the effectiveness of the imagery. And I'm a gal who loves her some figurative language, but watch for overusing it, which can grow cloying to readers, or slow pace, or call attention to itself rather than the story.

Are the narrative and dialogue consistent with each POV character?

This is part of characterization (see the Character and Point of View chapters), but as you're making your line-edit polish passes, keep an eagle eye on your characters' vernacular, in both their dialogue and the narrative that reflects their point of view and inner life. A high school dropout might not use elaborate language—but then again she might if you're using that to deliberately say something about who she is: for instance, broadly well-read or an autodidact. *How* and *why* she might use it also says something about her: Is she showing off to a colleague, a lover, a boss? Trying to convey her intelligence despite her lack of education?

Feeling insecure? Being ironic, or mocking another character, or trying to obfuscate or confuse? Everything your character does, thinks, and feels should be a choice you have made deliberately, and not only consistent with who that character is, but furthering the story in some way.

Is It Effective?

Great prose isn't just lean and precise; it's the fuel on which story runs. And just like when you fill up your car, using the most efficient fuel will let your story operate at peak performance. How effectively is your language working for your story?

Have you balanced the external with the internal?

A story that's all action or description can leave readers feeling as if we're skating on the surface of the story, held at a remove from what's going on below that surface level. But one that relies too much on a character's inner life, reflections, memories, thoughts can feel myopic and small. We need both elements in order to fully experience a story—on the surface and beneath it, the tangible and the intangible, the big picture and the close-ups.

I often see this balance slip in scenes that consist of mostly dialogue and stage direction. Without some glimpse into what's going on beneath the surface of the words, a story can read more like a screenplay. The author's intention may be spot-on—to streamline the story and keep pace clipping—but what people say is a fraction of what's going on in any human exchange. Pay attention to your next conversation with your partner or child or friend or a coworker: Besides the information you're conveying in your words, what else is going on? What are the nonverbals—expressions, tone, volume, demeanors, gestures, affects? What are you thinking beyond what you're saying about the topic? What about outside of it—is some part of you still stewing over a fight you had with your mother this morning? Thinking about all the emails piling up in your in-box while you have the conversation? Worrying whether you have kale in your teeth? What do you make of what the other person is saying—or doing, or how they are reacting to you?

Conversely, a story that's all internalization—reflection, impression, reaction, etc.—can quickly start to feel navel-gazey and slow; readers may feel removed or bored. Keep the story immediate and active.

Does it feel immediate and visceral?

In other chapters—Character, Showing and Telling, Point of View—we've talked about techniques to make sure you plunge the reader directly into the world of the story and the heads of your characters. The line edit is where you make sure you're doing that on a granular level: Is every development or description filtered through your POV character's perception? Do you have broad generalities that would be more effective as clear, concrete specifics? Have you summarized happenings that would have more impact if we see them directly? Are there events that happen "offstage" and are summed up in a scene after the fact that would be more effective unspooling on the page in front of us in "real time"? Do we see a character's reactions firsthand and viscerally (lizard-brain), rather than summed up with shorthand (intellectualization)?

Have you overdone it?

It's key to say what you mean to say in your prose, but have you *over-stated* it? Even otherwise compelling storytelling loses its effectiveness with hyperbole, purple prose, repetition, redundancy. "She was absolutely enraged, her face hot with rage" is redundant (being enraged is pretty all-consuming and "absolutely" is superfluous here, plus the sentence states basically the same thing twice), feels repetitious ("rage" echoes "enraged"), and is likely hyperbolic—is she really seething with violent, uncontrollable anger, or is she simply mad? (And is there a way you can *show* us her emotional state through her actions and behavior, rather than *telling* us, for bonus effectiveness?)

Does the music fit the mood?

Does the prose reflect the action, convey the feel of a scene, create the right pace, fit the character? Have you varied the rhythms throughout from line to line, paragraph to paragraph, scene to scene, to avoid a metronomic or repetitive feel to the story? Does your language suit the genre you're writing in?

Is your language culturally aware?

This isn't about being painstakingly PC—it's about reflecting the world you live in honestly, accurately, and uniquely, and respecting your readers. With the rising awareness of women's issues, for instance, defaulting to old sexist tropes—even ones that used to be broadly accepted in books, movies, TV, and other mediums—would alienate a good portion of modern audiences, like the "alpha men" of old in romances manhandling women or pressing themselves on the heroine despite her protests, or even the troubling lyrics of the holiday song "Baby, It's Cold Outside," with its overtones of coercion, shaming, and possibly drink tampering. (For a delightfully fun and enlightened version, check out John Legend and Kelly Clarkson's update of the song, where the man repeatedly respects the woman's cues and offers to call her a ride-share in case she's not okay to drive.)

Being culturally cognizant includes informing yourself about what is perceived as ignorant or offensive to historically marginalized groups—for instance, describing ethnic skin color or features in food terms (chocolate skin, almond eyes, etc.), or defaulting to stereotypes, like the inscrutable Asian or the mystical wise Native American or the sassy or catty gay man.

It also includes being vigilant in your prose for charged or pejorative words: "handicapped," "retarded," a character with "Mongoloid" features. And educate yourself to use proper terminology, like transgender, LGBTQ (or variations up to and including LGBTQIA), Latinx, "typical" versus "normal," etc.

Cultural norms are constantly evolving as society (hopefully) becomes more inclusive and enlightened. Staying aware of these shifts helps you keep your writing from causing you embarrassment or alienating readers or feeling dated—when we know better we can do better. And it might even allow you to help move the world in that direction: Throughout history the arts have been a powerful precursor of and voice for social justice, equality, and acceptance.

Is It Yours?

This is the most personal, individual, and empowering part of line editing—letting your writing reflect the vastness and color of who you are: your values, beliefs, perceptions, thoughts, imagination, and vision. This is where you make it unique, fresh, original—where you give your prose your singular expression, as we discussed in the Voice chapter.

With their permission I harvested some opening paragraphs from a few authors I've worked with, in varying genres, so we can analyze hands-on what gives their writing such strong, distinctive voice.

> Bigger Falkirk returned from South America missing a testicle and I envied him.
>
> He said he picked a fight with a surly muchacho at a seedy Colombian bar. The fight turned into a brawl when the muchacho's pals joined in. Bigger threw beer mugs and bar stools. He landed his fair share of punches until he got speared in the ball sac with a broken-off beer bottle and that was that. Bigger fell.

Aaron Brown has let me use this passage from his wonderful literary fiction story *Bigger* for years in my classes and workshops. This works so well on a storytelling level as an opening because from the very first line he catches the reader's attention with an upended expectation and a question (no one would expect envy as a reaction to a missing testicle, and why would anyone feel that?). It's replete with character, both Bigger and the narrator; starts on terrific action; and makes us want to know more.

But beyond the story strengths of this excerpt it's dripping with voice: from the distinctive phrasings and vernacular ("surly muchacho," "speared in the ball sac") to the effective alliteration (the repetition of the plosive "B" sound beautifully echoes the violence of the scene described) to the deliberate use of rhythm and meter that effortlessly carries the reader along on its melody and re-creates the rhythm of a bar fight that ends abruptly. This excerpt never fails to elicit overt reactions from the room as soon as I pull up the slide: smiles, laughter, and clear interest—the voice is so strong people immediately respond to it.

· · # · ·

There are, Monroe thought afterward, those moments in one's life when everything you've known until that point becomes incompatible with everything that follows, a kind of time warp, which, if you were inclined to believe in parallel universes, might very well convince you that you had jumped the track.

Twice in his fifty-six years this had happened to him. First when he saw the only woman he had ever truly loved shot to death. The second only hours before, when good Dr. O'Brien announced that he, Monroe Colson, had at best a year to live. The ghost of death itself, visible in the X-rays on his light box.

John Jones's literary novel *A Dignified Exit* is a departure from some of his other works, which feature the West Texas sensibility of his upbringing, and in it his voice takes on a different character as well, reflecting that of his protagonist, an older artist. John uses more complex sentences, literary imagery ("The ghost of death itself, visible in the X-rays on his light box"), and slightly more formal language ("if you were inclined to believe," "might very well convince you") to convey something of his protagonist's personality, creativity, and intelligence.

He uses varying rhythms as well: The first paragraph is one long compound sentence, but the following graf then contrasts with two shorter, simpler ones to convey the first startling piece of information (and story question): his wife being shot to death. Then John uses two more sentences that split the difference in length and complexity for the next provocative hook: Colson's terminal diagnosis. Read this excerpt aloud to see how he varies the music of the lines—and how he reflects the subject in the sound of the words: that first long, winding sentence, suggesting the time warp the protag mentions upon hearing his diagnosis; the hard, choppy consonants of "shot to death" like the rhythm of three sharp bullets; the character's dawning acceptance of his fate as his voice returns to what we soon realize is "normal": his innate decency (referring to the man who just gave him a terrible sentence as "good Dr. O'Brien"), and the artistic description of his CAT scan.

·· # ··

"If a frog didn't hop, he'd be dragging ass," Pete's grandfather used to say in his thick Italian accent. Nonno would say it as if to the room but with a side glance directed toward one individual in particular. He intended it to periodically motivate one of his grandkids when they put off raking the yard, taking the trash out, or some other mundane chore. It was an old saying that sounded funny to Pete. He didn't know anything about frogs but he was no stranger to dragging ass, at least in certain areas of his life. He stared out the car window thinking, *I need to hop,* as they pulled over to the side of the road.

Filmmaker Richard LeMay's story *Wrightsville* is his first foray into fiction writing, but from his earliest drafts his strong voice gave this coming-of-age drama with comedic elements a lot of appeal. Rich's humor—and his protagonist's, Pete—is evident right away, as are Pete's distinctive voice and perspective. We get a lot of information about his life and personality in just a few lines (magical multitasking again): the use of "Nonno" immediately suggests Pete's family is Italian, and the salty vernacular of his grandfather conveys something about the man—and about Pete, whose reaction to it is a bit more literal at first, it seems, but then Rich twists that around too, as Pete adopts the phrase and applies it to his current situation. Rich might have simply said something about Pete realizing he had to change his life, but instead he conveys that message in a distinct, original voice that creates a sense of character, hints at background, and moves the story forward. Revealing voice doesn't have to mean fancy writing or in-your-face imagery.

"The icy professional they called 'the Nazi' was the cruelest, most dangerous assassin in the world, a heartless madman whose sadistic fantasies could only be fulfilled by the darkest hobbies."—Jayna Devile, *From Russia with Lust*

I suppose I could start by explaining why my parents called me Island, or even dissert on the many reasons why being the daughter of a Frenchwoman and an American curmudgeon can traumatize a child for life . . . but I suspect no one really cares. So let's start with the day my apartment got cleaned—I promise this is more interesting than it sounds.

. It was a Friday in late October, and much like the rest of my colleagues in EMTech's R&D department, I had spent the entire day looking for a way to fix a major bug in our latest banking app. Around 5:20, I finished the floor's last Dr Pepper, pressed Enter, and announced to my colleagues that our software was back on track. I then proceeded to call them losers—in a common display of virile superiority over fellow engineers—and, for once, left early.

Camilla Monk is a voice chameleon, from her urban fantasy *Still* to her grimdark fantasy novel *Silverlegs* to her Spotless series, the first book of which the above opening excerpt is taken from. *Spotless* is an unusual genre that blends elements of humor, romance, parody, and suspense/thriller, and from the very beginning of the first novel Camilla lets the reader know they're not in for an average ride with her made-up over-the-top quote from a made-up romance novel; the humorous, intimate tone; the character's self-effacement and snark. From a storytelling standpoint she immediately creates a question in the reader's mind with "I suppose I could start"—start what?—juxtaposes the mundane apartment cleaning with the protag's promise that it's more than it seems, and segues into the punctilious delivery of a tech nerd (which Island is), all of which is again multitasking and letting voice serve story.

On a gummy August evening about ten p.m., an entirely naked man stood behind a red-tipped photinia in dire need of pruning and waggled his skinny hips, pelvis thrust slightly forward. His only audience, a three-foot green iguana sitting on a pillow

under the photinia, bobbed his head slightly but otherwise
paid no attention. The only way for the old frank 'n' beans to
live was unencumbered by the bondage of fabric, just like
nature intended. His first act as governor would be to issue
a proclamation that made all clothes optional, right down to
boxer shorts.

Kelly Harrell's story *All Bets Are Off* also bends genre—it's a humorous mystery in the vein of Carl Hiassen, and she makes the feel of her story crystal-clear from this very first paragraph. Readers know they're in for an irreverent, funny, off-the-wall story. She uses original, evocative descriptions using several senses—the August evening is "gummy," and she creates vivid setting with clear and specific descriptions of the foliage and the lizard—and she brings the character's voice into the narrative—"the old frank 'n' beans"—as well as his perspective: "unencumbered by the bondage of fabric, just like nature intended." She also sets a hook with story questions right away—why is the man naked? What is he doing in the bushes? Why is the iguana there…and on a pillow? And…"when he's governor"? Kelly upends our assumptions and keeps us delightfully off balance in this brief paragraph—a style the rest of the story maintains.

· · # · ·

Judith's mama didn't answer her daughter's strained good-bye.
Instead, she stood silent on the porch in a yellow shirtwaist
dress, clutching a tarnished pot that still needed washing from
the breakfast grits. With the bright blue house framing her,
Judith thought her mama looked like a black-eyed Susan, just
about to wilt against a Texas sky too clear and bright-hot not to
force a squint.

Amber Novak's *Haint Blue* is literary fiction with a Southern flavor and tinges of romantic, suspense, and paranormal elements. From the beginning she sets the story's tone, with her vivid descriptions of intense colors that evoke the feel of a brilliant clear day, contrasted with a sense of conflict and tension: the strained goodbye, the mother's silent reception to it. And Amber uses this contrast to great effect to convey mood and reaction: the bright, clear colors that set off the "black-eyed Susan" of her mama (note—not "mom" or "mother," another instance of using voice to convey character), and her mother's "wilt" against the crispness of the other imagery that connotes her disheartened reaction to Judith's leaving.

Voice brings nonfiction to memorable life as surely as it does fiction. The below excerpts are taken from various genres of nonfiction—memoir, psychology and self-help—but each one sets a clear, strong tone from the beginning with voice:

> In the early days of my family, before their hearts were broken, my mother and father liked to tell one story in particular about my childhood.
>
> I was just a baby in a crib, looking up at colorful mobiles and trying to grab something.
>
> "What is she trying to do?" my dad asked.
>
> "Oh, my . . . look!" my mom replied. "It's the sunlight. She's trying to grab the light."
>
> I saw the rays of sunlight as dust motes drifted through them, lighting up like fireflies. I grabbed at the sunbeams, trying to master the magic of these bright things. My parents watched as I flailed and grasped in my floundering attempts, entranced with the effort. To them, it was simple, sweet, and beautifully innocent in its futility. They knew sunbeams were not made to be caught.

This excerpt from T. M. Yates's *Signal Grace* (no relation) starts as the rest of her memoir continues: with a lyrical, literary style and an almost larger-than-life approach to her story about her relationship with her charismatic, enigmatic father. Does she truly remember this scene so vividly from her infancy? Who can say—but Yates lets us know right away with this opening that this is a Paul Bunyan kind of tale, and that's borne out as she paints a complex picture of a complicated man she never fully understood, but adored.

Fifty-three minutes into a fifty-five-minute counseling session, which we'd devoted fully to the question I'd been unable to answer for thirty-six years, Dr. Z offered his delicate assessment with a slight upward inflection at the end: "So, it seems like you're thinking 'no'?"

That sounded exceptionally definitive to a chronically indecisive person.

"No, no...I wouldn't say that. I'm not ready to say 'no.'"

Despite his best—and incredibly gentle and thoughtful—attempts to help me land on an answer once and for all, I still didn't know if I wanted to a have a child.

Ashley Brown's *Letters to the Daughter I'll Never Have* is an intimate and revealing exploration of her very mixed feelings about deciding with her husband never to have a child as her child-bearing window closes, and we know that clearly within the first three paragraphs—Brown gets right to the point in almost a thesis statement. Yet the narrative isn't dry or impersonal—the tone is accessible and chatty—and from the very beginning she shows us something of who she is: precise and deliberate (the exact counts of minutes and years), observant (noticing the doctor's demeanor and inflection), intelligent (her phrasings and words), and of course indecisive, which she not only tells us straight-up, but shows with her verbal vacillation at his question. Right away the reader's feet are planted—in Ashley herself and in the dilemma she's facing—in a way that makes her experience immediately understandable and relatable, a strong asset in a memoir.

Perhaps you've seen the bumper sticker: "Oh, no, not another %#*@ learning experience." And maybe, like me, you've lived it.

In 1997 I was closing in on a doctorate in psychology. My specialty wasn't relationships, but memory. If you were worried about it, wanted to know what changes are and aren't normal with age, wondered what causes memory decline, or needed to regain what you lost, I was your woman.

My unofficial occupation—what I spent at least as much time on as research—was finding Mr. Right. Like some of you, I knew unreservedly that I wanted one Love O' My Life, and I figured it was worth investing a lot of time and effort. I was working hard. But I was not working smart.

In her self-help book *Love Factually*, Dr. Duana Welch's voice as a psychologist who specializes in dating and relationships is one of a trusted confidante and caring friend, and she makes that utterly apparent in her opening paragraphs, adopting an intimate, confessional, casual tone that draws the reader in and creates instant rapport—she has been where readers are, she conveys right away. She also puts a just-outside-the-ordinary spin on her word choices—"unreservedly," "Love O' My Life," contrasting the implied formality of her doctoral studies in memory against the more casual "I was your woman." She knows where we're coming from if we picked up a book about finding love, her tone suggests, and we can trust her expertise and that she is on our side.

$$\cdot \cdot \# \cdot \cdot$$

Kiss and Tell imparts a reassuring truth about sex for all women to take away: You are normal.

Sadly, this is an affirmation many women have trouble internalizing, perhaps because we're all just a little bit worried that our insecurities and our preferences are just a little bit, well, odd.

The veil of secrecy that still exists when it comes to talking about sex doesn't help. Even close girlfriends tend to keep bedroom matters private. They'll crack a joke, sure, or tell

an occasional story, but genuine sharing about what goes
on sexually with their partners isn't an integral part of most
female friendships, despite what *Sex and the City* would have
us believe.

So it's a bit revolutionary to push past the focus on bedroom
techniques, positions and partners—and delve deeper to the
core issue of desire.

Anne Rodgers and Dr. Maureen Whelihan's exhaustively researched
book on women's sexuality, *Kiss and Tell*, could easily have been technical and dry—but that's not the approach they chose. Their book, based
on interviews with more than a hundred women, takes an anecdotal and
accessible tone, as if you're among close friends talking about the most
personal of subjects—"you are normal," "just a little bit, well, odd"—
but they also maintain an undertone of professionalism and authority so
readers feel they are in capable, experienced hands.

Even from just these brief excerpts, you wouldn't confuse any of
these writers for any of the others, fiction or nonfiction. Voice makes
story unique and personal.

Voice also sets our expectations of what we're about to read—and
is among the first impressions we have of the story and whether we are
drawn to it. Just as we draw conclusions fairly quickly when we meet people (seven seconds, according to studies) based on subconscious cues we
pick up, we do the same thing from the moment we open a book: What
do we think of this personality we'll be spending hours with? Do we like
it? Does it resonate? Suit our mood? Do we want to keep going, find out
more, spend more time together?

And just as in interpersonal relationships, not every author voice
will resonate with every reader, no matter how good the story sounds or
how much a reader may like that genre. Your job isn't to create the most
broadly appealing voice, but an authentic one that serves your story best.

· · # · ·

Line editing is all about the detail work. It's the final buff of the car as it comes off the assembly line, those last little tweaks in the mirror before a big meeting or interview or date—ensuring that you're putting forth the most precise, polished product you're capable of creating. Just as with the car or your appearance, these final details may ostensibly be only on the surface, but they're the first impression someone gets and often what will (or won't) grab their attention—and they set an expectation for what's underneath. After you've committed so much time, energy, and effort to the demanding, intricate work of editing the story, let it shine in its best light by giving that same level of dedication to polishing your prose.

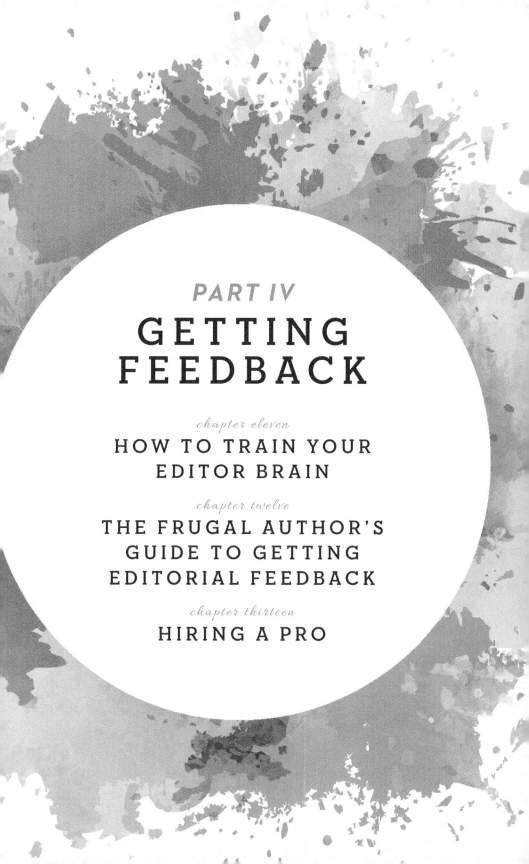

chapter eleven

how to train
YOUR EDITOR BRAIN

E ditor brain doesn't belong in the room when you're writing—he lurks over your shoulder, telling you everything you're writing is crap and stifling your creative freedom. Banish that judgy little bastard from the initial work of creating your story.

But once you're finished with a first draft and it's time to assess and revise, welcome him in; make him coffee. Give him a doughnut. Send writer brain out of the room while editor brain does his job—it's not writer brain's time anymore. This is when you need all the distance and objectivity you can summon, but given the difficulty of seeing your own work analytically, how can you learn to see what's actually on the page rather than what's in your head?

The more you can learn to divide these two parts of yourself—yes, like a low-grade mental illness, but one you control—the better you will get at editing your own work...and the better writer you'll be. And the most effective way I know to learn to objectively edit your own work—to switch on editor brain—is to see others' work edited and to edit it yourself.

That mental (and emotional) distance we struggle to achieve with our own work is far easier to achieve with others'. Because it isn't your story you aren't filling in the blanks as you go—presuming things a reader doesn't actually see on the page because you know your story so well. With someone else's you're seeing—and evaluating—only what's *there*, a crucial skill to develop in editing your own writing, spotting the things we're often initially blind to in our own work. Remember, once you've seen Waldo you can't unsee him.

As with learning any skill, the trick is to practice—as much as possible—editing others' work so that editing your own becomes second nature, and there are plenty of ways you can do that.

Find a crit group or partner

Participating in a critiquing relationship with other writers offers a regular opportunity to learn to analyze and assess effective writing (with a number of caveats, primarily that you find one that's supportive, positive, and constructive, among lots of other baseline requirements; a bad crit group can do more damage to writers than almost anything else).

While you'll get the chance to receive feedback on your own work—which is good—and gain direct experience critiquing others' work, the hidden value of this kind of group many writers overlook is the ample opportunities to listen to other authors' critiques. Pay at least as much attention to these—multiple critiques of the same submission are an invaluable way to see not only what objectively works and doesn't work in a piece of writing, but to notice the subjective differences as well—one reader's *Romeo and Juliet* is another's *Fifty Shades of Grey*. Learning to edit your own writing is also about knowing when to stick with your vision even if it doesn't work for every reader, and those variations of opinion are a great way to see that firsthand.

Having a critique partner is a great start, and one we'll talk more about in the next chapter, but there are many other ways you can gain experience with editing.

Seek out examples

Writing classes and workshops geared toward editing are a great way to see other authors' writing analyzed and revised—and you often get the chance to weigh in yourself and practice editing other authors' work.

But if time or financial commitments don't allow for that, you can find great examples of hands-on, granular editorial feedback in action online. Editor Margie Lawson offers specific prose examples, before and after editing, in her blog posts for Writers in the Storm (https://writersinthestormblog.com/), along with detailed analyses. Dave King, in his "All the King's Editors/Editor's Clinic" columns for Writer Unboxed (https://writerunboxed.com/), presents a page or more of a WIP with his editorial markup, and then specifies the reasoning behind all his suggestions; and in the "Flog a Pro" feature, also on Writer Unboxed, editor Ray Rhamey presents the first page of a bestselling novel and analyzes why he would or wouldn't turn the page, inviting reader feedback as well (and make sure you read the comments for more perspectives).

These types of editorial critique can be invaluable for learning to spot weaknesses in all areas of storytelling, macroedits, microedits, and line edits.

Binge-watch and binge-read, without guilt

This is an editorial training technique you can do every day, from the comfort of your sofa or mattress, to learn to analyze what you watch and read. Are you staying up late to keep turning pages of a book? Put it down (no, really) and grab the notebook that you *do* keep by your bed, don't you? (You should! Genius strikes at night.) Jot down—quickly, without thinking too hard about it—why you didn't want to stop reading (or did).

Be specific: What was keeping you hooked? Probably something you needed to know—will she escape? How is he going to solve this? What will happen next? Who is stalking him? That's suspense and tension, among the most useful tools in a writer's toolbox, and analyzing with your editor brain how other authors create it successfully is a powerfully visceral way to learn to do it in your own stories. And why did you care? Probably because you're invested in those characters. How did the writer create that in you? Write down exactly why this character—and her fate—matters to you.

Same with your favorite shows—binge-watching something? Take five minutes in between episodes and do the same thing—why are you compelled to start the next one? What—very specifically—is keeping you hooked, driving you forward? Something make you cry? Pause the movie or put the book down and write down what it was, and then analyze critically how the writer got you there, step by step. Same with when your heart is racing, or when you're on the edge of your seat with tension, or when you're bored or indifferent, or when you're angry (I watched the movie *Vice* with my heart at 96 bpm the whole last hour, I was so enraged).

Extra credit: Go back and *re*watch or *re*read with an objective, assessing eye, ruthlessly analyzing how the author/screenwriter elicits reaction and engages you. That's editing gold—figuring out with your analytical left-brain editor self what techniques to use when your right-brain writer self comes back into the room.

Attend writers conferences— and be a voyeur

Watching an experienced industry professional—an editor, an agent, an accomplished author—go over in detail what's not working in a story excerpt as well as it could, as well as what *is* working (equally important!)—is a great way to learn to see what they see. (You can see an example of one of mine here: https://vimeo.com/72851019.)

Read-and-critique sessions (R&Cs) are *fantastic* training for editor brain—and help you learn to separate the two when you aren't "on guard" as a writer being evaluated. Sit in on as many R&Cs as you can at these events—and focus as intently on other writers' submissions as you do your own.

Pay attention to what jumps out at these industry pros as they evaluate out loud. Often these R&Cs focus on the macroedit areas—the foundations of good storytelling. Notice, for instance, that the first thing many will point out is whether anything is actually *happening*, and if it is, whether they are invested enough in your characters to care. Notice how frequently they may point out that the story needs more suspense or momentum or higher stakes (or beautifully creates them). Those are the basic building blocks for effective writing, and you'll be surprised how readily you spot where these elements are and aren't working as you listen to other people's work read aloud.

· · # · ·

Experts always tell you writing doesn't just happen at your desk, but all the time, when you're showering or exercising or—annoyingly—sleeping. Editing is the same. If you learn to watch and read everything with an analytical eye, I promise you'll see your writing improve even more than the best book or workshop or webinar could ever offer. There's no substitute for training yourself "on the job" to see and think like an editor. (Just remember to leave that guy out of the room when you're writing—and apologize in advance to your loved ones for becoming intolerable to watch TV with.)

the *frugal author's guide*
TO GETTING
EDITORIAL FEEDBACK

I used to volunteer at our local animal shelter, and walking the dogs there and offering them company, attention, and warmth fed my soul. With hundreds of animals in their care and a relatively small staff, the shelter relies on its team of volunteers for everything from reporting on possible medical concerns and behavioral issues to being adoption ambassadors to fostering pets to helping train the animals so they are more adoptable, and so much more. The volunteers' work with them isn't just superfluous feel-good activity—it matters and is essential to the shelter and the animals, and I took that responsibility dead seriously.

However…this wasn't remunerative work, and oxytocin doesn't pay the bills. So as much as I wanted to do all that I could to help, there's only so much time and energy most of us can afford to donate. Sometimes I had to say no to shifts or to fostering when the shelter was overcrowded or animals needed a break from the shelter—and eventually I had to put my volunteering on hold for a while when other commitments over-crowded my schedule.

You have to know when to say no.

It's not always feasible to take on the expense of hiring a professional editor—but that doesn't mean you can't still move forward with your WIP. In addition to books like this one (and others I recommend on the Resources page of my website), there are a number of very good (mostly free!) options for getting the objective outside feedback that can help you hone your work.

Critique groups

A good critique group can offer you invaluable hands-on experience editing others' work that is often the most effective way to learn how to edit your own. (It's infinitely easier to evaluate a manuscript's strengths and weaknesses objectively when you aren't the one who wrote it.) It can also provide a wonderful array of feedback from a variety of perspectives and preferences that can help you see and assess your work through new eyes.

A bad crit group can do incalculable damage to your writing, your creativity in general, and your self-esteem.

That's a pretty broad spectrum of outcomes, so while I highly recommend exploring this option as an excellent way of getting the kind of objective insights that can help you edit your own work, I also strongly caution you to be an informed participant. The other members of the group may be knowledgeable, relatively experienced writers and readers, or they may not. They may be able to put aside their personal preferences and evaluate a manuscript objectively, or they may not. They may help you tell the story you envisioned the most effective way possible, or they may try to impose what *they* think would be a better story onto your idea. They may have good intentions, or they may be there to make themselves feel superior by tearing others down. (Here's a great article on red flags for unhelpful crit groups: www.writersdigest.com/editor-blogs/guide-to-literary-agents/ oct-2012-ready-the-top-10-worst-types-of-critique-partners.)

Manage your expectations and keep a healthy skepticism, but do go into a group with an open mind and receptivity. You won't like everything you hear—but I promise you that you also won't like everything you hear from a professional editor. Our creative efforts are the most tender, vulnerable parts of us. They are our babies—and our babies are perfect to us. Be willing to have others (gently and constructively) point out where your baby might benefit from a little improvement.

Keep in mind, however, that people's opinions are exactly that. We all see the world through our own unique lens, shaped by our history, our biases, our preferences. In a critique group you also tend to have people with a wide array of experience, skill level, and knowledge. Not everyone in the group is your target reader. Not everyone will offer you feedback that is specifically useful to you. It's tricky to find the balance between staying open and really hearing people's input, and knowing which of it resonates for you and the story you are telling—what to incorporate and what to disregard.

Remember Neil Gaiman's advice, which applies nowhere as thoroughly as to crit groups and beta readers: "When people tell you something's wrong or doesn't work for them, they are almost always right. When they tell you exactly what they think is wrong and how to fix it, they are almost always wrong." (I'd add my own admittedly biased addendum: "When an experienced professional editor suggests what may be wrong and how you might address it, at least consider it.")

HOW TO BE A GOOD CRIT GROUP MEMBER

I was once in a critique group where the head of the group used to begin her critiques by saying, "I stopped reading on page X...."

Her intentions may have been good—I suspect she meant to show where pace or tension lagged, or to help a writer see where an agent or publisher might decide to put the manuscript down—but her execution was totally counterproductive to the aims of a critique group. Not only was she the group's leader—the person others looked to, to set the tone—but her approach effectively started with the negative, instantly putting the author on the defensive and shutting her down. Her crits after that tended to be insightful and even positive, but it was unlikely the poor author on the end of her initial offensive was hearing it.

One author I worked with called the delicate art of critiquing "a negative sandwich on positive bread." She was talking about the time-honored approach of beginning a critique with a few things that work really well in an author's work or that you liked, and ending on the same and with encouragement and praise. If you lead and finish on the positive, an author is far more able to receive the "meat" of the critique that, by its nature, tends to focus on the areas that may not be working as well as they could. I often tell authors that an editor's job is like a building inspector's: The focus is on looking for areas that could use a bit of shoring up, and that means editors don't necessarily get to point out all the areas that are in wonderful working shape. But please do try in your own critiques of others' work! I've been told time and again by authors I've worked with that the smiley faces I insert or my reactions in comment bubbles to things that are working really well or are especially effective help them receive the other more diagnostic comments.

That said, the "negative filling" shouldn't actually be negative—in tone or in spirit. In editing I try to cast my feedback on the positive side: rather than "we're not seeing her motivations," for instance, I simply rephrase an observation like that to, "her motivations could be made clearer here." Small change, big subliminal impact. Even avoiding imperatives—"cut this passage"—sets a better tone for authors: "You might consider trimming this; this was established on the previous page and may feel redundant here." Note that I not only make the suggestion, but support why I made it. Does this careful and specific approach take longer? Yes. That's part of respecting an author's work and person, and that's the foundation of a good critique.

Here are a few others:

Show up for your group as regularly as you are able.
Don't be the guy who drops in only for his friends' critiques, or his own. Do your part to help create a sense of safety and support in the group.

Be positive and constructive with others' work.
That doesn't mean blowing smoke up anyone's hind end—that's not useful to a writer. It does mean approaching your feedback in a spirit of encouragement—as I am fond of saying, creativity responds only to the carrot, never to the stick. Rather than saying, "This isn't working,"

which will feel like a body blow to most authors, you can say, "This confrontation could be more effective if we saw more clearly what's at stake for the protagonist."

Critique the work, not the person.

This is the equivalent of the advice to offer "I feel" statements to your spouse instead of "you never." A good critique offers clear and insightful feedback without value judgment. Remember these are your opinions, regardless of how well informed or factual they may feel to you. Avoid absolutes—"You didn't make her actions believable." They may not be believable to you—but who knows how they strike another reader? Even if you're sure you're right (and you may be), be cognizant that you are offering your personal impressions, not an absolute truth...and always wield the carrot: "I wanted to invest more deeply in her choices, and for me that meant I needed to better understand what was motivating her."

Be generous and thorough.

Don't rush through someone's submitted pages. Remember how hard you have worked on your own, and how much they mean to you. Offer that same respect and consideration to your fellow writers.

Be specific.

It's not useful to offer vague or generic blanket statements. Dig deeper and be clear and specific. Instead of "I like this," try, "When the character wrestles with leaving her husband even though he is abusive, you really show clearly what's holding her there, as far as her worries about her children and her own insecurities." Rather than, "That part just didn't work for me," you could offer, "It wasn't clear to me why he would turn on his partner suddenly."

Don't try to change anyone's story, genre, or vision.

This isn't your story—you are simply a mirror reflecting back to the author what you saw on the page. You may hate visceral descriptions of gore, but if the author is writing in the horror genre (or about a serial killer or murderer), that may be entirely germane to the story. That said, if it was hard for you to read or pulled you out of the story, do tell the author that. That's useful feedback, provided you qualify it by sharing that this isn't your genre or comfort zone, or support why it doesn't feel to you as if it fits their story or scene.

Be quiet when it's your turn to be critiqued.
Don't waste time and breath arguing, defending, or denying. Readers' opinions aren't wrong—they are their impressions, and that is ideally what you're there to find out. And no matter how brilliantly you may have developed your character or plot or any other element of the story, if it isn't on the page, it isn't working. You won't be there with your readers filling them in on everything they need to know—it needs to all be on the page. Your crit partners are offering you invaluable insight as to whether it is or isn't. Be respectful of their time and effort, and take full advantage of the gift of varying perspectives by considering them.

Really, as with most areas of life, all the guidelines for crit groups can be summed up with the Golden Rule: "Do unto others…" And if you find yourself in a group that doesn't operate in this spirit, honor yourself and your own creative spirit by finding another one.

WHAT TO LOOK FOR IN A GOOD CRIT GROUP

It will have rules.
Here's the only instance in the book when I don't put that word in quotes. Clear guidelines keep a crit group from becoming a free-for-all and descending into chaos. They set expectations and structure, such as time limits for each person's critique to prevent anyone from presenting an impromptu seminar.

**New members will not be allowed to submit
work for critiques until they've been there
awhile, critiquing others' work.**
This protects all members and helps makes the group a safe, supportive, fair place. Some writers want to just drop in and have their own work

critiqued whenever they want to; they aren't interested in giving others feedback, just in taking what they need. Enforcing a minimum participation bar encourages regular attendance and creates a sense of fellowship and mutual support that allows every author to benefit from the group.

The group will be a manageable size.

What this is will vary for each group, and for each writer's preferences. I've been in effective groups of four and of fourteen. (The latter makes for long meetings, though.) I've also been in groups of twenty-four, and this can be unmanageable. Most of us have a "saturation point" where we can't absorb any more—it's like going to a museum; you have to take it in digestible chunks or after a while you just aren't seeing the art.

It will have a positive, constructive, respectful tone, without candycoating or empty praise.

The ways critiquers can hinder rather than help you in your writing are multitudinous: from an overly pedantic approach, to a negative or attacking tone, to someone rewriting your story, to blowing smoke up your nether region, and plenty more. None of these approaches are conducive to creating a safe and productive atmosphere for writers—negative, judgmental, or controlling comments will shut a writer down (remember the carrot, never the stick); adhering too closely to dogma about craft can strip everything unique and wonderful from a story; and meaningless praise is useless—it offers you no concrete, actionable feedback.

Members never, ever ridicule or denigrate a member's writing or person (and if they do the group takes action to stop it).

This is tied into the previous point, but merits a separate address. There are groups and individuals who think "critique" means "criticism." It does not. If mean-spiritedness, sarcasm, mockery, or even just unkind passive-aggressive "helpful suggestions" are tolerated in a group, get up and walk out. Which brings us to the last point:

It makes you excited to be there, not dreading it.
If you find yourself hating the drive to your meetings, or coming up with excuses why you have to miss a meeting, or just having a knot in your stomach when you're there (even when it's not you on the critique chopping block), trust your gut—that's a sure sign this group isn't for you; but keep looking! There are many options out there.

HOW TO FIND A CRIT GROUP
- Community listings in your local paper, especially alternative papers.
- Search on a site like NextDoor or MeetUps or craigslist for writers' groups near you, or post a listing yourself to create one.
- Ask at your local bookstore; post a notice if they have a community bulletin board.
- Check with the local chapters of national writers' groups like the Women's Fiction Writers Association or Sisters in Crime or the Science Fiction and Fantasy Writers of America (if these are your genres).
- Contact a local or state writers group and ask about critique groups. For instance, here in Texas we have the Writers' League of Texas; Colorado has the Rocky Mountain Fiction Writers, Pikes Peak Writers, Northern Colorado Writers, and more. Just do an online search for "[state or city or town] writers' group" or similar.
- Check with your local library.
- Online: There are many "virtual critique groups" in cyberspace; try searching through some of the above channels, on social media (lots of groups have Facebook pages, for instance), or do a search.

OTHER OPTIONS
Many of the guidelines for critique groups apply to the other good options for getting objective feedback on your work:

Trading edits with a writing partner
This can be a great way for both of you to get valuable feedback on what is and isn't working in your story—essentially a critique group of

two. To be most effective for both of you, it's helpful to pair up with an author in your genre (or genre-adjacent: women's fiction and romance, for instance, or mystery and suspense) and roughly at your level as far as where you are in your careers and experience levels.

One great way to hook up with a writing partner if you don't already have one is through writers' organizations, which often have programs for connecting members looking for crit partners. You might also find a like mind at your crit group, if you attend one; at meetings of local chapters of the national organizations or other writers' groups in your area; at conferences and other industry events; Facebook groups for writers; or workshops and classes.

Beta readers

Beta readers can offer excellent insight to authors even if they aren't necessarily authors themselves. The trick to making their feedback most useful to you is to offer some guidance as to what kind of input you're looking for, so you don't get generic comments but specific impressions of specific areas of the story. An easy way to do this is by providing them with a questionnaire along with the manuscript. (Author Kristen Kieffer offers great examples of these on her wonderful Well-Storied blog, www.well-storied.com/blog/how-writers-can-prepare-for-a-fantastic-beta-reader-experience.) You can tailor your questionnaire to your particular story, as well as areas you may already know need more development, like character arcs or sustaining tension or certain parts of the plot.

The ideal beta reader is a habitual reader—someone who loves books and has a broad perspective on fiction (or nonfiction, if that's what you're writing) from having read a lot of it. They will be readers in your genre— someone who loves military novels isn't going to offer you the most useful feedback on your Victorian romance. They may be writers themselves, but it's not necessary. They're usually *not* your best friends or your family, who will have a hard time offering objective analysis because they are too colored by their feelings for you (and concern about possibly hurting yours).

Make it "safe" for your readers to be honest with you by graciously accepting all of their feedback—even if they don't give you the heaps of praise you hoped for. A thorough beta read is a lot to ask of someone, and a generous thing for someone to do for you, so offer at the very least your gratitude. You could even sweeten the pot with a box of gourmet chocolates, or a coffee-shop gift card, or taking them out to dinner as a thank-you. And a shout-out in the acknowledgments is always— *always*—a huge thrill.

Find a bargain editor

I hesitated to include this option, because with editing I'm a big believer that you generally get what you pay for.

But here's where the proliferation of people wanting to get into the field can work to your advantage. An editor just starting out in this industry needs to establish herself and her credibility—and the number one way to do that is with a track record.

A little story: I started in the publishing business as a proofreader and copy editor, and had many years of solid experience with major publishing houses, including several of the Big Five (Big Six back then). My credibility for that type of edit was terrific—but I wanted to start working as a developmental editor. I'd done it for a number of author friends, and had seen the process fairly firsthand over nearly two decades, and I was confident I had the experience and knowledge to offer meaningful, informed editorial feedback.

But who was going to hire a totally untried developmental editor doing her first professional developmental edit?

Well, authors to whom I offered ridiculous fire-sale rates. I was lucky enough to have good contacts, through my work and some writers' organizations, with some well-established, fairly high-profile authors. They knew my work as a sharp-eyed copy editor firsthand, so they knew I had at least some clue what I was doing, and I offered my developmental-edit services to them so cheap (full disclosure—in the very first case free) there was little risk for them.

Fortunately things went well. The authors were happy with the work I did for them, passed on my name to fellow authors looking for a good dev editor, and even hired me again for subsequent manuscripts— and I got very kind blurbs and acknowledgments to post to my website from established authors touting my abilities. Which opened the door for more authors to take a chance on me…which got me more work and credibility…which gave me more credits and blurbs…and that lovely snowball kept expanding.

When editors ask me for advice on getting started, I always tout this advice to them: Offer a few edits on the cheap, like an internship or a residency.

So how can you find one of these hungry unicorns? Put the word out among your author friends, writer's groups and organizations. Check Reedsy. Post on the Editorial Freelancers Association's job boards with whatever rate you can afford to pay. Ask around at writers' conferences. Ask at your local college or university's English or writing department. Ask other professional editors—often they know someone starting out or can point you to where to find them.

By now it will come as no surprise to you that I have some caveats.

- Even though this is someone who may be starting out, you want them to have some experience in this field. Perhaps they've worked as a managing or production editor at a publishing house, or freelance copyedited or proofread for legitimate publishers, or worked as a magazine or newspaper editor, or taught creative writing at a legitimate outlet.
- Remember even those who have worked in adjacent fields may be learning the specific skill of developmental editing "on the job," so keep in mind that you are hiring an editor who is essentially in training. That doesn't mean they don't know what they're doing and can't help you hone your manuscript: When I lived in New York I enrolled in famed hair salon Bumble and Bumble's colorist training program as a living subject for the budding stylists to learn on. They'd been well trained, but we volunteers were their practicum, so while usually I got a gorgeous color for a fraction of the price of a regular customer at the tony salon I couldn't have otherwise afforded, occasionally there were mishaps. Luckily I learned anything could be fixed (one way or another, even if it meant an unexpected haircut now and then)—but it taught me

to manage my expectations. If you go into a bargain edit knowing it's a value-add to have an editor's feedback but realize that a newly minted dev editor may still be honing her approach and that her comments might not be as finessed as those of a more established editor, or he might not see everything a more experienced editor would spot, or she may not yet have mastered the art of helping to help improve a story without taking it over, you can still get some valuable objective professional feedback.

• Don't insult a professional editor by bargaining down her rates or asking for a discount. Most established editors have spent years honing their craft and most price themselves commensurate with their experience and in accordance with industry standards for the skill (see the next chapter, Hiring a Pro, for rate information), although as with any industry there are some who cite exorbitant rates. If a quote is too expensive, that may not be the editor for you—just let him know and keep looking. (And who knows? Perhaps he will offer a lower rate.)

It's important to spend only what you can fairly easily afford for a professional edit (or any expenses attached to your writing career). But a tight budget doesn't mean you're shut off from the resources that can help you put out the most polished version of your work. It just means you may have to be a bit more creative about finding those services.

Luckily you're a writer—creativity is what you do.

hiring a
PRO

The first time I read A. Scott Berg's biography *Max Perkins, Editor of Genius*, I felt giddy.

If the world of editing has rock-star equivalents, Perkins is it. The legendary editor at the legendary publishing house Charles Scribner's Sons for thirty-six years, Perkins edited—among many others—Ernest Hemingway, F. Scott Fitzgerald, and Thomas Wolfe (helping tame the latter's *Of Time and the River* from its original one-million word count—no, really—to a more manageable quarter million over a period of years; the original manuscript filled three crates: www.nchistoricsites.org/wolfe/bio.htm). If you have ever had a fantasy of working intimately with a clear-eyed expert who would toil side by side with you on your story, as invested as deeply as you are as they exhaustively help you polish every facet of your diamond, Perkins was the embodiment of that: as much psychologist, coach, cheerleader, and parental figure as he was an editor.

Today's publishing-industry realities are a bit different. Frequently understaffed, increasingly market-driven, and often tightly budgeted on both money and time, most publishers aren't able to offer the kind of intensive, collaborative editing process many authors crave. And authors who are indie publishing or publishing with small presses may not be guaranteed any editing at all. Sometimes, no matter how diligently you've self-edited, it's hard to objectively evaluate your manuscript and find the path forward, and you need to call in a pro. Even editors often hire editors!

The independent and freelance editing market has bourgeoned in recent years to fill the editorial gap, offering a mixed blessing. On the one hand, authors have access as never before to an incredibly broad field of editors from which to choose. (Post a job description on the Editorial Freelancers Association website and wait for the tidal wave of responses if you want to see what I mean.) On the other hand, their qualifications and experience vary just as widely.

On top of that, professional editing is usually expensive—you can expect to spend thousands of dollars for a developmental edit, and if you're self-publishing, more on top of that for a copy edit and proofread. And even if you find a knowledgeable, experienced editor and have the budget to hire one, there are the ephemeral considerations: Does this editor "get" what you're striving for with your story? Does she respect your voice? Will he help you actualize your vision, or impose his own? Does she work in a way that fits your writing "style"? And, important in a relationship that's so uniquely intimate, do you *like* each other?

By the time you've taken all these factors into consideration, trying to hire an editor can feel almost paralyzing.

Professional editing is likely the biggest single investment you will make with any manuscript. And as with any major investment, arming yourself with the right information beforehand offers you a much greater chance of making a choice that will pay off.

The first thing to determine is whether you're at the stage that a professional developmental edit will be most helpful to you. You're about to plunk down a significant chunk of change—make sure you're in a position to reap the benefits from it. You don't hire a midwife until you're ready to deliver the baby.

A developmental editor is different from a writing or story coach. The latter are generally process-oriented—their job is to help you create the story, and they're usually most effective to a writer in the first-draft stage; they can help you get the story onto the page if you're struggling to do so.

While developmental editing is very much a process as well—I've worked with many authors who swear that they "find" the book in editing—ultimately it's more *product*-oriented, meaning that until you have some sort of a workable first draft (which may in fact wind up being your second or third or tenth draft), paying for a professional edit may not be the best use of your money, time, or energy. If editors are midwives, book and story coaches are the fertility clinics. Having the former won't do you much good if you're in need of the latter.

Even if you have a completed manuscript, you may not necessarily be ready for a full developmental edit. You're making a big investment—make sure you're in a position for it to do you the most good. Here's a checklist for determining whether you need or are ready for a professional developmental edit:

Yes:
- Have you polished a draft to the best of your abilities, but know it's still not quite "there" yet?
- Have you received constructive feedback from beta readers, crit groups, or writing partners, but aren't sure how to incorporate it into revisions?
- Have you submitted to agents and gotten no nibbles?
- Have you submitted to agents and gotten some interest, but no offers?
- Are you self-publishing?

No:
- Are you stuck or "blocked"?
- Are you midway through a draft and need help finishing?
- Do you have a bunch of great material/scenes, but no idea how to knit them into a cohesive narrative?
- Do you have a great idea, and need help writing it?

I'm speaking exclusively of a developmental edit here, but there are several other types of edit you may have heard of as well. Knowing which one you're looking for is vital before you begin your hiring search.

What Kind of Edit Do You Need?

DEVELOPMENTAL/SUBSTANTIVE

A wide-ranging, comprehensive edit that exhaustively considers and evaluates all aspects of the story: structure, characterization, pacing, plot, dialogue, character, point of view, etc.

LINE EDIT

Addresses sentence by sentence the author's style, consistency, tone, and verbiage, keeping watch for things like echoed words/phrases, awkward or clunky narrative or dialogue, sentence organization, syntax, extraneous words, word choice, meaning, etc.

COPY EDIT

Sometimes called proofread, but not technically the same. This edit checks basic linguistic mechanics: grammar, punctuation, spelling, fact-checking (including all names, locations, and trademarks), consistency, tense agreement. *All* self-published manuscripts should have at least a professional copyedit; readers are eagle-eyed and unforgiving when it comes to errors, and regardless of the quality of your writing itself, you will come across as unprofessional if your book is riddled with mistakes.

PROOFREAD

A line-by-line comparison of the original manuscript to the final formatted galleys.

There's one other consideration that's delicate, but important: Is the money you will spend on a professional edit disposable income? If not, don't do it until it is. Don't deny yourself the necessities of life; don't go into debt; don't spend your children's college tuition.

Writing is a calling, a pleasure, a privilege—and for a few lucky authors it's also a living. But not for most—even if you're fortunate enough to garner a publishing contract, generally advances are well below even a modest annual salary. Factor in the costs of marketing—which authors are often expected to do the lion's share of in today's publishing environment regardless of whether they are self-publishing or with a major house—and writing books as a way to make a living or even augment your income begins to look a little bit like buying a lottery ticket for the same reason.

These hard facts aren't meant to discourage you from taking your writing dead seriously and pursuing it professionally. You have a unique voice, a story to tell that is exclusively and solely your own, and if you want to get your work out into the world, you should. Reaching another soul with your art is one of the noblest and most rewarding human experiences I can imagine.

But until your ship comes in (or at least your gravy boat), don't treat writing like any other investment, where the capital and other expenditures you pour into it will likely yield dividends down the road. The chances are that you may never make a living wage from your writing.

Don't make the mistake of thinking it's a hobby for that reason, or not taking yourself seriously—but as with any other endeavor, **do** consider what resources you can comfortably afford to delegate to its pursuit.

Finding an Editor

Once you've determined that you are ready to hire a professional editor, the most overwhelming step can be finding one. As editing became increasingly accessible and increasingly important with the advent of self- and indie publishing, a whole lot of people hung out their shingle as editors. Many of them have legitimate, pertinent experience and credentials; some don't. But there are great ways to sift through the clay for the gold and make sure you find a reputable, experienced professional in your genre.

Just like on Yelp or Amazon, often customer reviews are the gold standard of recommendations. And who are the "customers" of editors? Writers.

- If you're in a writing group or have author friends, especially those writing in your genre, ask them whether they've worked with an editor they liked.
- Try messaging or posting on a writers' group Facebook page—these proliferate now, a sort of virtual watercooler for writers.
- If you have an agent, ask her whether her clients have worked with freelance editors they rave about, or whether she herself has seen a particular editor's work she thought highly of. Agents often shepherd their clients' projects from a germ of an idea through multiple drafts to publication, and they know a good editor when they see one help a client transform his manuscript into a polished gem of a book. And with so many authors choosing to be "hybrid" (traditionally and self-published), many agents now offer self-publishing resource lists for their authors for everything from editors to cover designers to formatters to marketing experts. If you are unagented but have a friend or writing colleague who has an agent, try asking him to ask. (See caveat in the next bullet point, though.)
- If you are traditionally published and intending to hybrid with indie publishing, and you have a great relationship with your publisher, you can try asking. Some publishers have self-pub arms operating under their banner, and these will keep resource lists for authors. Some downsized or retired publishing-house editors become freelancers, and your editor may be willing to refer you. Some houses may even use freelance editors; even if they don't the publishing world can be small, and in-house editors may know of some of the more experienced and reputable freelancers. One caveat here, though—some less than ethical agents and publishers have been known to point clients toward editors with whom they have a kickback deal, meaning they get a percentage of the money you shell out for your edit or other "outside" services. Make sure you check out anyone you're hiring or partnering with thoroughly (more on how to do this below) before you sign or pay anything.

- Authors of blog posts and articles in writers' outlets like *Writer's Digest* or Writers in the Storm or Absolute Write (or hundreds of others) are often editors—contact them if you like their info, style, and tone.
- Writers' conferences are marvelous for so much more than pitching agents. They are a great way to expand your support circle of writer friends with people you meet there (whom you can then ask about their own editing experiences), as well as exposing yourself (not literally, please) to some of the industry's top professionals who are there as speakers, panelists, or presenters. Hear something you like from an editor leading a workshop or panel? Conferences are a delightfully democratic place where it's easy to approach most anyone directly. Stick around after the session and introduce yourself, or share a drink with her at the bar later. It's a rare opportunity to get to know an editor face-to-face in a process that's often conducted almost entirely virtually.

Even if you don't get a personal recommendation, knowing the right places to look for an editor will help you find a good one:

- Check the acknowledgments of published books you liked (particularly in your genre). Authors often thank their editors, and in today's publishing environment, even if the book was professionally published that may very often be someone who works freelance directly with authors.
- Check writers' organizations like the Science Fiction and Fantasy Writers of America (SFWA), the Women's Fiction Writers Association (WFWA), Sisters in Crime (SinC), etc. Many have Facebook pages for members to communicate, or chat boards on their sites to help connect members to one another and to industry professionals.
- Check writers' forums online. There are a proliferation of wonderful (and some not-so-wonderful) sites that have established threads on finding an editor, or where you can chat with

other writers. Some especially good ones are Absolute Write, Writing.com, NaNoWriMo, and Query Tracker.

Finally, there are a number of professional organizations where you can check out editors' listings and websites and contact them directly. A word of caution: Editors on these sites will come from all types of backgrounds and levels of experience. These sites are a starting point, but it's still up to you to do your due diligence—which I'll talk about below—to find a qualified, reputable editor who is a great fit for you.

- Editorial Freelancers Association (EFA): www.the-efa.org
  The EFA has a free job board where you can post—at no charge—
  a listing for your project. I recommend narrowing down the list
  based on some of the below criteria, and then asking your top two
  or three for sample edits. (I'll talk more about sample edits below.)
- Independent Editors Group (IEG): www.bookdocs.com
- National Association of Independent Writers and Editors:
  naiwe.com/
- Professional Editors Network: www.pensite.org
- Society for Editors and Proofreaders (UK): www.sfep.org.uk
- The Editors Association of Canada: www.editors.ca
- The Institute of Professional Editors Limited (Australia):
  iped-editors.org
- 5E Editors: www.5eeditors.com
- Bay Area Editors' Forum: www.editorsforum.org
- Northwest Independent Editors Guild www.edsguild.org
- Society of American Business Editors and Writers:
  www.sabew.com
- Western New England Editorial Freelancers Network:
  www.editorsplus.com
- The Editors Circle: www.theeditorscircle.com
- Words Into Print: www.wordsintoprint.org
- Book Editors Alliance: www.bookeditorsalliance.com
- Reedsy: www.reedsy.com

Vetting an Editor

Okay, you've found the mother lode of editors and you've got a list. Now what?

While I strongly recommend doing your due diligence, there's no need to make a long-term project out of finding the right editor. You can cull the list down to a manageable few fairly quickly, and then focus on deciding among those with a bit of a deeper dive. But this is a major investment of time and money in an undertaking that's extremely important to most authors—be prepared to give the process of finding the right editor at least as much effort as you'd give to buying a new mattress.

If you were lucky enough to get a personal recommendation from someone you know or an author you admire, ideally who writes in your genre, that editor's name can go at the top of your list. Same with any editors you found through seeing them speak at a conference or reading an article you liked.

After that, using editors' websites or industry-site listings, narrow the field based on genre—not every editor works well in every genre, and if they say they do, walk away. (That's like a brain surgeon saying he's also pretty good at heart surgery.) Good, experienced editors know their strengths, and most will have just a handful of genres they specialize in.

Now check that they have legitimate developmental editing credits in that genre, and in the publishing industry. This doesn't necessarily mean they've worked on books published with major publishers—plenty of great editors work with smaller pub houses or specialize in self-published authors. But you do want to make sure they have worked on *books*, rather than articles, essays, white papers, or ad copy. If you're looking for substantive feedback on your main story elements, you likely won't get what you need from an English teacher or librarian; a newspaper, magazine, or scholastic editor; or a copy editor or proofreader.

Testimonials are also useful—quotes from authors the editor has worked with—but you might look up the actual books the editor worked on (the "Look Inside" feature on Amazon is perfect for this) to make sure the story's standards are as high as you expect for your own.

Some authors like to ask for references and actually contact authors an editor has worked with. You're spending thousands of dollars on a very subjective, personal service, so I'll never discourage anyone from checking references (and if an editor balks at this, I'd call that a red flag), but often you can get an excellent idea of an editor's skill, experience, and credibility simply from checking the above areas.

There are a few other industry sites that can help you research an editor's reputation or track record as well. You may find information on any of the following chat boards:

- Preditors and Editors: www.pred-ed.com
- Absolute Write Water Cooler: www.absolutewrite.com/forums
- Writer Beware (through the Science Fiction and Fantasy Writers of America): www.sfwa.org/other-resources/for-authors/writer-beware/editors

A Word about Writer-Editors

I've seen a lot of advice for authors to seek editors who are also authors, or vice versa, apparently on the theory that anyone who has mastered one of these skills must also be an expert in the other, and I'm constantly startled to see how many people subscribe to this misbelief.

Steven Spielberg and George Lucas are by most estimations brilliant directors, but no one is hiring them to star in movies. Can they even act? We don't know—that isn't their skill set. Nor is every actor a great director (I'm looking at *you*, Steven Seagal). Legendary coaches aren't necessarily MVPs; great conductors likely never play Carnegie Hall.

Don't let this off-track advice keep you from hiring an excellent editor, or encourage you to hire a talented author who may not be as skilled as an editor. While related, these are very distinct

> skill sets, and being good at one doesn't necessarily make you good at the other.
>
> A good author is not necessarily a good editor—and vice versa.

Now that you've narrowed the very broad field a bit, you can contact the top handful on your list to winnow it down further. Send a brief email describing your manuscript and what you're looking for: "I've written a X-word fantasy YA story about a boy who can change shape into any animal, and how he saves his family's village. I'm ready to hire an editor for a full developmental edit prior to sending this out to agents/self-publishing, and I'm interested in finding out whether we'd be a good fit."

"A good fit" is a phrase I use a lot with new clients—finding the right editor is about much more than résumé, price point, and scheduling. It's an intimate relationship and, like any relationship, has a lot to do with personality and chemistry. You need to know whether this editor's "style" (and every editor has one) suits you—is he a minimalist, or exhaustively thorough? Some authors might prefer painstaking detail and hands-on suggestions for addressing any areas of concern; others may find that level of feedback pedantic, or overwhelming, or intrusive, and prefer a briefer bullet-point approach. Some authors may like a direct, pull-no-punches editing style that another author might find tactless or offensive.

On the other side, the editor needs to know whether your story is a good fit for her too—is it a genre she specializes in? Does she like it and feel enthusiastic about reading this story multiple times—sometimes as many as half a dozen times over months or even years, in some cases—and plunging deeply into it? Is the manuscript in a state where she feels it and the author are ready for a professional edit, or does she feel this is still a revision or two away from the editorial stage?

All these questions are subjective—as is so much in this field—which is why it's so important to do your homework and carefully search out the right editor for you and your story.

There's only one way to find all this out prior to hiring an editor, and that's with a sample edit.

The Sample Edit

You'd test-drive a car before you bought it, interview a photographer before hiring him to commemorate your wedding, have a house inspected before you signed the contract. As with any other significant, important investment, it's wise to "try before you buy." And there is simply no other way to really determine whether an editor is the right one for you and your manuscript.

Sample edits are usually short—I offer 1,000 to 1,500 words; I've seen editors offer as little as 250 words (a single standard page) and as much as 30 pages. With only a snippet of the manuscript it's impossible to offer as complete an edit as with a full manuscript (it's like reviewing a film from a five-minute scene), but a good editor should be able to see and offer enough to show you how they work, their approach, whether they get your style and voice—and respect it—and what you can expect from a full edit. I offer a mini version of what I'll do in a full dev edit: a brief editorial letter summing up the big-picture elements I see that might benefit from some polishing or developing, as well as embedded notes that clarify and build on those. These take at least an hour and often more, and that's unpaid time for me, but I wouldn't even bid on a project I hadn't done a sample edit for, at least with first-time clients. I need to know whether this project and this author are a good fit for me as much as the author needs to know, and it's also how I assess the amount of work we may be looking at and offer an accurate firm quote. The sample edit is a "trial run" for both author and editor, and if an editor balks at offering one—or offers you a generic one from someone else's project—again, my personal advice is to walk away. (Would you buy a car the salesman didn't want you to drive first, or after test-driving a different version of the same make and model on his assurances that it's just like the one you're looking at?)

As with hiring any contractor, my recommendation is to narrow the editing field to your top three, and ask for sample edits from those to make your final decision.

After the Sample

Now it's time to assess the feedback you received to see which editor is right for you. Chances are you'll have a gut reaction when you get the samples back and know immediately, intuitively, which one is most right for you and your manuscript. But here are some specific things to consider if you find yourself waffling:

Does the editor "get" your work—your genre, your style, your voice, and the story you are telling? Does he offer suggestions that make clear exactly what may not be working as well as it could, and why, in a way that helps you clearly see how to address it? Are her comments constructive and positive in tone—respectful of you and your work—without candycoating straightforward feedback? Does he offer solutions, or just point out problems? Do his edits "resonate" with you—do you find yourself nodding and thinking, "Yes, of course…" or shaking your head because that's not the direction you want the story to move in, or the comment feels off base for your intentions?

Is the editor offering feedback that shows she's interested in helping you clarify and develop *your* vision on the page, or does she seem to be trying to "take over" the story and impose her own preferences? This can be a fine line—an editor won't always tell you exactly what you want to hear. But the suggestions should be respectful (have I said that enough?), never condescending or controlling, and if they differ substantially from your intention, the editor should clearly support why she's making the suggestion—with solid, craft-based reasons, rather than subjective or personal ones. (For instance, I've suggested authors change a character's name because another character's name is too similar and it may confuse readers. But one author I know was told by her editor that her romantic lead's name didn't sound very sexy and she should change it. The former is objective and craft-based; the latter is entirely subjective.)

Are the editor's comments thorough and clearly actionable, or a bit vague and confusing? "It's not evident to me why she walks away here when she said she needs him to help her; can you let us see more clearly what makes her give up, or whether this is just a different tactic?" is very different from, "Motivation unclear." What motivation? Unclear how? What might the author do about it?

Are the comments positive and tactful, rather than dictatorial or high-handed? "Wordy—cut" may be a comment that rubs a lot of authors the wrong way (it would me). An editor can convey the same idea more constructively: "This feels as if you restate the same thing twice here; the first clause is stronger—you might consider cutting the second." The first suggestion may be subjective—the author has no way of knowing—and it's brusque. The second comment not only lets the author know what's not working as well as it could in the sentence, but why—which means that in the future she'll be more cognizant of this tendency in her writing and probably be able to spot similar redundancies on her own. Sugarcoating is counterproductive, but a bit of consideration and tact goes a long way—as does supported reasoning. This is a more labor-intensive approach for editors, but if you're investing thousands of dollars in a professional edit (and you will), you deserve someone who's willing to take the time and go a little deeper. You want an editor who helps you find solutions, rather than just pointing out problems.

Once you've assessed the samples in this way, chances are excellent you'll have a favorite. Now it's time for the nitty-gritty.

Rates

What should a full developmental cost?

In a subjective field populated with editors of all levels of experience and skill, rates are often all over the map. But established, reputable editors tend to fall within an industry-standard range. The Editorial Freelancers Association offers this rate chart to give you a rough idea of current rates: www.the-efa.org/rates. In the UK, the Society for Editors and Proofreaders offers this guideline: www.sfep.org.uk/resources/suggested-minimum-rates.

Editors with many years of experience in the publishing industry, especially at major houses and with titles by bestselling or critically acclaimed authors among their project list, will likely skew toward the high end of this range, and even beyond it. Newer or less proven editors may fall at the lower end. If you pay more, make sure you're getting more in terms of experience. If the rate seems too good to be true, it probably is—editing is a labor-intensive skill and art, and the best editors have honed their skills over years of experience and education; in this sense you get what you pay for. If a fee is astronomically out of the meaty part of the bell curve for the industry, I would strongly question whether that's a worthwhile use of an author's resources—you can get an extremely good edit without paying inflated rates for it.

The above charts suggest hourly rates; personally I much prefer a word rate, and many editors' sites show that they do too. But some editors favor an hourly rate, since it's impossible to know exactly how much work and time will be involved in the full manuscript until he or she has read it at least once in its entirety (a full "cold read" is my and many other editors' first step in a developmental edit, and a large time commitment very few editors would agree to prior to contracting for the full edit). To my mind a word rate benefits the author enormously—you know exactly what you will be paying the moment you turn in your completed draft to the editor, and can budget accordingly. I've heard horror stories from authors of very unpleasant surprises when their editor presents the final bill with an hourly rate.

A word rate seems fairer to me to both parties, and everyone's expectations are firm and finalized before we even embark on the first chapter. With a sample edit I'm generally able to assess the likely overall demands of a job and price my quote accordingly; I've been "burned" by too low a quote only a few times, but it's one reason I and many other editors tend to ask for a sample from a midpoint of the manuscript—authors often hone their early chapters to a diamond shine, and the later parts of the story are where the most significant edits may be needed. If editors quote on the revised, reworked, and often workshopped chapter one, we may severely underbid the work required by the time we realize the rest may not have received the same level of polish. A word rate also "levels the playing field" of variations in editors' speed. You'll notice on the EFA chart, for instance, that average editor speed on a developmental edit ranges from 1 to 5 pages per hour. That's a *wide* variation—on a 250-page manuscript at $50/hour, for example, it's the difference between a bill of $2,500 and one for $12,500. (And if anyone quotes you a five-figure developmental edit, unless you're Thomas Wolfe with his one-million-word draft of *Of Time and the River*, please feel free to head for the exit.)

Regardless of how an editor charges for her work, I offer one absolute piece of advice to authors: **The editor should offer you a firm quote in writing with the returned sample.**

If he's unwilling to do so, move on.

Contract

Finally, do not work without a contract that clearly spells out what is expected of each of you, including the rate, schedule, and payment terms. The contract should also spell out definitions of terms, and ideally contain clear termination, property rights, and confidentiality clauses. You and the editor should agree on a schedule in writing, and the contract should include a delineated firm deadline for the return of at least your first pass (if doing a multiple-pass edit), as well as a time frame for completion of all edit passes, and clear terms in case of breached deadlines by either party.

I once offered a sample edit and firm quote to an author who subsequently wanted us to work together on his story. We agreed on the schedule and I let him know the contract would be headed his way—and he immediately bristled. He'd worked with many editors, he said, and not one had ever suggested he sign a contract. Despite his telling me he was a lawyer himself, he expressed that signing a contract for our work together implied a mutual lack of trust. I explained that the contract was mostly designed to protect the author, spelling out our agreed-upon rate and deadlines and exactly what work would be performed and how. He very reluctantly agreed...but his continued irritation over signing a formal contract—especially as a lawyer, who might be expected to appreciate the value of clear expectations—raised a yellow flag for me, and I ultimately declined the job.

That brings me to my final piece of advice for choosing an editor after your due diligence and sample edit: What does your gut say? As I mentioned earlier, chances are great that the right editor for your story will be crystal-clear to you—it will resonate through your bones just as good edits will.

What Can You Expect from a Good Editor/Author Relationship?

After you find and choose your editor, the real work begins—and a successful working relationship involves more than an editor's skilled observations about your story. Every writer has her own personality, style, voice, and way of working—as does every editor—so the actual working relationship may look different for each pairing, but there is a baseline ethos you're entitled to expect from your editor to create a healthy, positive, helpful atmosphere:

- Respect—of your work, your voice, your story, and you as a person.
- Honesty and positivity—constructive critique, encouragement, and a positive approach, but without candycoating or "blowing smoke."
- Clarity and specificity—not just pointing out problem areas, but explaining why something isn't working and suggesting methods for addressing it.
- Accessibility—the level of contact you may have varies from editor to editor, but you should know what to expect up front, and ideally have some follow-up time built into the contract for the inevitable questions, clarifications, and concerns.
- Flexibility—preferred methods of contact may vary (e.g., email, phone, Skype, in person, etc.), but the editor should at least attempt to accommodate your requests (within reason).
- Professionalism—an editor should present a professional demeanor and approach to business as well as craft.

After the Edit

No matter how carefully you selected your editor, how constructive his approach may be, and even how much you might ultimately agree with his assessments, getting back what's often a voluminous amount of feedback all at once can be a plank in the face.

Offering up your manuscript for professional evaluation is like walking naked into a roomful of fashion designers and saying, "No, really, tell me exactly what you see." No matter how prepared you may think you are for honest, thorough evaluation and critique, it can hurt to receive a lengthy editorial letter (in my case usually around 5,000 or more words, and I've gone as high as 12K) and literally often hundreds of embedded notes on where your painstakingly written manuscript might benefit from a bit more development, clarification, or polish. It's easy to feel overwhelmed or daunted, or even paralyzed. Ideally your editor will also point out the strengths of your story, but trust me, it's going to feel like, as one author I worked with memorably put it, a literary root canal.

So be good and gentle to yourself. Pour a glass of wine or a really good cup of coffee or tea. Sit somewhere relaxing—a comfortable easy chair, your back porch, a bathtub. Put your dog (or cat) on your lap. *Then* open up the files from your editor and read.

When I first return edits to an author I always suggest he read through the editorial letter first, then the embedded notes—then sit with it for at least a day or two before diving back in. Let the feedback percolate in your mind for a while before you try to put it into action—you need time first of all to recover from the impact.

But there's also magic in the subconscious. Thousands of words of editorial letter and hundreds of manuscript pages studded with embedded notes feels like staring up the sheer face of Revision Mountain and thinking there's no way you'll make it to the top. But a day or two of letting the feedback simmer at the back of your mind has an astonishing way of showing you the path and the footholds, and by the time you actually sit down and start working you've got your route mapped out one doable step at a time till you reach the summit.

Last, but truly not least, remember that editorial feedback, like any feedback—even by a professional—is one person's opinion. Granted, hopefully it's based on a lot of experience in and knowledge of the industry, but this is your manuscript, and you should take the suggestions that work for you and leave those that don't. Ultimately this is *your* story, *your* voice.

The only thing I would add is that if there is a suggestion that really rankles, that makes you knee-jerk resist, you might just sit with it for a while. Sometimes those are little red flags for "darlings" that aren't serving your story and may need killing. You may still decide that the editor's feedback is off-track—or you might see things from a fresh, objective angle you never would have considered on your own.

And ultimately, that's exactly what an edit is for.

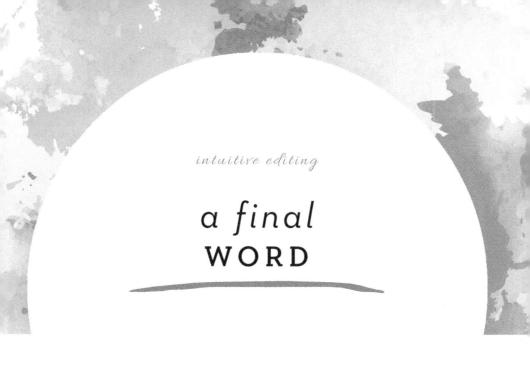

a *final* WORD

There's a feeling I get whenever I read an author's final edited version of a manuscript that's come together to create the seamless, impactful, satisfying story he set out to tell in the first place: sort of a steady mental smile, my joyful inner version of Walt Whitman's yawp sounded over the roofs of the world—a resounding feeling of *yes*.

That's the feeling I hope you come away with from your own manuscript after you've applied the techniques and theories in this book toward making your story the one you dreamed of telling. Editing can be a challenging road, and while you're traveling it the journey may not feel nearly as fun as the thrilling ride of a first draft. But stay the course, friend. The books that feel most effortlessly, deeply engaging for readers almost always grew from painstaking, determined, intensive work on the part of the author. Your art, your vision, your message matter enormously to you or you wouldn't be reading a book like this. They matter to humanity, too. Stories are the engine of the world— where we find comfort, knowledge, connection, understanding, hope, and so much more.

As master editor Maxwell Perkins said (I'd be remiss if I didn't end my book on editing with a quote from my greatest editing idol): "If you get discouraged it is not a bad sign, but a good one. If you think you are not doing it well, you are thinking the way real novelists do. I never knew one who did not feel greatly discouraged at times, and some get desperate, and I have always found that to be a good symptom."

May your good symptoms remind you that your stories are worth the effort, and help you shepherd them into the world.

For a list of additional resources and recommendations, visit my website at www.foxprinteditorial.com. And to be notified about future supplemental materials, webinars, upcoming workshops and presentations, and more, sign up for my newsletter at www.foxprinteditorial.com/contact.

ACKNOWLEDGMENTS

Twenty-eight years ago, living in a women's residence New York as a struggling actor, I spent $25 I could ill afford on a pamphlet advertised in the *New York Times* classifieds: "Get Paid for Reading Books!" I was pretty sure it was a scam...but I'd adored reading, books, words, and language all my life, and with a freshly minted English lit degree (my subconscious apparently knew where my true passions lay even before I realized it), I took the long-shot hope that the booklet might actually lead me to a way to make ends meet as an actor while doing something I loved, rather than waiting tables forever.

To my shock the pamphlet was full of specific, useful advice on how to approach major publishers about working as a freelance proof-reader and copy editor. Armed with its information, I pored through the enormous spiral-bound *Literary Marketplace*—a huge compendium of every publisher's info, stats, employees, and contact information—sitting for hours on end at the reference desk of the New York Public Library because you weren't allowed to check the behemoth out. (This was pre-internet, kids....) Once I had a long list of potential publishers to contact, I mailed out my résumé, took proofreading tests from those who responded, and hoped.

A few weeks later I got my first call and assignment—proofing a romance novel for Leisure Books (defunct now)—and I remember clutching it to my chest after I picked up the towering stack of manuscript pages and galleys from the publisher, hoping with all my heart that it was the start of the end of my waitressing career.

Back then I worked with a red pencil on actual paper pages, and fact-checking meant going back to my perch at the New York Public Library for hours at a time, painstakingly hauling out reference books and thumbing through the card catalog to hunt down endless source books for an insane array of arcana that needed verifying. In many ways I feel I came into the business just in time to be part of the "old guard," and I'm grateful to have experienced that.

It took just a few years for me to realize my "side hustle" was actually my calling, and I quit acting to dedicate myself to a career in publishing, eventually moving from copyediting to developmental editing. Everything I have learned in my years in the business since the beginning has been with the help of others, and the list of people I want to thank is long.

To the publishing-house editors who took a chance on an untried copyeditor when I first started out—especially Frank Walgren, who gave me that very first job; Nora Reichard, who always taught me so much; Adrian Wood Liang, who became a friend and valued sounding board; Dan Walsh; Kathleen Fridella; Nancy Delia; Megan Gerrity; Mark Rifkin for also letting me write about movies, one of my favorite things; Ellen Scordato; Rachel Granfield; Gwen Morton—thank you all for allowing me to work in the field I loved, with the top publishing houses in the business, and for your tutelage and advice that helped me learn and grow. And to the editors who have helped me hone my knowledge as a developmental editor: Danielle Marshall, Chris Werner, Liz Pearsons, Jodi Warshaw, Jessica Tribble, Kelli, Martin, Lindsay Guzzardo, JoVon Sotak, Alicia Clancy, Victoria Pepe, Terry Goodman, working with you is a joy and an ongoing education.

Thank you to the hundreds of authors who have trusted me with their stories over the years. When I tell you it's one of the great honors of my life, I'm not overstating. Thanks to the publishers who have offered me the opportunity to do what I love on a wide stage, with some of the best authors, editors, and agents in the business.

To Camille LeMoine, as gifted as you are as an author, your gorgeous designs for my website and social media make me look so good.

And you handle my neuroses, obsessiveness, endless questions, and OCD tweaks with unflappable grace and warmth. I'm so glad you're French... and I'm so glad I was lucky enough our paths crossed all those years ago, my friend.

Domini Dragoone, your beautiful cover captured exactly the feel I wanted for this book, and your interior design made it feel as navigable and professional as I'd dreamed. Thanks for your patience, care, and professionalism.

Thank you, Kristen Kieffer, for your warmth and receptiveness to a complete stranger seeking advice and guidance on the publishing journey, and your encouragement and kind words as you generously shared your knowledge and time with me.

When I finished this book I asked a number of people whose opinions I greatly valued about reading it and offering their thoughts, and the reception I received outstripped my wildest hopes. Almost without exception, the authors, editors, and agents I approached replied to me nearly immediately with not just a yes, but a warm, enthusiastic, supportive yes—despite their own towering to-do lists and projects, and the many other commitments each of them had (and even as a global health crisis sent everyone's world sideways). It was a bit overwhelming to be on the receiving end of so much kindness and generosity, and I want to thank the following people with all my heart:

Lainey Cameron! How do I begin to thank you? You generously took on the potentially thankless task of offering edits to the editor, and *boy*, are you good at it. Your observations were so thoughtful and reasoned and insightful, they gave me a little editor envy. ☺ I am so grateful for how much better and clearer you made the book, and the way you made me think even more deeply about what I wanted to convey, as the best edits do. Plus you offered your brilliant market-research magic! How lucky am I that our working relationship turned into a friendship?

Thank you to my first readers, who let me know whether this concept was working: Karin Gillespie, who offers as much moral, marketing, and personal support as she does excellent feedback; Camille LeMoine, Dr. Duana Welch, Kathryn Hera Haydn, Richard LeMay, Kelly Harrell, and Sarah Bird. Thanks to the authors who graciously allowed me to use their work directly: Aaron Brown, Richard LeMay, John Jones, Kelly Harrell, Amber Novak, Camilla Monk, Dr. Duana Welch, Anne Rodgers and Dr. Maureen Whelihan, T. M. Yates, and Ashley Brown.

Amid their own towering reading lists, full client slates, and a pandemic, literary agents Elisabeth Weed and Annelise Robey took time to read and offer a few words of support for this book, a magnanimity of spirit I will not forget.

Thank you to the authors who took time away from their own book projects to generously give their time and attention to mine—and didn't even take advantage of the chance to get back at the editor who routinely sends them reams of story notes: Andy Abramowitz, Ania Ahlborn, Sejal Badani, Sarah Bird, Bette Lee Crosby, Camille Di Maio, Liz Fenton, Karin Gillespie, Kelly Harms, Steena Holmes, Laila Ibrahim, Joy Jordan-Lake, Kerry Lonsdale, Elisa Lorello, Camilla Monk, Amy Sue Nathan, Barbara O'Neal, Camille Pagán, Amanda Prowse, Marilyn Simon Rothstein, Kaira Rouda, Allison Winn Scotch, Sharon Short (writing as Jess Montgomery), Barbara Taylor Sissel, Lisa Steinke, Victoria Helen Stone, Sherry Thomas, Rochelle Weinstein, Sonja Yoerg. Your generosity, kind words, and feedback mean the world to me. And your skill, talent, and vision make me a better editor. Thank you.

Word nerds aren't always so up on technological advances, but luckily I married a tech geek, and over the years my husband, Joel, has helped keep me on the vanguard of the ongoing evolution of the publishing world and allowed me to stay deeply involved in it even as the industry experienced enormous change. From the very beginning he has believed in me on every level, sometimes more than I believed in myself, and pushed me to trust myself. This book, a career-long dream I've held, exists in your hands in no small part because of that, and because of him.

about the
AUTHOR

Developmental editor Tiffany Yates Martin has the great good fortune of helping authors tell their stories as effectively, compellingly, and truthfully as possible. In nearly 30 rewarding years in the publishing industry she's worked both with major publishing houses and directly with authors (through her company FoxPrint Editorial), on titles by *New York Times, USA Today, Washington Post*, and *Wall Street Journal* bestsellers and award winners as well as newer authors. She presents editing and writing workshops for writers' groups, organizations, and conferences across the country, and writes for numerous writers' sites and publications. Connect with her at www.foxprinteditorial.com for additional resources and information, and to sign up for updates on supplemental materials and future publications, presentations and workshops, and links to her articles and other writing.

Made in the USA
Coppell, TX
11 February 2021